THE HIDDEN SPRINGS

A flight of migrating Snow Buntings over Fair Isle

THE HIDDEN SPRINGS

An Enquiry into
Extra-Sensory Perception

REVISED EDITION

RENÉE HAYNES

Little, Brown and Company • Boston • Toronto

#618472

REVISED AMERICAN EDITION

A

Library of Congress Cataloging in Publication Data

Haynes, Renée, 1906–
   The hidden springs: an enquiry into extra-sensory perception.

   1. Extrasensory perception.   I.   Title.
BF1171.H33 1973   133.8   73-6691
ISBN 0-316-35226-8
ISBN 0-316-35227-6 (pbk.)

PRINTED IN THE UNITED STATES OF AMERICA

FOR

Crispin, Patrick and Thomas

Contents

Note		9
One	Definitions	15
Two	The Psi-function in animals	31
Three	Amateur and specialist in primitive human groups	60
Four	Organized divination: the ancient Mediterranean cults	83
Five	Sage, clairvoyant and magician in Asia	108
Six	Psi and Miracle	128
Seven	Philosophical assessments: from the World Soul to Prophecy	157
Eight	The Enlightenment: "What I don't know isn't knowledge"	180
Nine	Spirits or Electricity	209
Ten	A New Interpretation	237
Appendix	The Evil Eye	253
Index		256

Illustrations

A flight of migrating Snow Buntings over
    Fair Isle   *Frontispiece*

Nests of the Termites from *The World in
    Miniature — Africa,* by Ackerman   *Facing page* 32

A Soothsayer (The Flyer)   33

Model of a Liver used for instructing students
    in the art of divination   64

Cover of a contemporary pamphlet describing
    the strange phenomena at Edge Hill   65

St Joseph of Cupertino in flight   192

Prosper Lambertini, Pope Benedict XIV   193

Dr Mesmer
"Count" Cagliostro
Dr Mesmer's Tub as contemporaries saw it   224

The Mystic Rose from Dante's *Paradiso*   225

Note

IT has been suggested that I should indicate exactly what I myself believe to be proven about psychical phenomena. This necessitates a personal note.

I have been interested in psychical research ever since, as a child, I read Sinel's study of telepathy in animals and men, *The Sixth Sense*, of which I recollect two things: that certain tribes of American Indians recognized it under the name of *chumfo*, and that the author believed it to be a true sense, whose organ was the pineal gland.

As a result partly of reading, thinking and discussion, partly of studying experimental work, and partly of personal experience I have come to the following conclusions:

1. That spontaneous telepathy probably occurs among most living creatures, and certainly in human beings, and that among them it does so far more often than is generally realized, particularly between mothers and young children.

2. That willed telepathy can occur, among both sophisticated and unsophisticated peoples; witness on the one hand, say, the various experiments recorded in the *Proceedings of the Society for Psychical Research* from 1882 onwards, and on the other, for instance, the reply of an Australian aboriginal to a query from the anthropologist Ronald Rose as to how he conveyed detailed messages by smoke signals. He said he would attract the attention of another man miles away by making a smoky fire of green boughs and ". . . when he sees it, he knows it is not a campfire, and he gets to thinking. And I am thinking too, so he thinks my thoughts".

3. That experiences of time-displacement occur, in the form of retrocognition, which is probably the basis of many "hauntings": and that they also, though more rarely, occur in the form of precognition. St Thomas Aquinas recognized this in certain

species as "natural prophecy", while the Biblical Pharaoh (not to mention his baker and butler), J. W. Dunne and many others have observed it operating in dreams, sometimes straight-forwardly and sometimes in symbolic form. It has also been recorded in large-scale card experiments.

4. That cumulative evidence, both from the "field natura-list" study of poltergeist outbreaks and kindred phenomena in different parts of the world, and from the experimental angle, seems to warrant the assumption that telekinesis (or psycho-kinesis) may occur; the movement, that is, of physical objects, animate or inanimate, by an unknown energy exerted by the psyche for the most part in accordance with some motive operating below the level of consciousness, and just conceivably —though not in Western cultures—by the voluntary use of psycho-physical techniques. Much investigation remains to be done here.

5. That the success of dowsing or water divining cannot always be explained by coincidence, fraud, imagination or a shrewd assessment of "the lie of the land" (but *not* that the myths in accordance with which some dowsers project and rationalize their curious gift have any necessary connexion with reality). Those interested in pursuing the question may care to consult the British Society of Dowsers.

A list of some of the books which have led me to form these conclusions is appended, and footnotes in the text refer to others from which material currently discussed is drawn. Contemporary anecdotes have been taken from sources known to me at first hand.

As I accept that such psychical phenomena as have been listed can and do occur, I have not rejected out of hand traditions, legends and historical incidents that can no longer be investi-gated, but have instanced and discussed them as worthy of con-sideration and have tentatively put forward hypotheses that may serve to account for them.

I should like to thank all the people who have helped me in

connexion with this book, and to remark at the same time that they must not be held responsible for the uses to which I have put their kindness.

Among them are my mother and sisters, in whose gardens much of it was written; the late Miss Theodora Bosanquet, who first introduced me to the Society for Psychical Research; Fr Joseph Crehan, S.J., who read and commented on Chapter Six, and spent valuable time in answering questions in his special field; Mr J. H. Cutten, who patiently made clear some points about electricity and magnetism; Dr E. J. Dingwall, for the loan of photographs and for his insistence that I must consult the work of that great pioneer in psychical research Pope Benedict XIV in its original form instead of relying on a truncated translation; my family, for their forbearance while I was working; Miss Celia Green, for allowing me to read a proof copy of her translation of René Sudre's *Treatise on Parapsychology*; Professor Sir Alister Hardy F.R.S., who most kindly answered some complicated questions; Mrs Rosalind Heywood, who lent me the typescript of her brilliant study *The Sixth Sense* before its publication, and gave me references to work published in current overseas periodicals which I should not otherwise have seen; Mr Francis Huxley, for finding the picture of The Flyer; the late Dr E. B. Strauss, who read and commented on Chapter Two, lent me many books and spared time to discuss various points with me; and the Society for Psychical Research for leave to quote from its records. It should be made clear that the Society as such holds no corporate views and is in no way committed to mine.

R. H.

Basic Sources of Information

BENDIT, LAURENCE, M.D., *Paranormal Cognition*. London, 1944.

BROAD, C. D., *Lectures in Psychical Research*. London, 1962.

CARINGTON, WHATELY, *Telepathy*. London, 1945.

DUNNE, J.W., *An Experiment with Time*. London, 1934.

HARDY, SIR ALISTER, F.R.S. *Biology and Psychical Research*. Proc. S.P.R. Vol. 50 1953. Gifford Lectures Vol. I *The Living Stream*. London, 1965.

HEYWOOD, ROSALIND, *The Sixth Sense*. London, 1959.

KOESTLER, ARTHUR,*T The o Roots (of n Coincidence.*lc London, 1972.

LAMBERTINI, PROSPERO, (later Pope Benedict XIV) *De Servorum Dei Beatificatione et Beatorum Canonizatione Liber Quartus*. Bologna, 1737.

MCCREERY, CHARLES, *Science, Philosophy and E.S.P.* London, 1967.

MACKENZIE, ANDREW, *The Unexplained*. London, 1966.

OWEN, A. R. G., *Can We Explain The Poltergeist?* New York, 1964.

RAO, K. RAMAKRISHNA,.*Experimental Parapsychology*. Illinois, U.S.A., 1966.

RHINE, J. B., *Extrasensory Perception*. Boston, U.S.A., 1934.

RHINE, J. B., *The Reach of the Mind*. London, 1948.

RHINE, J.1 B. AND PRATT, J. G., *Parapsychology*. London, 1968.

RHINE, LOUISA, *E.S.P. in Life and Lab*. London, 1969.

ROSE, RONALD, *Living Magic*. London, 1957.

SCHWARTZ, BERTHOLD ERIC, *Parent–Child Telepathy*. New York, 1971.

SOAL, S. G., AND BATEMAN, F., *Modern Experiments in Telepathy*, London 1954.

THURSTON, HERBERT, S.J. ed CREHAN, J. H., S.J., *The Physical Phenomena of Mysticism*. London, 1952. *Ghosts and Poltergeists*. London, 1953.

TYRRELL, G. N. M., *Science and Psychical Phenomena*. London, 1938. *Apparitions*. London, 1953.

WEST, D. J., *Psychical Research Today*. Revised edition. London, 1962.

WHITE, VICTOR, O.P., *God and the Unconscious*. London, 1952.

THE HIDDEN SPRINGS

Chapter One

DEFINITIONS

PSI is the word currently used to indicate an energy which—like electricity, with which some useful and other extremely misleading analogies can be drawn—must for the present be defined in terms of what it does rather than of what it is. It is postulated as the activity at work in an enormous, mixed mass of phenomena, from whose flowering tangles, luxuriant as bindweed, one constant characteristic emerges—the communication of imagery and of impulse from one self to another without the use of the senses or of any secondary mechanical devices, a communication which is usually independent of distance in space, and occasionally of distance in time. Such phenomena have been recognized with a variety of emotions—acceptance, awe, superstition, respect, fear, credulity, defensive ridicule, and fascinated interest—all over the world and throughout recorded history. They are taken for granted even now by such remaining primitive peoples as remain unable to record their beliefs and practices.

There is still, of course, considerable opposition to the idea that psi exists at all. My reasons for accepting it as a fact which cannot be ignored will become apparent. Much resistance to the idea springs from dread of the acute intellectual discomfort involved in recognizing its implications, an intellectual discomfort worked out with slow, painful, vivid honesty in such essays as Dr Jung devotes to his theory of synchronicity.[1] These implications are, of course, almost impossible to reconcile with the neat, mechanist conceptions of causality, and of the nature and working of the universe upon which so much scientific experiment and brilliant achievement have been based over the last four centuries.

[1] *The Interpretation of Nature and the Psyche* (London, 1955).

Such conceptions have become preconceptions. The mind craves security, the support of things taken for granted. This craving leads it to seek protection in intellectual constructs against the frightening impact of the strange, the unknown, the imperfectly understood. Such constructs, however, are all too frequently no more than hypotheses into which, so to speak, reinforced concrete has been poured. Found valid in some circumstances, they have been used as axiomatic in all. But however much reinforced concrete is poured into them, they do not become self-evident truths even though an earthquake may be needed to break them down, an earthquake which is indeed a large-scale example of what was defined by Herbert Spencer (quoted by T. H. Huxley) as the principal tragedy of scientific work, a hypothesis demolished by a fact.

There are several methods of classifying psi-phenomena.

They can for instance be divided into the spontaneous, the induced and the experimental.

Among the spontaneous kind come flashes of unexpected and unaccountable knowledge that something significant has happened, is happening or is about to happen. This knowledge is sometimes conveyed in clear, detailed, sensory terms, apparently external to the percipient, as when a voice is "heard" or the apparition of a living, dying, or dead person is "seen".

The psycho-physical process involved in producing such knowledge in "external" imagery of this kind is pretty certainly the same as that which produces ordinary hallucinations. The difference lies in the stimulus which sets the process going, in the one case some physical accident or disease, some electrical device or some mental or emotional abnormality, in the other the psi-factor in connexion with an objective event occurring quite independently of the observer. Psychical research workers have used the phrase "veridical hallucination" to indicate occurrences of this sort. It is useful and accurate within its own framework but is vitiated in everyday parlance by the fact that "hallucination" is semi-automatically associated in the general reader's mind with mental instability.

Urban civilization stimulates the senses of sight and hearing with so many irrelevancies that those who live in it tend to develop a certain general numbness to all that does not immediately concern them; not only to the sight of moving traffic, red buses, black, green, blue, and parti-coloured Siamese-cat cars, and the noise of electric drills and changing gears and aeroplane engines, which have no individual meaning, but also to the sound of voices on next door's wireless, voices which expect a hearer, and to the sight of advertisements, which presuppose a buyer. The city dweller, then, tends to withdraw attention from most sensory stimuli, heeding only those with which his feelings are already involved. In this withdrawal of attention, this self-defensive numbness to the images presented by sight and hearing, lies the probable explanation of an odd fact. In contemporary urban cultures, and in waking hours (the imagery of dreams remains uninhibited), knowledge obtained through spontaneous psi activity tends to reach consciousness much more in terms of a generalized awareness, a "hunch", than through veridical hallucinations, though the subconscious has been known, on occasion, to attract notice by using, say, such contemporary projected imagery as that of a strident telephone bell insistently ringing, to be followed by a warning "voice".

The "hunch" may be tantalizingly vague or have a certain amount of detail. Its owner may be suffused with the unwelcome knowledge that something is wrong at home, or that so-and-so is ill or hurt, or perceive with clarity that a boy has got a scholarship, or that Daddy Long Legs will win the 2.30. The knowledge may come through as no more than a dim sense of relief or apprehension or inexplicable happiness, or even in the form of an unaccountable impulse, almost a compulsion, to do something that may seem quite absurd; to leave, perhaps, an air-raid shelter which is giving some measure of protection and to go out into the dangers of the street five minutes before that shelter gets a direct hit; or to cancel a ticket on some aircraft which in fact crashes on that particular journey.

It may be noted how closely such feelings can be paralleled in

those of people suffering from various neuroses, and here
again the difference lies in the fact that where psi is at work
these feelings tend to be unexpected and are set going by events
outside the psyche. It is true that psi is sometimes operative in
persons subject to neurotic disturbances, but such people seem
for the most part to be able to differentiate in some way between
the kinds of stimuli that have released their emotions, to distinguish, so to speak, between the sudden, startling flash of psi
darting and zig-zagging like a brilliant, blue dragonfly into the
field of consciousness and the familiar fluttering of those "butterflies" in the stomach which arise from conscious or unconscious
anxiety. I heard the difference neatly summed up in a conversation between a grandmother and a mother, both of anxious
dispositions, about a child at school. The mother spoke of
worries about health and of the difficulty of being sure the child
was being properly looked after. The grandmother, with an
admirable briskness, said, "Well, my dear, is it a hunch or a
cark? If you are *sure* it is a hunch, act on it; if you are not sure,
then it is no more than a cark, and you must not torment yourself about it any longer. You have already taken all reasonable
precautions."

Among the insane, of course, no such distinction is possible.
Recent small-scale investigations seem to show that psi-phenomena do occasionally occur amongst them, probably with about
the same frequency as they occur amongst the sane, but in such
a jumble that only the most careful observer already interested
in the matter could hope to sort them out. A good example of
what such an observer can glean is to be found in Dr Lawrence
Bendit's thesis on *Paranormal Cognition*.[1] He describes an odd
episode in which he was called twenty miles into the country
one afternoon to see a woman suffering from violent auditory
hallucinations. When he asked her what the voices said, she
repeated the conversation at a lunch party from which he had
come to see her.

Induced psi-phenomena are those deliberately sought. Some-

[1] London, 1944.

one—oracle, medium, soothsayer, wise woman, scryer, palmist, fortune-teller—attempts to make himself or herself aware of knowledge only to be acquired through the use of the psi-function. This is a very chancy business, for psi seems to work best when it is unobserved. It is like something seen out of the corner of your eye that vanishes when you turn to look at it, like a child playing tricks; or again, like good talk at a dinner party full of relaxed congenial people, talk which cannot be deliberately engineered. All the methods used to set the psi-function to work are based on what is called dissociation: the lulling or distraction of the conscious mind so that the unconscious through which psi wells up can have free play. Many activities other than psi however arise in the unconscious—desires, phobias, superstitions, forgotten associations. It is by no means easy, under induced conditions, to be sure which is which.

Where the conscious mind is lulled, the techniques employed are usually either chemical or hypnotic. That of the priestess of Delphi was quieted, it is said, by the fumes of gases from the volcanic crevice over which she sat. The Mexicans used the sacred peyotl plant, the Lapps a fungus which produced delirium. The surface consciousness of Eskimo shaman or African fetish priest is rhythmically soothed by the pulsations of drumming, singing or dancing; that of the scryer is fixed, like his gaze, on the bright crystal which will reflect the secret imagery of his thoughts back to his eyes.

Where, on the contrary, the technique used is that of distracting and preoccupying surface attention by various means, there is an insidious tendency to rationalize and systematize those means, to regard them as if they had an inherent and magical significance of their own. This accounts for a great deal of that nonsense which so repels many intelligent investigators that they are inclined to dismiss the whole subject. Thus the Roman haruspices came to think that there was some fixed equivalence, as between map and terrain, between the colour and pattern of the entrails of animals sacrificed for prophetic purposes and the colour and pattern of future events; the for-

tune-teller ascribes a constant symbolism to the random sequence
of cards drawn from the pack by her client, and the palmist, out
to justify her procedures, claims that the future is recorded in
the actual lines of the hand like a page of manuscript in a micro-
film. Even the teacup reader may look for objects whose allegorical sense she believes to be absolute instead of using the
swirled design of leaves to stimulate percipience, percipience
which may of course be exercised on the most trivial events.

All these methods of attempting to induce psi—palmistry,
tea leaves, coffee grounds, cards, shapes of molten lead flung
into cold water on New Year's Eve—have much in common
with that used by the psychologist when he employs the Rorschach test to assess the personality, interests and preoccupations of a candidate for some special type of work. He asks him
what he thinks two irregular ink blobs are intended to represent;
the candidate, concentrating conscious attention on these intriguing shapes "sees" in them his own revealing imagery.

It would be interesting to know whether this test, intended
as it is for totally different purposes, has ever shown evidence of
psi activity. It should not be impossible to devise a series of
experiments based upon it.

Experimental psi-phenomena are those elicited and tested
under laboratory conditions with elaborate precautionary measures to eliminate all possibility of fraud, collusion, hyperaesthesia and so on. Experiments of this kind can be either qualitative or quantitative.

The former are directly concerned with thoughts, feelings,
images. They are interesting both to do and to read about, and
usually convince those who examine the evidence for psi without any preconceived idea that it must be explicable in terms of
hoaxing, cheating, coincidence, self-deception, or insanity. A
fascinating series of private, qualitative experiments was carried
out by Gilbert Murray and his daughter some years ago, the one
describing various scenes of history, literature and drama, the
other, who came in from a different room, stumbling almost unerringly towards a full description of them. Whately Carington,

in pre-television times, conducted a public broadcast series in which listeners were asked to "guess", sketch and send in a copy of a drawing being shown in the studio that night. This had some very interesting results. In a number of cases listeners reproduced the shape of the drawing but put their own interpretations upon it, so that, for instance, a pair of cutting-out scissors might appear as a geometrical study of lines and curves[1]; while others might send in drawings of something associated but not identical with the theme of the picture being shown (as it might be, a flock of lost sheep instead of the harassed Bo-Peep herself, or a giant spider instead of Miss Muffet).

Quantitative experiments are often made by arranging for percipients to "guess", under controlled conditions which totally preclude all possibility of their acquiring the knowledge in any sensory way, the order in which five cards will occur. These cards are usually a series of five designs made by Dr Zener, but for children pictures are often used.

Dr J. B. Rhine, of Duke University, North Carolina, was of course the pioneer in research of this kind. His first book, *Extrasensory Perception*, published in 1934, described the experimental work, running into thousands of trials, which he had undertaken with his students, in a number of whom he found psi, or extra-sensory perception (E.S.P.) as it was then called, in a marked degree. The book aroused widespread interest, as it was the first account ever written of the first attempt ever made to study psi in the laboratory, using the methods of the exact sciences both to organize the experiments and to check their results. A few years later, in England, Mr G. N. M. Tyrrell, a psychical research worker who was also an electrical engineer, perfected an ingenious self-recording electrical apparatus. The percipient using this had to guess, by opening the appropriate

[1] For an interesting assessment of the observer's part in moulding the information presented to him, see M. L. Johnson Abercrombie, *An Anatomy of Judgement* (London, 1960). It contains a series of drawings with the different interpretations placed upon them by different persons which have much in common with the Whately Carington series.

lid, in which of five closed and light-proof boxes an electric bulb had been switched on. He too found persons who showed marked E.S.P. ability. Dr Soal, then Senior Lecturer in Pure Mathematics at the University of London, carried out in the nineteen-forties a long and remarkable series of card experiments, with Mrs Stewart and the distinguished photographer, Mr Basil Shackleton, and after an initial setback obtained startling results.[1]

The advantage of quantitative experiments from the scientific point of view is that they can be evaluated statistically. It can be determined, in accordance with the calculus of probability, what the chance average of success would be, and from this can be assessed the objective significance of scores which consistently exceed this average and, indeed, of scores which fall consistently below it, which are psychologically extremely interesting. The mathematical techniques used in this work are also used to test metal stresses in engineering; upon their accuracy and reliability the safety of millions of human lives depend. There is no reason to doubt their usefulness in any field of scientific investigation.

The disadvantage of quantitative experiments in psychical research lies in the fact that, to achieve numerical significance, infinite patience is needed in experimenter, agent and percipient. If the last (who will obviously be influenced by the two others) gets really bored, the psi-faculty ceases to work, and no amount of dogged perseverance can take its place.

Psi-phenomena can also be grouped in accordance with their subject matter, though this may turn out to be an unexpectedly complex business, as the different categories are by no means watertight.

Thus, the phenomena can be labelled telepathic in instances where one centre of consciousness, human or animal, seems to be immediately aware, without direct or indirect sensory communication, of what is going on in another.

They can be called time-displacing in cases where it is clear

[1] S. G. Soal and F. Bateman, *Modern Experiments in Telepathy* (London, 1954).

that events are being perceived out of their temporal sequence. Such occurrences may be precognitive, as happened when, in Dr Soal's series of experiments, Mr Shackleton began to guess the card ahead of the one being shown: "not the one the 'sender' or agent was looking at but the one she was going to look at in about two and a half seconds time"[1]; and again in the Whately Carington broadcasts, when one or two of the listeners described not the picture in the B.B.C. studio at the moment when they were tuned in, but one which was to be shown on the following evening. There are also post-cognitive experiences; these appear to be involved in many cases of "haunting", where the percipient becomes aware of scenes in the near or remote past as if they were occurring in the present; witness the curious and well-authenticated accounts of the re-enactment of the Battle of Edge Hill in the Civil War; and the recent account published in the *Journal of the Society for Psychical Research* of sisters-in-law on holiday in Normandy together, who were awoken with a start from their sleep at a very early hour in the morning by the sounds of the D-Day landings of years before, sounds to which they listened, fully awake, for a long while.

This category of time-displacement tends, like water flowing into the base of a sandcastle, to crumble and melt away the older category of clairvoyance, a term for psi-phenomena in which objects and scenes far off in space or duration seem to be perceived directly and without reference to other minds. It is plain, however, that those objects and scenes must at some moment, past, present or future, be or become known to other minds, otherwise it would be impossible to record the clairvoyant's impressions and find out if they corresponded with reality. Then, if precognition and post-cognition are recognized as possible, many forms of clairvoyance might more accurately be considered as a form of precognitive or post-cognitive telepathy.

Psycho-kinesis (or telekinesis) is another category into which psi-phenomena may fall. This, perhaps the strangest of all, con-

[1] Soal and Bateman, *op. cit.*

cerns instances in which the psyche seems to be able to affect physical matter without being in any sort of contact with it. Either concentrated volition—as in Rhine's experiments in "willing" dice to fall with such and such faces upwards—or, more often, intense interior conflict, appears to have the power of moving, cracking and possibly setting on fire exterior objects, large and small, stones, furniture, crockery, coal, saucepans. Dr Jung has described the cracking of a massive wooden table at the moment when one of his patients reached a psychological crisis; and poltergeist "hauntings" seem frequ ᵢᵢy to be connected with the temporary, acute emotional tensions of an adolescent, who is clearly seen to be taking no voluntary part in the first disturbances, though later, pleased by the attention they attract, he or she may clumsily fake phenomena, in the same way as what is called a "physical" medium, in whose presence objects may occasionally show spontaneous movement, may feel that he must always produce results, and use all sorts of ingenious artifices in order to do so. The reader interested in the possible connexion between psycho-kinesis and the Evil Eye is referred to the Appendix.

There is some temptation to regard psycho-kinesis as a process reversing that involved in egg-sexing or dowsing, two activities in which a hidden physical object seems to affect human muscles irrespective of any direct or indirect sensory contact. In egg-sexing, a technique used for agricultural purposes by the Japanese before poultry breeders had succeeded in producing chicks whose sex is indicated by their colour, the operator holds over each egg a strong thread weighted by a ring which presently begins to rotate, from left to right where a male is concerned, and widdershins for a female.

With dowsing, the unknown presence of underground water, and sometimes of minerals, is signalized by the violent twitching of the forked hazel twig or rod held in the hands of a diviner as he walks above it. This diviner or dowser must be a person with a natural gift for such work, as specialized as a "born" musician or poet or gardener with "green fingers". Professor Yves

Rocard suggested in *Le Secret du Sourcier* (Paris 1962) that this gift might well be an especial sensitivity to the variations in electromagnetic fields produced by running water as by other factors. The independent experience of Mr H. L. Wendell, an English public health inspector who is also a dowser, fits this theory rather well. In a letter published in *Country Life,* December 30 1965 he said that he was accustomed to use his divining rod to detect underground field drains, and later found that it reacted in exactly the same way to the radio-active buttons then used for civil defence exercises, and never needed to carry a Geiger counter to trace them.

The mode of apprehending information about hidden material objects, streams of water, veins of ore, embryos walled up in egg shells, information unknown to other living minds, remains complex and mysterious; and here, perhaps, it is legitimate to draw a comparison with psycho-kinesis in reverse. There is some interchange between the living unconscious and the world of inanimate objects in both kinds of activity.

But to extend this comparison to the actual processes involved would be a misleading over-simplification. It is plainly not only the proximity of the water itself that brings about the movement of the fork in the dowser's hands, for many dowsers seem able to work just as well with a pendulum and a large-scale map as with twig or rod at the actual place concerned. Thus the dowser's muscles do not necessarily react automatically to some "influence" emanating from the water itself as the eyelid automatically reacts to a sudden flash of light by blinking. It may be that information received, possibly through more than one channel, is being brought to the attention of the dowser not through the projection of sensory imagery familiar in other contexts as the voice "heard" or the figure "seen", but through a perhaps more primitive mechanism, as it were a veridical hallucination of the muscles, the nerves of arms and fingers being provoked by the stimulus of this unrealized knowledge to produce as a reflex action the recognized symbolic gesture, the traditional signal, "There is water here".

Perhaps I may illustrate what I mean by an hallucination of the muscles by citing an instance[1] known to me where a premonition, a piece of precognitive psi, seems to have made itself felt in this kind of way.

An undergraduate who had occasional bouts of somnambulism at times of stress, but had no worries that he knew of when this incident took place, twice walked in his sleep from his bedroom to his sitting-room, where he awoke with a start to find himself staring apprehensively out of the window. He was standing by that same window a day or so later, talking to a friend in the quad below, when he saw the body of the man who lived in the rooms above him hurtle past his eyes. He had thrown himself out, attempting suicide. With the odd shock of recognition that accompanies a dream come true, the sleep-walker realized in that instant that here was the reason for his unconscious excursions to the window, the fulfilment of his fear.

Incidentally, this incident is interesting not only as an example of how psi can express its message in terms of muscular automatism, but also as an illustration of how ineffectual that message can be. The premonition was strong enough to arouse anxiety and to make the body respond to this in a symbolic variation of its usual way, but it was not sufficiently detailed to give any useful indication of what exactly was going to happen, so that help could be given to the suicidal student. Perhaps, however, from certain philosophical points of view, it is surprising that any instance of precognition should enable any percipient to modify, by withdrawing from his own share in it, a future event of which he is aware as a given fact, already whole and complete. That this does sometimes happen—as when a passenger, acting on a hunch, cancelled his reservation for that particular voyage of a steamship line on which the *Lusitania* sailed her last—shows how much more complex than has ever been realized is the issue between freewill and determinism.

It would seem that the psycho-physical mechanism involved in dowsing may be a more primitive form of that involved in the

[1] Personal communication.

muscular activities of automatic writing and painting, activities once frequently ascribed wholesale to the directing influence of "the spirits" but now seen as the work of the unconscious mind when the guiding, directing and sometimes cramping and inhibiting strength of the daylight self is fully relaxed.

Here, as in other fields, the enormous advances made over the last eighty years in the study of psychology and psychosomatics have usefully narrowed down the range of psychical research, enabling investigators to differentiate more sharply between the psi-function and the psychological activities through which it may manifest itself. It can rarely be crystallized out in pure form from the rich mixed currents of human thought, emotion, sensation and desire; but it is now easier to see what it is not, to distinguish between its activity and data, and the feelings and physical reactions intermingled with them.

There has been some tendency to assume that because it is now possible to plot out the psychological mechanics of such formerly mysterious phenomena as, for instance, dissociation, trance states and the automatic production of vivid imagery in verse, prose or paint, there is no need to investigate further. But to know how a thing works is not to explain why it works, or to understand the source and significance of all the material it works on and produces. It is true that these mechanisms can and do exist without any necessary connexion with psi, and that they can and do convey emotional and instinctive images and compulsions whose sources are well known or easily found out. It is also true that they can and do contain and express images and compulsions whose source can at present only be indicated by the word psi.

This colourless word has of late years been used to indicate whatever energy underlies that extra-sensory, extra-spatial, extra-temporal mode of knowledge and communication, some of whose protean forms have just been adumbrated.

The choice of a colourless term was deliberate. Its use ensures, as far as this is humanly possible, that no preconceived ideas generated by verbal imagery should direct, condition, delimit or flavour investigation into the nature and workings of this energy. The earlier "thought transference" suggested a telephone exchange. "Mental radio" falsely assumed that "brain waves" have something to do with "wireless waves", and that broadcasting and television, whose accuracy is modified by distance, can usefully be compared with telepathy whose intensity is modified by conscious or unconscious emotion. "Extrasensory perception" indicated no more than the acquisition of sense data without the use of the senses, and did not cover either time-displacement or psycho-kinesis. Worst of all, "the psychic sense" has sent all too many, investigators and theorizers alike, off on a wild goose chase after some as yet unrecognized physical or "astral" organ for psi. Descartes believed that the pincal gland was the site where soul and body interacted. Certain nineteenth-century writers revived this idea, and maintained that this gland was a "third eye" open on a non-physical world. Theosophists have elaborated[1] a detailed concept of a hypothetical "astral body" (based in all probability upon the body-image which every human being frames of himself) composed of "more tenuous matter" than that of the ordinary body and have fitted it out with cornucopia-shaped organs called *chakras* especially designed to receive and to transmit psi.

It is clear that verbal imagery is fatally prone to engender unnecessary hypotheses or analogies, those brood-nightmares of the mind. One may well hazard the conclusion that the workings of psi are as fundamentally mysterious as those of other commonplace everyday occurrences taken for granted because of their very familiarity. There is, for instance, that inexplicable, continual interaction between physical processes and human consciousness which from minute to minute all day long transmutes the impact of electrical waves of different frequencies upon the nerves of ear and eye into, say, the sound of swans' wings creaking in flight and the slap-slap-slap of water under a punt, and the sight of white may be reflected in the rippled golden network of the stream.

[1] On a basis of Indian thought.

Again, there is the interchange between emotional and organic states which can, on the one hand, make anxiety take physical form in a gastric ulcer or, on the other, relax tense muscles in the tranquil awe inspired in the mind by a still night of stars.

The interaction between psyche and body is incessant and complete. Each can affect or express the activities of the other in a generalized way. This holds good of psi, as of the other functions, though it seems possible that in certain instances a special part of the brain may be used, as Professor Eccles postulated in an article published in *Nature* for July, 1951. Here he outlined a theory that the mind is not identical with brain activity, but an independent entity in which the psi-factor is included, and that "mind achieves liaison with brain by exerting spatio-temporal fields of influence that become effective through the unique detector function of the cerebral cortex".

This concept of mind clearly presents it as something which has enough in common with energy in the physicist's sense to set off some form of electrical stimulus, though Professor Eccles was careful to say that the brain's sensitivity to this particular stimulus differs from that evoked by any other kind, and that no artefact such as an electronic brain or "thinking machine" could receive or register it. It might be thought that the electro-encephalograph, which measures and records the variations of the low-powered electrical waves generated by the brain, might produce some relevant information here, but the evidence to be drawn from it is doubtful and contradictory. Professor Eccles maintained that "only when there is a high level of activity in the cortex, as revealed by the electro-encephalograph, is liaison with the mind possible". This high level of activity shows itself in a specific tracing in such states of concentrated attention as are necessary, say, for mathematical calculations. Yet, though a mind-brain liaison of this kind may be necessary for experimental work with psi, information spontaneously received by this channel usually comes through, as has been mentioned above, in states of dissociation, or when attention is relaxed and the percipient is, say, listening to music, or thinking of nothing in particular, or lying between sleeping and waking in the early morning.

If the theory that psi operates *only* through a "mind-brain" relationship maintained in a state of intense intellectual activity fails to cover all the observable facts, so does the alternative hypothesis put forward at the other end of the scale by Fr Réginald-Omez, O.P., who concludes in his interesting but hesitant essay *Psychical Phenomena*[1] that psi is no more than the vestigial remnant of a primitive faculty, more important among animals and primitive tribes than in that reasoning being civilized man. A third explanation, most recently formulated by an Austrian writer,[2] to the effect that psi is the survival of a power vivid in the state of man's innocence, before the Fall, is again inadequate, in that it fails to take into account its presence among non-human creatures.

It looks, then, as if psi can interpenetrate all the activities of the living being, mind, emotion and instinct, getting through to the brain at moments of intense concentration, but also bringing it about that *le corps, autant que "le coeur, a ses raisons que la raison ne connait pas"*; as if the extra-sensory, extra-spatial, extra-temporal mode of knowledge and communication which is to be examined, were operative at all biological levels above that of plant life, from ants to eels, from birds to mammals, from household animals to man, patterning itself in accordance with the life style of each species, and reaching consciousness in our own.

[1] London, 1959.
[2] Abbot Weisinger, *Occult Phenomena in the Light of Theology* (London, 1957).

Chapter Two

THE PSI-FUNCTION IN ANIMALS

THERE have been a great many theories, speculations, proverbs and legends about the occurrence of psi in animals, insects, birds and fish as well as mammals. Psi is sometimes believed to play a part in directing the migration of eels and butterflies and salmon and swallows; and to underlie the marvellously co-ordinated behaviour, in routine and emergency alike, of the members of termitaries and bee communities and ant hills. It is said that in the days when rats were to be found in the hold of every seafaring vessel they showed evidence of some form of precognition by quitting at its last port of call the ship that would never see land again; and that the wolf separated from the pack seems to have some clairvoyant faculty in that it rejoins its fellows not by following their track by scent and sight but by taking a direct short-cut across country. And so on.

There are also innumerable anecdotes, whose cumulative effect is impressive, about the incidence of psi in animals connected with men; the cats that find their way home though they have been lost hundreds of miles away after journeys by car or train, the dogs that howl at the time of their master's death, the creatures aware of their owners' impending return, from the swan that used eight centuries ago to herald the coming of St Hugh by flying about the grounds of his palace in Lincoln, to the little dachshund Charlotte who, in the nineteen-thirties, unconsciously ensured that the painter Philip Steegmann should always have a hot meal waiting for him when he returned from his various voyagings, by trotting down to the front gate of his house and sitting there precisely four hours before his arrival, so that his observant Chinese cook always knew when to begin preparing something to eat.

There are legends of creatures whose appearance is said to presage death to a member of a certain family or calling; witness the "white bird" of the Oxenhams in the sixteenth century, and the flight of enormous swans (once observed by Edith Olivier without any previous knowledge of its significance) "seen" over the plain at the time when a Bishop of Salisbury dies. It seems unlikely however that stories such as these have any connexion with psi in animals. It is more probable that they are symbolic hallucinations in which the knowledge of such a death is projected and recognized; or in Miss Olivier's case projected and seen, but not understood, as might happen to a man who accurately receives a message in a cipher he cannot decode.

Ronald Rose's fascinating study of psi among an aboriginal tribe in Australia[1] cites a number of instances in which knowledge received by means of extra-sensory perception was formulated in a symbolic way, using imagery connected with the percipient's tribal totem-animal, which might, for instance, appear in a dream to warn him of danger, or tell him to go home because his father was ill. It is tempting to think that a mechanism of the same sort is involved in these English stories. Heraldry, which looks very much like a sophisticated allegorical form of totemism, may well have supplied the symbolic beasts. As late as the Wars of the Roses it was common parlance to allude to a family by the name of its crest, so that, for instance, the political couplet—

> The Cat, the Rat and Lovel our Dog
> Rule all England under the Hog

was perfectly comprehensible to those who heard it at the time. It should also be noted, in passing, that lively and lingering traditions survive, not only in primitive cultures but in western Europe, that certain stretches of countryside are haunted by uncanny animals. This is a different thing from the last flickerings of the ancient and widespread belief that some humans can leave their own bodies and roam about in the shapes of beasts,

[1] *Living Magic* (London, 1957).

Nest of the Termites from *The World in Miniature — Africa*, by Ackerman.

The termitary is opened to show the interior, with its fungus gardens between the central cavity and the outer surface, its brood chambers, store houses and galleries. Towards the base, in the cell she never leaves, is the queen, looking rather like a slim slug. If she dies, the co-ordinated life of the community — soldiers, builders, gardeners, food gatherers, nurses and those who sink shafts for water —is disrupted

Radio Times
Hulton Picture Library

A Soothsayer (The Flyer)

Drawn *c.* 1585–90 in Virginia by John White, an early traveller who
spent a considerable period among the Indian tribes

such as the man who turns at dusk, the hour *entre chien et loup*, into a werewolf thirsting for children's blood, or the black hare which, hit by the silver bullet that alone can harm it, disappears to leave the body of its tranced witch-double wounded at the corresponding spot. These strange survivals are still actual enough to frighten the twilight mind. Algernon Blackwood's stories used them well and, in 1956, a company of strolling players was thrilling village audiences in the West of Ireland with a revival of a gothic *roman-policier* French drama of the eighteen-thirties woven round the werewolf theme.

This territory is in the main, however, the hunting ground of anthropologist and psychiatrist, relevant in only one point to the general theme of this book. That point lies in the possible connexion between the apparition of someone living, dying or dead, and the body-image formed by that someone of himself; an image so persistent that in those who have lost an arm or leg it may long remain intact, giving rise, as happened with Nelson, to the sensation of a phantom limb. If, as seems probable, it can be established that such a connexion between apparition and body-image does in fact exist, there appears to be no logical reason why a person genuinely convinced of his nocturnal transformation into the furred, clawed shape of wolf or cat or hare should not form a body-image of himself in that shape and be perceived as such.

The animal apparitions that I have most in mind, however, come into a different and an even more puzzling category. It looks as if they had some connexion with ancient pagan cults, yet there is reason to believe that they are "seen" by persons who have never heard either of the cults themselves or of local legends that the creatures appear in certain places. The English story of a spectral black dog—Conan Doyle based *The Hound of the Baskervilles* upon a Dorset variant of it—forms a case in point. It is supposed to have originated in a Saxon or Danish belief in the Hound of Odin, the wild hunter; and it is widespread both in East Anglia (where the creature is variously known as the Colley Trot, Old Shuck, and the Shug monster) and in the West Country. If it were simply a tale told to frighten children or to add interest to a familiar landscape it would be no more than a stimulating piece of folk-lore, useful perhaps for purposes of archaeological research, but chiefly remarkable for having survived at all. Yet Mr J. Wentworth Day, who has done a good deal of useful field naturalist work on the subject, collecting instances as Cecil Sharp collected folk songs, has published in his *Ghost Hunter's Game Book* (London, 1958) a number of fairly recent stories of occasions on which the black ghost-dog "as big as a calf and with glaring yellow eyes" has been observed: "in the nineteen-twenties" by a Lady Walsingham, near Norwich; in 1921 by a startled young man of twenty-four; in 1946, in Essex, by a gamekeeper named William Fell, of Tolleshunt D'Arcy. In the West, he cites one case in which it was seen quite frequently by a man of sixty-five, a teetotaller, who drove a van regularly between Copplestone Mills and Torrington, and who, though alarmed at first, got quite used to the apparition. It is also said to have been seen—and heard baying—near the smithy at Down St. Mary and at Week Hill; and there is a well-supported story that in January 1932 it appeared "out of nowhere" on the Torrington-Bideford road, caused some frenzied braking among motorists, and vanished again. Mr Wentworth Day quotes a local investigator, Mrs Carbonnel, as giving reasons to suppose that the hound is "seen" at various points along a prehistoric track that runs in a direct line between Copplestone and Torrington.

Such apparitions, spontaneous, unexpected and unaccountable, are very curious. It may be hazarded that post-cognition is at work and that contemporary percipients may become aware in flashes either of some mental image which had an intense emotional content for our ancestors, or of some primitive rite in which the figure of a hound played a vividly significant part, as did the figure of the sacred horse, the Mari Llwd, in Wales. It is interesting that in England, Dogs' Paradise where Cerberus himself would be fed with vitaminized biscuits, it should be a sacred hound that walks the moors.

Plainly, however, neither warning heraldic or totem-creatures, nor post-cognitive experiences of beast-figures once the objects of numinous dread, have anything to do with the possibility that psi may exist in animals themselves, regarded not as symbol-fodder for human minds but as objective beings with their own lives, natures and habits.

It is of course very difficult indeed to estimate, appraise or define the working of psi in animals, and even to discover whether it does in fact occur. There are three main reasons for this. The first is that we know so little of their mode of consciousness; what they are aware of, and how they feel about it. The child's question, "Does the spider know he is a spider as I know I am a boy?" can probably be answered accurately in the negative. Though individual chimpanzees are said to recognise their own reflections in a mirror, it seems most unlikely that any creature but man is sufficiently individuated to be conscious of his own identity. But what, how much and how vividly the spider or any other non-human animal does know remains inevitably mysterious. The making of the web, an activity even more automatic perhaps than the movements of a woman shifting her weight backwards and forwards from foot to foot as she rocks a fretful baby; the sight, from the centre, of that web's lovely linear pattern, quivering on September mornings with enormous, limpid, prismatic globes of dew, less satisfying than the joints of lardered fly; the attraction of the small mate who, having finished the ritual of fertilization, is no longer recognized as anything but a quick snack, and is treated as such; what can we know of these events as experienced? What indeed can we understand of how a blue-bottle perceives the world from his many-faceted eyes as he walks upside down along the ceiling, with tacky feet that enable him to ignore the force of gravity?

The second reason is connected with the first. Animals have no means of precise communication with us. They can signal what they feel to one another; though those signals may indeed be given if there is no one to receive them (just as someone alone in a dark house may scream if suddenly frightened). If these signals are received by a member of the same species it will be with an intense and detailed delicacy of perception, atrophied in those accustomed to use such intellectual media of communication as spoken words, printed pages or mathematical symbols.

Humans can observe in a rough and ready way that, say, certain creatures yawn when they are sleepy or in want of air, make one kind of noise or tail-gesture when angry or alarmed and a different kind when they are pleased or contented, wash behind the ears when it is going to rain or, in another species, lie calm in the grass when the weather is to be fair. They may also observe that very few domestic animals can understand the human gesture of the pointing finger; cats and dogs alike may sniff or lick that finger, but hardly ever follow the line it indicates towards a bone or dish of milk.

Specialized students of animal behaviour can, of course, record much more. They may take the line of least intellectual resistance and formulate their observations, experiments and conclusions in the terms employed in the disciplines of physical science, using such thought-deflecting analogies as those of electronic stimulus and response, analogies which may insidiously bring about the habit of thinking of an animal as a robot. They may note without comment, say, that sticklebacks conduct one sort of prescribed ritual dance of courtship and cranes another, that hedgebirds are moved to satisfy first the gaping mouth and urgent chirp of the largest, loudest nestling, whether or no it is a cuckoo ousting their own young, while gull chicks are sensitized to accept food not by the call or presence of their parents but by the patch of red on the beak that opens to feed them, and will reject a real or realistically modelled beak lacking colour in favour of the roughest splodge of scarlet on a piece of cardboard. Others, like Lorenz, may combine an exquisitely detailed awareness of the nature and limitations of animal understanding with an equally vivid appreciation of the fact that these limitations are compatible with emotional sensibility.

Nevertheless, neither the amateur nor the professional observer, neither the scientist who thinks in electronic analogies nor the student who realizes that behaviour and consciousness are Siamese twins, can wholly understand of what animals are aware, or by what means they are aware of it. This leads to the third reason why it is so difficult to estimate the incidence of animal psi. It is that animals' senses are developed in other directions and degrees than ours, and that many of the sensory means of perception and communication natural to them are incomprehensible in terms of direct human experience. Scientific discovery, deduction and experiment have enabled us to have an intellectual knowledge of some of the occurrences of which they are immediately aware; but there may still be others of which we know nothing. Thus dogs, whose sight is inferior to ours, are infinitely superior in the acuteness of their sense of smell, and are able (as the blessed invention of the "inaudible whistle" shows) to hear sounds far beyond the range of ears which can at their keenest appreciate the squeak of the bat, vanishing into the void like a shooting star. Fish perceive the vibrations of voices or footfalls with acute delicacy. The colour vision of bees has been proved to extend into the ultra-violet range of the spectrum and they are immediately aware of the polarization of light (which we can only observe by using specialized optical instruments) and employ this awareness to guide their flights, orientating themselves with reference to the sun in a way which is not yet fully understood by man. They can moreover, by varying the pattern of their elaborate dances, give one another accurate and detailed messages mapping out the route to a newly discovered honey supply. It is almost impossible to conceive how such messages are formulated and understood. If we think of mime; of ballet; of dancing "Gathering Peascods" or "Hey Boys Up Go We" with small but infinitely significant variations of step and of setting with regard to the magnetic north; of gesticulation as simply made and recognized as we might make and recognize a smile; of the ideas of stimulus and response as woven into a pattern of infinitely varied traffic lights; of an automatic code of signalling built into the psyche; then, recognizing the significance of each analogy and accumulating the weight of them all, we might have some confused impression of what goes on, but we should not yet have all the truth. It is hard enough to communicate or to receive indications of much more than friendliness, enmity or the desire to eat, drink and sleep, to other humans whose language one does not know, although one shares their physical, mental and sensory make-up. It is infinitely harder to know what goes on in the lives of creatures who are organized along alien lines.

Nevertheless it may be both legitimate and useful to make a few generalizations about the probable quality of those lives. It may fairly be said that though animal perceptions are normally more vivid and often more extensive than ours, their power of standing away from these perceptions is almost nil, that their awareness is more general and less selective than ours, since it is unaccompanied by the ability to focus attention on single points to the exclusion of others (compare in human experience the generalized awareness necessary to the mother of a young family with the focused attention of a mathematician, blind and deaf to the distractions of the outside world in his concentration upon a single problem); that they live very much more by a pattern of conditioned reflexes than we, form habits more quickly, more deeply and more permanently than we, and react automatically to the majority of situations, having little, if any, capacity for choice though much for sensation.

Perhaps such a mode of "being that moves in predestinate grooves" can be most easily understood by humans if they deliberately imagine themselves as living permanently and completely at the levels upon which so much of their daily activity is indeed conducted: the utterly involuntary level at which one sneezes or blinks or turns, without knowing why one does so, to find and confront a stare; the level of breathing, eating, walking, swimming, activities which all had once to be learnt and are now known by muscle; the level at which yawning is "caught", or one is impelled to whistle a catchy tune because everyone else is doing so, or panic spreads in a crowd; and the level at which instant hostilities or overwhelming attractions are felt. It is not hard to realize that such an unwilled, unthought kind of existence is compatible with intense feelings of all sorts if we recollect the experiences of breathing mountain air, community singing, yielding to irrational anger, alarm at an unpleasant "hunch" or falling violently in love.

The extreme difficulty of examining the occurrence of psi in wild creatures, still more of attempting to gauge its extent, should now be clear. Nevertheless there is strong evidence that it exists, and some extremely interesting hypotheses as to its nature and working have been put forward for discussion, notably by the late Mr Whately Carington in his concentrated study, *Telepathy*,[1] and by Professor Sir Alister Hardy, F.R.S., in papers read to various specialist associations, including the Society for Psychical Research, and in the first volume of his Gifford Lectures, *The Living Stream*.[2]

With animals, as with human beings, it is of course necessary to look for every conceivable normal explanation of a phenomenon before admitting the possibility that psi may be at work. Where wild creatures are concerned, one way of doing this is to examine their behaviour in the attempt to find all the usual types of stimulus to which they respond and if—and only if— none can be discovered, then to posit and test the hypothesis that the unknown stimulus is given through psi.

In this connexion it may be useful to examine some of the facts of animal migration, such a familiar thing to all who see the swallows fly away in the autumn and hear the cuckoo calling in the spring that its strangeness is often forgotten. The eels come eastward from the Sargasso Sea and the salmon from the other side of the Atlantic, and up the rivers of England and Scotland to breed, leaping in curves of silver up the waterfalls. One generation of the Monarch butterfly migrates outward to a breeding ground, mates, lays eggs and dies, those eggs hatch into caterpillars which feed, weave cocoons, emerge as butterflies and return to the home of the parents they have never seen. With several breeds of migrant bird, again, it is the young, hatched and fledged in northern latitudes, who set forth first on

[1] London, 1945.

the long journey southwards along a route that they have never known. The older ones follow later. No one knows for certain how either group takes its bearings or finds its way though American experiments with a rotating planetarium, which could be put into reverse, show that willow warblers at any rate seem to have a built-in response to certain star patterns, which they keep on their left as they fly. The basic question as to how that response came to *be* built in will be discussed later in this chapter.

Numerous experiments have been carried out in the hope of discovering something about this faculty for direction finding. They have achieved little more than the establishment of the fact that it can be exercised in other circumstances than those of migration. Thus, it was found that the majority of starlings, swallows, storks, tern and petrels removed from their nests, taken in various different directions and released, flew straight home over distances of up to a thousand miles. It made no difference if they were doped during the outward journey. It made no difference if they were rotated, so that all sense of balance was disturbed. It made no difference if they were transported over a route that formed two sides of a triangle. They still flew the shortest way home.

Work done with carrier pigeons—who will fly back as fast by night as by day—seems to show that they do not use landmarks and are not aware of the plane of the polarization of light. There is still discussion as to whether they are affected by the earth's magnetic field. These three modes of direction finding are moreover ruled out in the case of insects, according to C. B. Williams, who in his study *Insect Migration*[1] carefully examines a number of hypotheses put forward to account for this faculty. He also dismisses the use of the sense of smell, orientation by the sun or moon (many species travel both day and night) and sensitiveness to wind, temperature, humidity, barometric pressure and the rotation of the earth.

It is hard not to conclude that some form of paranormal

[1] London, 1958.

cognition must be involved in this direction finding, though it must of course work in accordance with the make-up of the creature involved, as deep below the level of consciousness as we know it as is any reflex action.

If it seems difficult to imagine psi operating in this very simple and primitive way, it is worth reiterating that, as has already been noted, humans share with many animals, both wild and tame, at least one psi response which works precisely at this level. Occasionally indeed the experience breaks through into consciousness and is realized as "someone is looking at me"; or even, as travellers have found in instances where the experience has saved their lives, "some *thing*", leopard, wolf, snake. More usually, in familiar urban life, nothing more is felt and followed than an impulse to turn in a certain direction; and, walking along the road, or standing at a party, or strap-hanging in the tube, one's head moves as simply as a crossed leg jerks when tapped above the knee, to see that someone is staring, sometimes with interest or hostility, sometimes quite simply because the eyes must rest somewhere.

The impulse to turn is not equally strong in everyone, and there will be instances—as with waiters—when it is probably atrophied, ignored or directly resisted. A little mild experimenting though, say at a boring lecture or in a crowded canteen, will show that in the majority of cases to gaze intently at the back of someone's head will provoke a fidget and an uneasy turn and glance. This can also be done with sleeping cats or dogs—not to mention children who may be roused thus more humanely than with a cold sponge—and with birds in the garden.

I do not know whether it applies to creatures less highly organized as individuals than are mammals and birds. It would seem unlikely to work as between, say, human beings and insects living in communities, like ants and termites, because such communities do not appear to have much unitary consciousness. The individual creatures, each class with its own highly specialized function, seem to resemble standardized and automatically replaced spare parts in a living machine entirely concerned with self-maintenance, a machine in which a certain diffused awareness of the outside world may exist, but only in connexion with food, building materials and defence.

The peasant tradition that bees will not thrive unless they are told the news might seem to be evidence to the contrary, implying as it does that some sort of communication can occur between humans and insects (though plainly not at the verbal level). This and other traditions should be examined very closely before they are dismissed as meaningless. Bees which are kept informed of war and peace and the state of the harvest, births and deaths and weddings, are to a certain extent domestic creatures involved in human households and human lives; and I hope to make it plain when I come to outline and discuss Whately Carington's fruitful theory of how telepathy works, why psi in domestic creatures should be examined from a slightly different angle from psi in totally wild ones.

It will in fact be useful to bear in mind in all investigations of animal psi a general distinction between three sorts of animal group: those whose existence has no direct connexion with that of human beings, such as ants, and the blind white fish of subterranean lakes; those which have a sort of symbiotic relationship with man, like bees, pigs, sheep, cattle and carrier pigeons; and domestic pets, dogs, cats, budgerigars, whose behaviour is modified and whose consciousness is probably extended and sensitized by daily assimilation into the human way of life. Lorenz[1] has described, in this connexion, how one kind of dog has come to transfer to its owner the loyalty educed in the wild state by the leader of the pack.

Among creatures which live in communities—such as ants, termites and wild bees—the evidence for some sort of telepathic communication is considerable. The problem of inherited instinct, the drive to carry out certain activities in certain pre-determined ways at certain equally predetermined stages of the cycle of individual life, is not of course peculiar to these com-

[1] *Man Meets Dog*, translated by Marjorie Kerr Wilson (London, 1954).

munities and will be discussed in a more general context later on. It is matters of co-ordination and synchronization which are relevant here. What is it that will set a group of bees to manufacturing the royal jelly which will so change the anonymous larva fed upon it that it will develop not into a sexless worker but into a queen, potential leader of a new swarm, potential mother of a new city of "singing masons building roofs of gold"; how is it that another group of bees becomes aware of the need for wax so that they gorge themselves with the honey that their bodies will transmute into this building material; what impels the mobilization to sting to death the invading snail or mouse, and the waxing over of the corpse (too large to move away) so that its decay may not pollute the nest? How is it that the whole composite existence of the termitary (with its gardeners and warriors, nurses and builders, masseurs and bodyguards and civil engineers sinking those shafts for water which may be over fifty feet deep) depends on the vitality of the mature termite queen, a swollen white body unable to move from the dark tomb in which she fulfils without ceasing her function of laying eggs? As long as she is well, even though she is experimentally screened from half of the community by a sheet of steel, the work of the corporate organism continues in widespread, ceaseless and perfectly co-ordinated activity. But if she is injured, work is immediately disrupted even in the most distant regions of the termitary, as Marais notes in a description of such an incident in the last chapter of his book *The Soul of the White Ant*.

The hypothesis that the psi-factor is at work is the most plausible explanation of this instant response to the stimulus to order or chaos provided by the queen's condition, a response which can be observed at a considerable distance from her; considerable even by human standards, and much more so in relation to the size of the various working termites. This response is moreover just as vivid and immediate in that section of the community which has been cut off from her by the insertion of the steel sheet, a barrier which would quite certainly affect communication by sound, sight, touch, smell and, if properly earthed, electrical activity.

Marais and others have pointed out that whereas in mammals, birds, fish and reptiles the body is mobile and compact, composed of cells which fulfil their different interacting functions within it, dying and being replaced without affecting its continuous identity, in termitaries it can be said that the body is immobile, and that its component cells, the differentiated insects go in and out of it, also fulfilling their various interacting functions and also dying and being replaced without affecting its continuous identity. Marais cites evidence moreover to support the hypothesis that this static composite body is a comparatively late development in the history of the termite, which was once in all probability an unspecialized free-flying creature; that groups of these creatures grew up around their parents in sheltered breeding places; and that in the harsh surroundings of the South African *veldt* those groups survived best whose members most speedily developed an intensely communal life in whose service their functions became rigidly and exquisitely specialized, even though many of their powers as complete individuals were lost, the queen losing that of free movement once her nuptial flight was over and her egg-laying career was begun, the workers losing that of reproduction, the various castes losing those senses not absolutely necessary to the performance of their different duties. It seems reasonable to hazard that such a progressive atrophy of the sense must have necessitated a progressive compensatory development of extra-sensory perception.

If the communal activities of such insect groups are indeed co-ordinated and synchronized by telepathy, defined as a mode of communication independent of the sense organs of the individual ant or termite or wild bee, then telepathy as it operates in this field seems to have a marked likeness to two other modes of communication conducted below the level of consciousness; a fact which may suggest some useful ideas as to the workings of psi in different contexts.

One of these modes of communication is very clearly described in a passage from R. J. Harrison's *Man the Peculiar Animal*.[1] As this was written before the cracking of the genetic code, the author did not of course use the technical idiom in which this discovery has been set out. Plainly, however, the "chemical signalling system" at work in "embryonic growth" corresponds with what would now be seen in terms of molecular biology as the code mechanism of DNA molecules.

The communication of messages, signals or information is taking place continually in biological systems. . . . One can even argue that some kind of chemical signalling system exists within cells between the cell-membrane and the nucleus, or even probably within the nucleus. There is undeniable evidence that it exists in neurones and ample evidence that the cells of endocrine organs signal to various other organs and themselves receive orders. The whole of embryonic growth would appear to be similarly subject to control by some such system.

It is incidentally interesting to observe how well the use of the word "system" (comfortably associated with efficiently planned engineering) to indicate whatever controls the transmission, reception and co-ordination of these signals, camouflages the uncomfortable fact that almost nothing is known about that "whatever". It can also be called, in contemporary parlance, a "co-ordinating principle"; it is probably what medieval thinkers meant when they wrote of "the animal soul".

It looks, then, as if a striking resemblance existed between the workings of the psi-factor at insect-community level in synchronizing and co-ordinating the activities of the large visible "cells" moving in and out of their static body, the termitary, and the workings of that equally mysterious factor which synchronizes and co-ordinates the activities of the minute invisible component cells of the mobile and self-contained mammalian body. This factor, animal soul, co-ordinating principle, or "field

[1] London, 1958.

of force" in Professor Gardner Murphy's phrase, not only develops the embryonic structure towards its final form, but even ensures that in certain circumstances if "a cell be grafted from one part of one embryo to a different part of another, it will become, as required by its environment, a skin, a muscle or a nerve-cell". In the completed creature this principle co-ordinates all those teeming physical activities which normally never rise above the threshold of consciousness: the circulation, the transformation of food into body tissue, the mobilization of white blood corpuscles to defend a wound against invading germs, the release of adrenalin to supply energy in emergencies, and so on.

If it is this field of force or animal soul (each metaphorical phrase is valid and valuable in the context of its own intellectual discipline, its own idiom of thought) which co-ordinates the work both of the cohering cells of mobile bodies and of the in-and-out cells of immobile bodies, can it also be the energy that co-ordinates the communal activities of groups of warm-blooded creatures whose mobile bodies, though capable of individual life, are also members of a flock or pack or herd (starlings, wolves, buffaloes)?

In a fascinating paper, *Biology and Psychical Research*[1] as later in *The Living Stream*[2] Sir Alister Hardy gives good reasons for believing that this is so. Indeed, he goes so far as to maintain that it is psi in some form which determines the instinctive drives, the inherent behaviour patterns, of all animal species.

After describing in detail experiments in which a series of drawings exhibited at a given time in a closed room were simultaneously sketched by percipients at a distance, some reproducing the pattern and some the subject, he continues:

"If... we can definitely establish that impressions of design, form and experience such as" these "can occasionally be consciously transmitted by telepathy from one individual to another, is it not possible that there may be a general *subconscious* sharing of a form and behaviour design—a sort of

[1] Proceedings of the Society for Psychical Research Volso London 1953.
[2] Op cit.

psychic blue-print—between members of a species? This telepathic plan . . . would be a racial experience of habit, form and development open subconsciously to all members of the species, as in Whately Carington's group mind," which will be discussed later. "It acts by selection; external conditions being equal, those animals with gene complexes which allow a better incarnation of the specific plan will tend to survive. . . . I am suggesting a group mind holding the whole plan of structural form, and particularly development. . . . The mathematical plan of growth", in the embryo, and the young animal developing towards maturity, "seems to me to have all the appearance of a definite mental conception . . . a pattern outside the physical world, which has served as a gauge for selective action. It is suggested . . . that it is this plan in the group mind which indirectly *selects* those gene complexes presenting its best expression. It is a species plan mirrored in each individual . . . like one artist who is making thousands of reproductions of one picture—a miniature self-portrait if you like—but each time with a slightly different paint-box: the paints of course are the genes." . . . Whereas "the biology of the last century has been engrossed in the study of the pigments and their interaction as they are mixed in the painting, in the coming half-century . . . psychical research may show biologists something of the artist as well."

He quotes, in this connexion, a sentence from E. S. Russell, *The Study of Living Things*:[1] "As works of art are static organisms, so organisms are dynamic works of art"; and suggests that there are "as many species-minds as there are species", giving another definition of such a mind as a "unit of life beyond that of the transient individuals of the species . . . which develops as it goes along, building itself up from the unconsciously shared experience of all the members of the race".

Elsewhere again he notes that "the racial plan, telepathically linking all the members of a race, might gradually change as the

[1] London, 1924.

population was modified by external selection" and points out that "If the concept of the racial plan were true, then the old ideas of a 'morph', 'form' or archetype would not seem quite so quaint as we have sometimes thought them".

I have quoted at some length from Sir Alister Hardy's brilliant and original paper because of its startling relevance to a number of problems; and first of all, of course, to that of animal psi as it shows itself both in that telepathic relationship between individual and group which has been discussed earlier in this chapter, and in the apparently precognitive and clairvoyant activities of migrant creatures, leaving the familiar surroundings which are all that their senses have ever known to launch themselves into an uncharted void of winds and currents in the driving assurance that this must be done and that all will be well in an unknown and inconceivable fulfilment of their mysterious desire; that desire which is carried in the germ plasm and stimulated by climatic conditions. Considered in connexion with the human race, moreover, Sir Alister Hardy's concept of a group mind of every species "building itself up from the unconsciously shared experience of all" its members and telepathically operative in them all, is strikingly like Jung's concept of the collective unconscious of mankind. It may be noted in passing that in human experience information recognized as being received by means of psi is found to well up through the individual subconscious, which is believed to interact with the collective unconscious as does a tidal river with the sea.

Seen together, these concepts may throw some light on the doctrine of original sin, intellectually so baffling when it is formulated in legal terminology. It is perhaps more comprehensible if it is realized as a taint affecting the whole group mind of humanity, a taint "building itself up in the unconsciously shared experience" of our species and corrupting it; a taint open to and active in every human creature. Given that the "morph", the "form and behaviour design", of the race in which we are bred and born and conditioned was once wholly good and harmonious (and still indeed retains traces of its former state in the traditions of a golden age, of natural religion and of a natural law intellectually known where that of other creatures is instinctively followed), and given that the experience of its members can alter the group mind of a race, it is not hard to see how the human "morph", once distorted by the chosen activity of Adam, remains powerless to undo this past and ever-developing experience of its corporate self, and can only be altered by an outside intervention. It is fascinating to observe in this connexion how St Paul, formed in the discipline of law, finds himself using the names of Adam and of Christ not only as those of persons but as collective biological nouns, as when he says for instance that "as in Adam all die so in Christ shall all be made alive". He is speaking of the two morphs of the human species, the one unable to liberate itself from the distortion of the unit of life in which all its members are patterned, the other in which individual and racial being alike are transmuted in the mystical Body of Christ. An ever-accumulating pressure of evil experience and action subconsciously conditions every being born into the first, as to every being reborn into the second there is open the ever-accumulating "treasury of merits".

This is not however the place for a long discussion of the value of using biological or parapsychological concepts in communicating the teachings of theology. They are, of course, like all other concepts, inadequate; and in this particular context they are inadequate in failing to stress the fact that humans are individuals capable of choosing whether they will respond to the incessant stimulus of grace or lapse along the line of least resistance into the crooked pattern of their species.

Returning to the general theme of animal psi, the argument so far may thus be summarized: it looks as if psi in certain insect communities closely resembles that "animal soul" which co-ordinates the growth and functioning of fish, bird and mammalian bodies. It looks also as if both insect psi and the "animal soul" have some connexion with the "field of force" that unites the members of a flock, herd or pack in collective activity from time to time. And it looks as if all three might in these contexts be manifestations of some "unit of life beyond that of the transient individuals" of each species.

It is at the level of the flock that it becomes possible to study psi as it appears in creatures which have some individual awareness and are capable of some individual, if highly ritualized, activity; rearing young, fighting, searching for food. They are capable too of meeting new circumstances, in youth, with a modicum of adaptation; of moving short distances to and fro across the frontier between innate instinct and acquired conditioning, if only to the degree of the orphaned nestling described by Konrad Lorenz in *King Solomon's Ring*[1] which, reared by a human instead of a bird, grew up without interest in its own kind and in maturity danced attendance and hopeless courtship upon humans, like some poor mortal swan without a Leda. It is also in connexion with the activities of creatures differentiated enough to have both individual and communal lives that Whately Carington's theory of telepathy can first be fruitfully examined and discussed. Its primary reference is of course to the phenomenon as it occurs in human beings; but he also applies it to animals.

Carington accepts the force at work in telepathy as "a fact in nature", maintaining that there is no longer any doubt "that cognizance or awareness of events or objects can occur otherwise than by any sensory process or rational inference, and in a degree not reasonably ascribable to chance"; and he puts forward a most useful working hypothesis as to the way in which it works, a process closely akin to that of memory. According to this hypothesis, telepathy is "explicable as a kind of special case of the well-known phenomenon of the association of ideas, operating through a common subconscious".

He posits that mind and brain are different entities, so that "though A's mind has an especial relationship to A's brain, and B's mind to B's brain", and "both *brains* are localized in different

[1] *King Solomon's Ring*, translated by Marjorie Kerr Wilson; Foreword by Julian Huxley (London, 1952).

positions in space . . . spatial concepts do not necessarily apply to the minds themselves". It may be useful to compare this idea with Erwin Schroedinger's remarks in *Mind and Matter*[1] that "while the stuff from which our world picture is built is yielded exclusively by the sense-organs as organs of the mind . . . yet the conscious mind itself . . . has no living-space" in that world picture. "We do not usually realize this fact because we have taken to thinking of the personality of a human being, or, for that matter, of an animal, as located . . . say an inch or two behind the mid-point of the eyes. But . . . the localization of the personality . . . within the body is only symbolic, just an aid for practical use."

One may, then, think of the mind as related to but not spatially confined by the brain. Its content, in Carington's view, "consists in part of images and percepts, some in the field of consciousness and some not". These, together with ideas and concepts, are linked by association into what he calls psychons, so that "the mind is an organized system of psychons as a galaxy is a star system". (It may be noted in passing, though it is not relevant to the present argument, that this picture of the mind's equipment, machinery and stock does not include its user.)

Now some of these psychons are not peculiar to a single mind, but are shared by many; they are common say to a family, to a group of people working in the same office, even to a nation. Thus, for instance, Englishmen share a psychon in which the tune of "God Save the Queen" is closely associated with rising to stand to attention, a psychon non-existent in Americans to whom that sequence of sounds recalls the words "My country, 'tis of thee", which elicit no such muscular readjustment. In this instance of course the psychon is activated by a sensory stimulus applied to the hearing; but Carington contends that a non-sensory stimulus can produce a similar effect so that "if Mr Jones thinks of fish and has a communal subconscious with Mr Smith, they may simultaneously think of chips".

There is usually, of course, some particular image which

[1] London, 1958.

serves as a link between the two or more minds involved in any actual instance of telepathy. How this works may be observed in Carington's account of that series of experiments in the extra sensory transmission of drawings cited in Professor Hardy's paper to which I have lately referred. He pictures the transmitter, sitting at his desk and drawing "an object, O, say a jug. If he has put an unusual thing, K, on his desk at the same time, say a bootlace, then as he works he will associate K with O, and both with the experiment, X. The sight of K in the same place will later tend to remind him of O". Now, if we have a communal subconscious, the idea of the experiment, on which both transmitter and percipients are concentrated, will call up in the minds of the latter as well as the former the associated images of the jug and the bootlace; and conversely the images of the bootlace or of the jug may of course call up the idea of the experiment. Carington calls such evocative objects K objects, and notes that their use is probably exemplified in a different kind of way in what is called psychometry, where a percipient handles something—a ring, a seal, a lock of hair—belonging to someone unknown, and describes its associations. In this instance, seal, ring or tress is the K object. He notes too the possibility that in certain hauntings, the room or garden or building concerned may act as a K object; if this be so, the reason why only certain persons perceive the haunting would not only be that they had a temperament in which the consciousness of psi is uninhibited, but also that they shared a number of associations with the mind connected with the place.

Carington maintains moreover that individual minds or psychon-systems tend to become integrated, sometimes only partially or temporarily, into group-systems. In support of this he cites the well-known way in which a crowd tends to behave not like an aggregate of different individuals, but like a unit whose collective intelligence is much lower than that of its component parts; this is, he says, because in a fortuitous concourse of persons, only simple primitive ideas will be held in common, and telepathic associations will necessarily be at a simple and primitive level too.

Of such group psychon-systems, both in men and in other creatures, he writes that "if one had an aggregate of organisms that were identical, and living identically similar lives, there would be perfect telepathic interaction as they would all have the same associations". He cites a bed of oysters as an example of such an aggregate; but as oysters of different ages would be changing their sex at different times, perhaps an agglomeration of amoebas, who reproduce their species simply by splitting into halves, would be a more exact instance.

If, however, "the members of the aggregate were totally different in constitution, and underwent totally different experiences, there could be no telepathic interaction between them"; a theory which, if it is valid, puts paid to the horrid science-fiction myth of invasion by mind-reading monsters from outer space. "Telepathic interaction" should however "be at its most vivid where members of the aggregate have much in common, but display a moderate diversity in constitution or experience" and "we should expect to find the maximum of telepathic processes and consequent psychic integration just about where we do find them, namely among animals lower in the intellectual scale than man, but above the lowest forms of life".

It is indeed clear that any theory based on the data of human experience needs modification if it is to hold good of telepathy in animals, even if those are ruled out whose activity varies from that rigidly patterned by unalterable instinct to that capable of responding to changing circumstance through the formation of conditioned reflexes. Little, moreover, can be known with certainty of the mode of consciousness prevalent in creatures whose behaviour swings forward to oscillate between conditioned reflex and habit, habit which the individual creature can change until he becomes "set in his ways" by old age. It may fairly be said, though, that directly remembrance comes into play, however rudimentary it may be, the psyche must contain images and chains of association of the kind postulated by Carington; and that his hypothesis can therefore be applied usefully to all animals with memories, especially to those which can be observed to learn by experience through a process of trial and error (such as the rats whose behaviour in finding their way through mazes has been so closely studied), and of course to those whose activities have been enlarged by human training and are often reinforced by the affection which seems sometimes to produce a measure of true understanding, spontaneity and choice. Among such activities are the work of sheepdogs and of those Alsatians who guide the blind.

Writing of group movements among fairly undifferentiated creatures, Carington says that "no one who has observed a wheeling flock of starlings . . . or even a shoal of minnows can fail to have been struck by the extraordinary unanimity displayed. In the absence of any alternative we should have to suppose this due solely to the incidence of like stimuli on like organisms . . . but it is often a strain to do so in cases where no overt stimulus is perceptible and the density of the flock is such that all its members could hardly have sensed it simultaneously. To ordinary observation such aggregates certainly behave as if animated by a single mind; and since we know of the occurrence of telepathy and the conditions are favourable—an aggregate whose members have much in common but a certain scope for independent individual experience—the natural thing is to conclude that they are so animated". Since the writer's death, a good deal of new work in the field of animal communications has been published; but given that in creatures at this level his "system of psychons" can possibly be likened at least analogically to what Tinbergen calls "releasors", ritual movements eliciting a given response, there seems to be a significant similarity between the latter's concept of "sympathetic induction" of collective activity, Lorenz's idea of "mood convection" and Carington's "temporarily integrated group mind".

There is a certain amount of sporadic evidence, scattered and anecdotal but intriguing, for the existence of some sort of psi communication between human beings and animals living in a symbiotic relationship with them. The Moslem Emperor Akbar's curious power over flights of the palace doves, which are reported by two historians of his reign to have danced a kind of aerial ballet in response to the gestures of his conducting hands, may have been no more than an extension of the principle of the "releasor" movement. Nevertheless certain individuals do evince an innate power over animals which might suggest some sort of extra-sensory communication with them, a communication often, of course, supported by various quite deliberate objective techniques. Such individuals—lion-tamers, gipsy horse-copers—tend to be forceful rather than intellectual. Like that water-boatman of whom Belloc wrote that

> If the beetle stopped to think
> Of how he did it, he would sink

they work uninhibited by much care to rationalize what they are at. Indeed, it is the "natural", to use the gentle old term for the mentally defective, who is traditionally "good with bees".

The widespread belief that witches could "ill-wish" cattle and fowls might be dismissed as the purest superstition but for the fact that cases of a reverse nature are still to be found, in which animals appear to respond well to the ministrations of "healers". I came across the traces of one myself in Aberystwyth in 1945. He had a normal job of his own—something to do with domestic geysers—for which a little car was needed, and he combined this work with driving from farm to farm to treat sick animals. He was apparently very successful and much respected; and by all accounts his treatment was conducted entirely by suggestion.

Now it is an accepted fact that certain ailments in human beings, notably warts, can be cured by suggestion, whether that suggestion is carried out as it was by Tom Sawyer and Huck Finn in terms of sympathetic magic with stump water, or halved beans dipped in blood; or by a "wise woman" who prescribes certain rituals; or by a dermatologist using hypnotic methods. But human beings are aware that they have warts, and are also aware of the suggestion to which they yield; the process is a psycho-somatic one and the mysterious part of it lies in the mode of interaction between mind and body. It is however extremely unlikely that animals can have any concept of illness, still less recognize any name for it. It follows that no verbal suggestion could possibly set going a healing process in them as it does in human beings. If the suggestion works, it can only be through some form of psi. And it does seem to work, not only in the case of country healers whose patients are mainly farmyard animals, but also with the more sophisticated types of suggestion exerted by those who own Abrams Boxes and similar pseudo-electrical mechanisms which are reputed to work through devices which "tune in to the wavelength" of a drop of the patient's blood, and transmit "healing vibrations" through the earth. Those "treated" by such methods include hunters and race-horses. The only fundamental difference probably lies in the fact that the country healer may exert his powers of suggestion directly upon the sick beast, while those who use mystagogical boxes and "machines" exert those powers upon the sick beast through its owners.

Domestic animals living in a household and trained from youth by humans plainly share a very large number of sensory and habitual associations with them, and are moreover linked with the family group by strong affection; and, as Rosalind Heywood points out in her admirable study *The Sixth Sense*[1] telepathy seems to work best where a strong emotional element is involved. This probably accounts for the many and apparently reliable anecdotes of telepathic interaction between humans and pet animals; humans, who may be substitute pack-leaders or parents to their pets; pets who may be substitute or additional children to their humans.

In the majority of such stories the animal is the percipient. It howls at the moment when its master, near or far away, is in fact dying. It shows fear in a place he believes to be haunted; as did a black spaniel of my acquaintance, Judy, who refused to be left alone in the rooms in a house where people had experienced inexplicable noises and a sense of "a presence" for which

[1] London, 1959. new edition with additional chapter, paperback London, 1971.

there seemed to be no natural explanation. Or again, it behaves (as has been noted in the instance of the dachshund Charlotte) as if it knew that its master were unexpectedly returning at a certain time at which he did in fact arrive; this seems to happen with both dogs and cats, and in cases both where the owner is by nature or calling erratic, and where normal routine is interrupted, as it is by the absences and unexpected leaves of wartime.

There are however some instances in which the human is the percipient. Mr Osbert Wyndham Hewitt has very kindly given me leave to quote an interesting one in which he was himself involved; and for which two witnesses can vouch.

During the early nineteen-thirties, he lived in a house at Headington and owned a black and white cat named Mitzi, of whom he was very fond. He went one night to stay with some friends in London, and spent the evening in discussing the rights and wrongs of the Spanish Civil War. The discussion was heated and wearisome, and he went to bed late. Presently he began to dream that Mitzi came into the room, dressed as a volunteer for the Spanish war, and badly hurt. Her ear was almost torn off. She cried and sobbed and asked him to kill her, for the pain was more than she could bear. Not in the least surprised that she could talk, he tried to comfort her and told her he would take her to hospital; but she went on sobbing and screaming, and he woke up, in a cold sweat, to find that it was four in the morning. Rather shaken, he did not go to sleep again, and at breakfast told his hostess about his vivid dream. He had just finished when the telephone rang; she answered it. It was his housekeeper at Headington, who knew how devoted he was to the cat; she asked if he could come home early, as Mitzi had been badly hurt. She had come in through his bedroom window about four in the morning and had wakened the household with her screams; they had found her on his pillow with her ear torn nearly off. (He did go home, bringing a skilful vet; and Mitzi was cured.)

I cite this story out of many others partly as a well-authenticated instance of telepathy from animal to man, and partly because it illustrates so neatly what Rosalind Heywood calls the process of "surfacing along the nearest channel of association". The Spanish Civil War, with its volunteers, its wounds, pain, and blood, was vivid in the dreamer's memory; the cat's pain linked itself on to these thoughts, and its plight was stated in the imagery of that war.

Carington's theory, reinforced by that of strong emotional pressure, seems to illuminate the process involved in this and many other cases. It cannot, however, be accepted as final. It must remain a useful and stimulating basis for argument, elaboration and modification. Thus, for instance, Hardy's concept of a "psychic blue print" for each species contains but reorientates it; and it is not always applicable to those curious incidents to be found in Hindu and Buddhist traditions as well as our own, where wild creatures, birds, otters, seals, deer, wolves, even, in the case of St Gerasimus, a lion, show a strong and spontaneous attraction to contemplatives. If these are hermits, living alone in forest mountain or desert, then plainly they come to be regarded as part of the landscape, and their quietness, gentleness and calm must be reassuring; but these facts could not produce much more than a negative impression of habitual harmlessness. Moreover, they are not always hermits. St Hugh of Lincoln, to whom reference was made at the beginning of this chapter, was obliged to travel continually about his vast diocese, accompanied by his chaplain and various attendants; yet the fierce wild swan not only awaited his coming but would not be parted from him when he came, "plunging its head into his wide sleeves as if it were drinking cool water" as the chronicler writes. St Francis of Assisi and St Antony of Padua were always on the move, preaching, and were often followed by crowds of people.

This attraction differs in a marked way from that deliberately exerted and cultivated by animal-tamers (though some form of extra-sensory communication is probably at work in both instances). It is, that is to say, an incidental thing, a by-product of something else. There is no question, for the contemplative, of the willed exercise of power over animals for its own sake. Orpheus plays his lute not for the forest creatures but to God; and the creatures come to listen. The tamer exploits a natural kinship and insight. The contemplative living from moment to moment in the Divine Presence understands more fully with every breath he draws that he is a created and dependent being, finds happy peace in that humility and accepts with fellow feeling all other created beings made in love, rejoicing in their identities as in his own.

Here emerges that need to distinguish between three contexts of psi-communication which will recur time and again; psi as a natural and spontaneous phenomenon; psi as a faculty deliberately developed and used for ends that may be either good or evil; and psi sparked off by sanctity, as spring light makes the grass grow green.

It must be noted, too, that though they seek no power, contemplatives seem sometimes to use authority, as in the account of St Francis' dealings with the wolf that terrorized Gubbio; an incident which is plainly based on fact and is moreover very much in character, in that the public rebuke of the animal and its sorrowful dog-like gestures in the market place were followed by a request that the citizens of the little town should feed it regularly so that it might never again be tempted by hunger to attack them and their children. It would be very unlike a medieval—or a modern—man to spare the life of an extremely dangerous wild beast without good reason; and still more improbable would be the idea of trusting it, feeding it and allowing it to trot about as a town pet.

In instances such as these, as to a lesser degree in the relationship between families and their domestic creatures, C. S. Lewis's dictum in *The Problem of Pain*[1] echoes in the mind: "man was made to be the priest of the animals, the mediator through whom they apprehend as much of the Divine splendour as their irrational nature allows".

[1] London, 1940.

Chapter Three

AMATEUR AND SPECIALIST IN PRIMITIVE HUMAN GROUPS

THE fundamental difference between human and animal psi lies in the fact that humans are capable of becoming conscious of this as of their other functions, and that they can accept, cultivate, reject or repress it, as they can accept, cultivate, reject or repress the rest. (Thus, for instance, one may hear music casually, cultivate an aptitude for it, refuse to listen, or stubbornly deny the possibility of being anything but tone-deaf.)

Such a statement about psi may seem very odd to twentieth-century western man, end-product of three hundred years of the assumption that whatever cannot easily be classified, apprehended in quantitative terms, and interpreted in mechanomorphic imagery, is of no particular significance; an interior assumption projected in the exterior development of the industrial revolution, and reinforced and reflected inwards again by the habits of living and methods of working which that revolution brought and brings about. Yet twentieth-century western man's own ability to accept or to refuse recognition to this means of knowledge, flashing so disconcertingly across the categories of space, time and physical causation with which we are cosily familiar, has been statistically demonstrated by Dr Rhine and his colleagues.

They were of course primarily interested in the cumulative evidence furnished by their long, patient and scrupulously careful card experiments that certain volunteers were able to score, a proportion of "correct guesses" that was significantly, and sometimes startlingly, above chance average; evidence whence it was possible to deduce that extra-sensory perception was indeed at work. Their investigations, however, also yielded an unsuspected by-product. Examination of the scores recorded on work with other volunteers showed that while many of them seemed to obtain no more than the chance average of successes, there were also people who tended to score consistently and with a statistical significance *below* chance average.

Investigations[1] conducted into the views of these "negative scorers" showed that many of them had made up their minds that the psi-factor could not exist. The notion did not make sense. It was not intellectually respectable. Acute discomfort and insecurity would arise if its possibility were even envisaged.

It seems clear that, unconsciously aware of a high proportion of correct results, they equally unconsciously resolved not to recognize this awareness, and carried out this resolve with such a degree of over-compensation as to betray themselves. Uncle Remus-lovers may remember in this connexion how Brer Fox shammed dead in order to deceive Brer Rabbit: how Brer Rabbit, cautiously approaching the "corpse", remarked loudly and repeatedly to his children that though Brer Fox seemed to be dead this could not in fact be so, since it was well known that from time to time "dead folks hoist up deir behime leg and holler *Wahoo*"; and how in the end, hoping thereby to lull Brer Rabbit's suspicions, Brer Fox duly did that very thing.

In markedly unsophisticated communities, where verbal formulae are at a minimum, and the power of analytical thought has not developed even so far as to admit of differentiation between custom and law, there is no difficulty about acknowledging extra-sensory perception. It just is so; a fact of nature undeniable as a giraffe, or Mount Everest, or the green phosphorescence of soft roes in a dark larder. Its manifestations are mentioned with the same matter of fact simplicity with which, without realizing the full implication of her remarks, a woman might say today of her children that John has always had a

[1] *E.S.P. and Personality Patterns*, Schmeidler and McConnell (London, 1958).

marvellous bump of locality while Ted has amazing luck spotting winners.

Colonel van der Post's fascinating book about the vanishing Bushman tribes of South Africa[1] gives admirable instances both of a "homing" sense very much like that shown by birds, and of telepathy. He writes of his various journeyings with a group of Bushmen, that "Nxou and his companions were always centred. They knew without conscious effort where their home was. . . . Once indeed, more than a hundred and fifty miles from home, when asked where it lay they instantly turned and pointed out the direction. I had taken a compass bearing of our course, and checked it. Nxou's pointing arm might have been the magnetic needle of the instrument itself." On a hunting expedition that made a kill some fifty miles from the sipwells where the rest of the tribe had camped, he remarked, "I wonder what they'll say at the sipwells when they know we've killed an eland," only to be told that they already knew. He asked *how* they knew, and a Bushman named Dobe replied that "they know by wire". To quote directly from Colonel van der Post: "the English word 'wire' on his Bushman tongue made me start with its unexpectedness. 'Wire?' I exclaimed. 'Yes, a wire, Master. I have seen my own master . . . go to the District Commissioner . . . and get him to send a wire. . . . We Bushmen have a wire here;' he tapped his chest, 'that brings us news'." On their way back to the camp, long before even the fires were visible in the darkness, they heard the women singing the Eland Song.

To raise for a moment a curious side issue, why did the Bushman locate his "wire" in his chest, while any contemporary Englishman who went so far as to admit that he "had a hunch" would almost certainly locate it in his head ("I've an idea in my head" . . . "I can't get it out of my head that . . .")? This attribution is of course closely connected with the habit of thinking, noted in the last chapter, that personality indwells a man or animal "some two inches behind the midpoint of the eyes".[2]

---

[1] *The Lost World of the Kalahari* (London, 1958).
[2] E. Schroedinger, *op. cit.*

It is however a fairly new development. Some primitive peoples, as will be seen, go so far as to attribute the "hunch" to a spirit inhabiting foot or leg. Biblical writers tend to centre awareness in their bowels: Victorians knew "in their heart of hearts"; foreboding women "feel in their bones". It is possible that the unthinking association of the self with the head is due to the anatomical knowledge that the skull contains the apparatus in which the powers of perception, association, memory, thought and movement are centralized and co-ordinated. It is also possible that it reflects, as did the earlier associations, the importance attributed to a single function, an importance which has considerable emotional implications. Thus, the digestive system, accepting and incorporating what is given to it from the outside world, is essentially humble in its dependence on exterior powers and expresses itself in primeval terms, equating joy with fullness and fear with pain and nausea. The heart is less immediately concerned with physical substances which must be transmuted into the living entity; beating calmly in happy times, "standing still" at the shock of love or panic, "turning over" at some dreadful realization, thumping like a high-powered car in a traffic block in periods of anxiety and stress, it remains private in its cage of latticed bone and can endure or rejoice with a certain degree of secrecy. The self in the head, arguing "*je pense, donc je suis*", tends to argue further that those things not subject to its thought need not, for all practical purposes, be considered to exist.

These parallels cannot of course be drawn too far, but they must be useful in suggesting the difference between the contemporary point of view and the primitive point of feeling, and in showing why psi phenomena are more easily recognized from the latter.

It is human to try to fit experience into a logical pattern. Primitive humans, like the rest of us, attempt to do this. But the pattern into which they fit it is very unlike any of those generally accepted in the cultures of our age, though it has perhaps something in common with philosophical idealism on the one hand

and the tenets of Christian Science on the other. The contrast is vividly illustrated by Geoffrey Gorer's *Africa Dances* (London 1935). Describing his expedition to study the dances of West Africa, he wrote with an odd mixture of human sympathy and intellectual frustration that "if we are sane, all primitive negroes are raving mad". He pointed out that "in a community which has not been destroyed by outside influence" they *know* that the world is entirely spiritual; what we treat as the physical universe, bound by certain laws, and producing predictable effects, is to them nothing but clots of matter entirely neutral in themselves and only taking on the qualities of the spirit, whether human or inhuman, that inhabits them. "For us it is axiomatic that if you drink . . . poison, it is bound to disagree with you; but for the negro the poison has no specifiic qualities. If . . . a spell has been put on you or on the substance, then the spirit will make your body unwell; but if . . . you have the proper magic, a diet of this substance will nourish you." Again:

> if a man is hurt by a falling bough or drowned in a river, we speak of an "accident" but for the negro "either a sorcerer has entered the wood or the water" or worse still "the victim has angered the gods or the ancestors" and must therefore be shunned. Moreover "the negro's . . . idea of time is extremely peculiar . . . the present, the past and the future are inextricably mingled . . . most dream experiences are believed in as implicitly as physical ones. . . . It is my belief that negroes, without the inhibitions which our view of time and a causal universe impose upon us, regularly dream the future as much as the past, and as vividly, with the result that the ideas 'present' 'past' and 'future' have no meaning to them as they have to us."

This is a telling description of a state of mind still extraordinarily alien to our own; though perhaps not quite so alien as it was to that of 1935. Since then a number of experiments already described have demonstrated that there are persons who

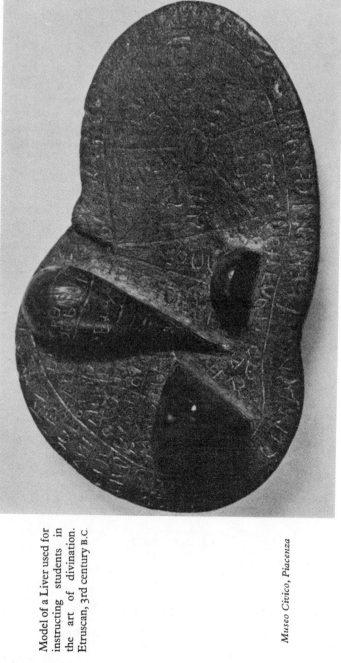

Model of a Liver used for instructing students in the art of divination. Etruscan, 3rd century B.C.

Museo Civico, Piacenza

A Great

VVONDER

IN

HEAVEN:

SHEWING

The late Apparitions and prodigious
noyses of War and Battels, seen on *Edge-Hill*
neere *Keinton* in *Northampton-shire*.

Certified under the hands of *William Wood*
Esquire, and Iustice for the *Peace* in the said
Countie, *Samuel Marshall* Preacher
of Gods Word in *Keinton*,
and other persons of
qualitie.

LONDON,
Printed for Tho. Iackson,
Ian. 23. *Anno Dom.* 1642.

Cover of a contemporary pamphlet, now in the British Museum,
describing the strange phenomena at Edge Hill

British Museum

have an ability for small-scale precognition; or "time-displacement" if that is a term with fewer philosophical implications. Again, the industrial psychologist's association of "accident-proneness" with an unconscious sense of guilt has bridged the gulf between modern ascription of damage by falling bough or rising river to chance, and the primitive conviction that the sufferer is being punished for offending the spirits of his ancestors. Moreover, it is possible to see that Mr Gorer was mistaken in reiterating that his primitives "did not recognize a causal universe". Plainly they did not think existence was a mere dazzle of unrelated events. They had the same concept of cause and effect as we have, but assumed that it operated in a different framework, that of a volitional rather than an automatic universe. As worked out in animist terms this assumption is plainly untenable; but that it cannot in itself be dismissed as pure moonshine, by even the most empiricist of thinkers, has been shown by Jung's recent learned, difficult and rewarding essay[1] on the theme of what he calls synchronicity. Here he acknowledges the objective existence both of the chain of physical causation with which our culture is preoccupied and of that given thunderstorm of phenomena—flashes of insight, gratuitous but apparently significant coincidences, rumbling premonitions, darting telepathic awareness—which provides the primitive with data whence he draws different conclusions.

Jung traces both back to the workings of a force he calls by a Chinese name which carries for the rest of the world no emotional, theological or philosophical associations, the Tao; a force which is presented as the First Cause at once of the physical universe, with its definite and predictable behaviour, and of consciousness, with which it is in continual and spontaneous inter-action. In the Tao, a name pointing to a reality, simple, powerful and elusive as water, of which no one can hold a handful, the Christian may seem to see scattered reflections of the Holy Spirit of God "mightily and sweetly ordering all

[1] *Op. cit.*

things". In some of its multiple aspects, however, the Polynesian might equally well recognize his own idea of *mana*, the power indwelling sacred places or objects; the pantheist the world soul; and all who have read Rudolf Otto the cold breath of the Numinous.

This is perhaps an appropriate point at which to remark that though it is advisable in theory and convenient in practice to separate out the subject matter of theology, of psychical research, of psychology and indeed of biology, in actual experience they tend to occur as a simultaneous mixture, just as eggs and flour and butter and sugar and fruit occur in the rich simultaneous unity of a slice of plum-cake. Analytically considered this stuff is the result of the assembling and processing of various easily recognized components. As tasted, it is simply and gloriously cake. I stress this lest students of any of the highly specialized subjects which have been mentioned should conclude that their data are being carelessly confused. There may in fact be times when it is necessary to lump all such data together simply because they are perceived in a lump, as cake. It should also be noted that among unsophisticated peoples this cake may contain as well as the ingredients just enumerated, others which may seem unpleasant, phoney, incongruous, or irrelevant ("foot of toad or ear of bat" as it were), and the most surprising beliefs and tabus. Yet we ought not automatically to doubt the authenticity of psi material recurring in such a context, any more than we should in our own medley of subcultural groups automatically doubt the authenticity of psi material supplied on the evidence of someone who threw a pinch of spilled salt over his left shoulder and did not really like walking under a ladder.

I know of no anthropological study of comparative psi; that is, of the psi factor as it operates and as it reaches consciousness in different sorts of human groups at varying cultural levels. Such evidence as is available seems to indicate that it is widely diffused, as common and as commonplace as the sense of smell, among such hunting and food-gathering tribes, living from moment to moment and from hand to mouth, as are described by Colonel van der Post in the Kalahari desert and by Ronald Rose in Australia. For them psi is merely one among many ingredients of quotidian experience, whether it is apprehended as a matter of course knowledge of the only possible direction in which the camp could lie; or as a "wire", a piece of definite unexpected information flashed on to the mental screen about events happening to people at a distance too great to be spanned by senses or signals; or as in symbolic form (like Pharaoh's dream of the seven fat cows and the seven thin cows, indicating seven years of plenty and seven years of famine); or as a message from the creature who is one's tribal totem (thus "I have seen (or heard) my rooster (or plover, or waterhen, or crow) and it told me of the death" of some close relation. The man it concerns often knows that "it is not real, you see it with your mind", but bystanders may also "see" it and think it objective).[1]

It seems likely that among those nomads—Lapps with their reindeer, gypsies with their horses—who own animals whose care and breeding demands a certain sense of the future, a certain ability to calculate time and to plan ahead, extra-sensory perception, though still vivid, will be very slightly less continuous, just because attention has to be concentrated on this or that piece of necessary routine and no longer flows widespread mirroring the world at large.

Here it may be useful to recall the odd but stimulating theory that one of the functions of the specialized senses is precisely to filter or focus attention and to concentrate it on particular objects, a process which makes the living organism more efficient at its primary task of keeping alive and reproducing itself than would a general diffused awareness. Parallel to this theory in its application to specifically human experience is the argument put forward by G. N. M. Tyrrell in his *Homo Faber* that too great and widespread an absorption in the general information received through psi may tend to distract men from the struggle to live, and that those who relegate it to a mental

[1] R. Rose, *op. cit.*

junk cupboard or glory hole where it can be safely disregarded are the most likely to survive and to train their children in the same psychological technique.

It should be added that such a training will not necessarily be a deliberate one, consciously undertaken: it is much more likely to be at the level of "Come along and don't moon about like that", "If you've nothing better to do, get some sewing but don't sit idle", "Everyone ought to have some handicraft hobby", and above all, "Stop dreaming and get on with your work".

This will tend to atrophy all inconvenient consciousness of the psi function except among those children in whom it is inherently strong; these may be set apart, tested, and trained as specialists. Even these may need some stimulus to "set them going"; thus Alfred Boeldeke describes methods used to induce the functioning of psi by tribes of Indians near Chuc Rurras, in Peru, in his oddly titled but fascinating book *With Graciela to the Head-Hunters*.[1] "The art of clairvoyance," he writes, "is taken seriously, and every tribe has its experts who are consulted. . . . One way of telling the future . . . is to mix coca leaves with lime and with a tree bark called chamayo, chew the mixture, spit it into your hand, shake it well three times, open your hand, and interpret the pattern made by the juice" (a technique neatly combining the use of a hallucinogenic drug, a magical gesture and the principle upon which the Rorschach test is based). This method was adopted when the clairvoyant attached to his party of tribesmen was consulted because a group they were to have met failed to turn up. After following out his ritual, the clairvoyant said, "the others would never reach us, and suggested that we should stop and force our way through the jungle. Before nightfall we should meet the other party. One of the men would have an injured leg and another a hurt back." The Indians insisted on following this advice and everything worked out as had been foretold. Mr Boeldeke also describes an Indian of another tribe, a Quechua who "special-

[1] Translated edition (London, 1958).

ized in telling the future from the smoke of his cigar" (another Rorschach-type technique) and gives an instance in which his verdict was accurate and unexpected.

It is when specialization begins, however faintly, that the real break with primitive psi is made. There may still be a general awareness of psi diffused throughout the community, showing itself sporadically, and recognized in such sayings as Homer quoted to distinguish between the untrustworthy dreams that come into the sleeper's mind through ivory gates, and are a jumble of imagery and wish fulfilment, and the true dreams that enter through the gates of horn. But there will also be one man, or a group of men, or more rarely men and women, set aside and trained to achieve and interpret it. Of course the primitive specialist in psi will not simply be a consultant, so to speak, in problems upon which precognitive and telepathic powers can usefully be brought to bear. In order to lay himself open to the reception of knowledge through psi, he will take steps to lose all sense of himself as an individual, to abandon thought and foresight and memory and choice: in so doing he will often sink into a state in which, like eel or swallow or bee, he will be lived by the morph of his species. Since that species is articulate and capable of imagery, what he perceives will be in imaged form, the figures of gods and ancestors will seem to speak to him, and the push towards certain activities will appear not as an impulse to be followed but as a command to be obeyed. Where the morph of another species, its life pattern modified by natural selection and reinforced by the reiterations of generation after generation, will produce psi-transmitted instinctive behaviour, the human morph, modified in any given tribe by the accumulating pressure of its collective unconscious, may understandably be interpreted as the will and wisdom of ancestral spirits showing their descendants what is right and what is wrong. The psi-specialist then, medicine man, shaman, angokok, by whatever name he is called, will become, among other things, a speaking link between the invisible dead, still exerting their parental authority, and their living progeny.

He is not, of course, to be thought of as a sort of chairman at an old-fashioned French *conseil de famille* to which a long genealogy of ghosts has been invited, nor even as the speaker who formulates "the sense of the meeting" at a Quaker assembly. He is a numinous figure, through whose mouth custom is re-charged with magic and tradition becomes sacrosanct. Since the morph of his species is distorted by original sin, he will not always be able to distinguish actual good from actual evil; but he will have these concepts, to whatever modes of behaviour he may attach them.

Roman jurists thought they could detect in the customs of the barbarian peoples brought slowly under the control of the Empire a common factor whence they could deduce the existence of a natural law recognized though not obeyed by all mankind, just as the law of nature is obeyed though not recognized by other species. Modern anthropological findings may make this appear somewhat of an oversimplification; but it remains true that in all culture patterns the idea that it is right to do one sort of thing and wrong to do another persists strong, urgent and distinct, however many variations there may be in the way in which it is applied. Even brain-washing can only deflect it. if one may judge from Dr William Sargent's terrifying study[1]; the idea itself seems to be ineradicable.

The primitive specialist in psi then will almost of necessity be a mediator between his fellows and the human morph, as modified by their collective tribal unconscious. He will also attempt to foretell the future and to discover the cause of this or that instance of illness or accident or death in a context of thought which sees in such misfortunes either a punishment for having infringed some prohibition or the result of witchcraft. This kind of thought, by the way, is not so very remote from us even now. Thus there was a case in the nineteen-twenties, of an old country woman being assaulted for her supposed "ill-wishing" of a neighbour's children. As a result of sleeping on the luggage rack in a train to Cologne in the late nineteen-

[1] *Battle for the Mind* (London, 1958).

thirties I was painfully enabled to find out that the German word for a stiff neck is a *hexen-schuss*, a witch-shot: and within the last two years I have heard a woman attribute the death of her pet cat to "evil absent treatment" on the part of her enemies.

The problem of how the psi specialist in primitive communities is chosen, trained and tested is of the greatest possible interest, both intrinsically and because it may throw some light upon the nature of psi.

Schmeidler and McConnell[1] put forward the idea that extra-sensory perception may be as normal in human beings as colour vision, with its wide range of intensity from colour blindness to the acute sensitiveness of the painter or, as they say themselves, from the level of the primary memory image to the extraordinary living vividness of the eidetic image. Whether extra-sensory perception is recognized and manifested seems to depend not only upon the individual's intellectual environment and beliefs, but upon the kind of person he is. Those who regard the world and its inhabitants as material upon which to exert their powers—technicians, engineers, administrators, organizers and "bossy" persons—are less likely to notice the workings of psi because their time and attention are otherwise occupied. Those who look at the world with wonder and acceptance, without any over-riding desire to master, classify, tidy and alter things and people, are more likely to realize the fact that they are receiving psi impressions. It seems probable, moreover, that children of this kind may unconsciously cultivate and develop psi ability as a means of compensation for their sense of inferiority in other directions, as Ronald Edwin suggests in his fascinating autobiography.[2]

Both colour-blindness and colour-sensitivity seem to "run in families": and tradition and personal observation support the idea that the same thing is true of psi-sensitivity; witness the tradition that those of Celtic descent are likely to display it, the Highland tales of "second sight" appearing again and again in

[1] *Op. cit.*
[2] *Clock Without Hands* (London, 1955).

a specific line, the African idea that "witch-substance"[1] is inherited (though it need not be used, and may remain "cool") and the fact to be elicited in conversation by anyone known to be sympathetically interested, that those who themselves acknowledge to having had "hunches", or telepathic or precognitive experiences, will often spontaneously mention that a sister, aunt, mother or grandmother has had them too (brothers, uncles, fathers and grandfathers less often appear, whether because they do not recognize having had such experiences, or because they do not like talking about them).

The choice of candidates to be trained as specialists in psi—shamans, angokoks, obi-men, medicine-men, witch-doctors, or whatever they may be called—has varied very much in different times and places. Many of the methods used, however, seem to accord with the ideas just outlined, that heredity, temperament, and individual circumstance may all play some part in developing the function. It may be expected to turn up again in generation after generation of some family. It may be anticipated in gentle, reflective misfits from an activist society. (Little has so far been done to investigate whether it is linked with any special somatotype; but to judge from personal impressions—a rash procedure—it seems in modern Britain to appear just as often among short, fat, emotional persons as in long, thin, withdrawn ones.) It may also develop as a compensation for a feeling of inferiority induced by the sense of being different from other people.

This last process should perhaps be outlined. It is very a simple one; a school child with flashes of extra-sensory perception may well ignore them if he or she is, say, a "fine athlete", a "good mixer" with quantities of friends, or a Meccano-addict who spends every spare moment constructing cranes and bridges. If he is clumsy and solitary, and has plenty of time to think about these flashes, and if in speaking of them he can create a sensation —as Ronald Edwin did in saying that a neighbour would die

[1] E. E. Evans-Pritchard, *Witchcraft Oracles and Magic among the Azande* (London, 1937).

next day, as die she did—then he will tend to concentrate attention and interest upon them. The same considerations are likely to apply to a boy in an unsophisticated culture who has little ability for hunting or weapon making or the arts of war; and, *mutatis mutandis*, to a girl bored with pounding mealie meal and tending babies. The idea that psi-ability is inherited must govern the practice of choosing candidates to be trained in extra-sensory perception only from certain families, a practice noted by John Lee Maddox[1] as prevalent among the Zulu and Bechuana in South Africa, and among many tribes in Borneo, Peru, Paraguay and Siberia. Among the Western Inuits the angokoks earmarked the children of certain parents, sometimes even before they were born, to be brought up as candidates for their ranks; each child was known as "one set apart" and conditioned from earliest years for its future career.

The hypothesis that extra-sensory perception is likely to come to the surface most easily and vividly among aesthetic temperaments not primarily concerned to enforce their will upon their surroundings is reflected in the selection (recorded by Edward Carpenter[2] and others) of boys of a gentle and feminine disposition as candidates. Carpenter quotes passages from Thomas Falkner's *Description of Patagonia* (1775) showing that the local "wizards" were recruited in this way, and cites a Russian writer, Davidoff, writing in 1800, to the effect that the Konyagas in Alaska also selected such children for training as what they called Achnutschik. John Lee Maddox too records this Alaskan custom, and notes that similar ones obtained in certain North American Indian tribes, in Korea, and among the Dyaks of Borneo. Among the latter's neighbours, the Sea-Dyaks, the principle of developing psi-sensitivity as a compensation for inferiority at other levels is to be seen at work in the practice of training blind men to be what are called spirit-doctors.

In other tribes more empirical methods are used. Maddox quotes from Mary Kingsley's West African studies a paragraph

[1] *The Medicine Man* (New York, 1923).
[2] *Intermediate Types among Primitive Folk* (London, 1914).

showing that in Calabar "every free man has to pass through the secret society of his tribe. If during his education the elders of the tribe discover . . . that a boy is *ebumtup*, that is, a person who can see spirits, he is usually apprenticed to a witch doctor. He . . . learns the difference between the dream soul, and the one in which *sisa* are kept" (a phrase of which no explanation is forthcoming; can it perhaps signalize the difference between fantasies and precognitive or telepathic dreams ?). In one part of Australia the Makjanawant aborigines say that if an orphaned boy can see the ghost of his mother sitting beside her grave, the medicine man will recognize and train him: and in another tribe in Southern Australia, boys who "dream of the devil" (whatever that means in the original idiom) are said to be good candidates.

Among yet other peoples a man feels "called" by his dreams; or falls into a sickness during which the ancestral spirits tell him what to do; or is marked by the medicine men as a suitable candidate because—as Maddox notes among the Kaffirs—he is prone to vague longings, deep melancholy, unaccountable restlessness, and the mood known to the German Romantics as *Weltschmerz*.

It is clear that young men and women such as these are likely to be Outsiders from the normal tribal life in which their contemporaries are absorbed and satisfied. They may often be mad, seen in relation to the standards of our culture pattern, and sometimes in relation to the standards of their own. They will find it easy to fall into states of trance or of somnambulism, in which the conscious mind is dissociated from the unconscious. They will be likely to project their inner ideas in the form of eidetic imagery or of actual hallucinations; though they may nevertheless be perfectly well aware of the distinction between what is perceived by the physical senses, and what is not[1]: as in

---

[1] Monk Gibbon says in his study of W. B. Yeats (*The Masterpiece and the Man*, London, 1959) that the poet's sister Lily, who sometimes saw very vivid visions, "never lost touch completely with her environment" but had a curious "dual functioning of consciousness".

the case Maddox[1] quotes from Powers' *Tribes of California*, in which a shaman of the Kelta tribe "cried out suddenly that he saw a certain murderer *with his spiritual eyes*" (my italics). He then told his hearers where the murderer was hidden and gave details as to how long he had been there. The information, which could not have been received through normal channels, was later "found to be correct". Such people will also be quick to apprehend and formulate the K-ideas of a tribal assembly. The majority of them will—as will the majority of other men—interpret their experiences in terms of their own preconceived ideas, formed by their own physical and intellectual environment, and assume that they are possessed by the spirits of their ancestors, or of the tribal totems from which they believe those ancestors to be descended, or of gods and goddesses, or even, in modern Voodoo, by that of a railway engine[2] on the local line (a really terrifying instance of being dominated by the machine, beside which the idea of the Robot seems to have no more than an abstract horror).

The training to which these candidates are subjected will develop their capacities still further. They may often have to be much alone. They must be chaste. They must avoid certain sorts of food. They must frequently fast even from that, a process which, by depleting the body's reserves of calcium, in some way renders the psyche more apt to perceive its own thoughts in the form of living images thrown on the screen of the exterior world. A person may even perceive his own body-image or *doppelgänger* in this way and experience a sensation of being literally beside himself if one may trust, in spite of its floral style, to the description written by Elie Reclus and cited by Edward Carpenter[3] of the training of the Choupan or aspirant to the office of angokok. "Disciplined by abstinence and prolonged vigils . . . he must learn to endure pain stoically and to subdue his bodily desires. . . . He must be silent. . . . He courts

[1] *Op. cit.*
[2] Maya Deren, *Divine Horsemen: The Living Gods of Haiti* (London, 1953).
[3] *Op. cit.*

solitude. He must absorb . . . the splendours of the aurora borealis, that ardently sought occasion for 'drinking in the light' " until at last he sees "his own genius which says 'Behold me, what does thou desire?' Uniting himself with the Double from beyond the grave, the soul of the angokok can quit the body at will, and sail through the universe" seeking "the knowledge of all mysteries that they may be revealed to those who have remained mortal".

Various techniques of dissociation may be taught and their success is taken to prove the sacredness of the object or method employed. These include fixed gazing at a narwhal tooth, listening to the reiteration of a single note or rhythmic chord of music, dancing and the use of drugs, eaten or drunk or rubbed into the skin in ointment form (these last seem to have been used in Europe by members of witch covens as late as the six-teenth century). In Arizona "concoctions of datura" were con-sumed, in Mexico peyotl or coca, among the Samoyeds a poisonous toadstool and, in the more familiar cult of Dionysos, wine. *In vino veritas*; and perhaps also *in peyotl*. Among the procession of archetypal images, and personified ideas and emo-tions streaming with fearful vividness across the subject's sky, flashes of psi may well have played their part.

In many areas of the world, the long training culminated in an ordeal or series of ordeals. Maddox writes that among the Tshi-speaking peoples of Africa a candidate had to do a success-ful fire-walk over hot embers[1]; had to show publicly that he was possessed by a god (throwing a fit was considered an adequate proof of this); and had to make predictions which were even-tually fulfilled. Sometimes these showed genuine precognition, but a formula such as, "If the gods do not intervene there will soon be sickness," was often employed to the satisfaction of all

[1] This phenomenon has been watched by trained observers. Explana-tions of how it is done range from the use of some form of protective ointment to that of hypnotic suggestion. The latter has certainly been used to the reverse effect in modern civilization, causing the formation of blisters in a hypnotized patient told that he was being touched by a red-hot poker.

concerned. Evans-Pritchard notes among the Azande that a public burial formed part of the initiation ceremonies. He also notes that, though the witch doctors did from time to time succeed in producing genuinely precognitive dreams, they were considered to be less reliable, on the whole, than the "oracles", which included a "rubbing board" of which questions were asked and whose simple mechanism slid or stuck for yes or no.

Human beings seem to be profoundly reluctant to acknowledge the existence of psi as one of their own functions. They prefer to attribute its workings, as in this instance, to a machine operated at a somnambulist level by their own muscles or to a "message" mysteriously received from some exterior entity (compare the early attribution of "falling in love" to the wounds caused by "Cupid's arrows", which were not always an elegant literary convention by any means). They will even, on occasion, believe that paranormal knowledge is conveyed to them by a "ghost" inhabiting a part of their own bodies: witness Peter Freuchen's[1] description of how Anawree, an Eskimo girl travelling with his party in the Arctic, consulted her "foot-ghost". She *said* her method was to tie a string round her foot and ask it a question. If the answer were yes, she could lift her foot; if it were no, no power on earth could raise it from the ground. In this particular instance, however, she divined—correctly—that a murder had been committed in the wild territory through which they were to pass; and this without asking her foot any questions at all. All that happened was that "she could not get her foot off the ground, and she said she could tell by this that someone had been killed". It looks as if a psi-experience had flashed into her mind, as the answer to a sum does, without the preliminary stages having had to be worked out.

Elsewhere[2] he mentions a professional fortune teller, old Asivak, who had a more elaborate method. She used to tie her right foot with string, sing magic songs, and lift the bound foot

[1] *Arctic Adventure*, English edition (London, 1935).
[2] *It's All Adventure*, English edition (London, 1953).

to communicate with a leg spirit, which would tell her with accuracy when the expected steamer would arrive. (She was put out of business by the radio.) Though Peter Freuchen is a popular writer, his accounts of such processes are borne out by those of more scientific observers. Thus Maddox refers to a similar process used for medical divining; here the "ghost" was in the head of a man. The head was bound with a thong, the man lay down by the patient, and the angokok asked him leading questions about the disease. If the answer were yes, he could not lift his head, if no, he could.

Even in our own time and culture sayings and half beliefs survive to illustrate this curious reference to the feelings or reactions of some bodily area, as if it could itself receive and convey some simplified message. Thus, if both ears "burn" "someone is talking about you"; if one alone, then either someone specific is indicated, or something specific is being said; "left for your lover, right for your mother" or "left for love and right for spite". Again, an irritation of the lining of the nose "makes" the Azande sneeze once if people are speaking well of him, and twice if they are speaking ill; while it compels the Dane to "sneeze to the truth" of some remark. It is of course quite possible and even probable that the psi-function may from time to time work through some psycho-somatic mechanism, attracting conscious attention by operating a generally accepted code of symbolic physical signals. If the skin of neck and face can reflect the upsurge of anger or embarrassment or joy by becoming hot and red in a blush, there is no reason why the skin of the ears should not communicate to consciousness the realization of some emotional stimulus received by way of psi. If the eyes can dazzle with tears at feelings unexpectedly aroused by something sensorily perceived—the hearing of four lines of verse, the sight of a small boy on horseback—why should not the nose be the site of the same sort of reflex action, of a rather more explosive variety, at equally unexpected feelings induced by way of extra-sensory perception?

This rough sketch may serve to show something of the different ways in which primitive peoples choose, train and test their psi-specialists, in so far as their capacity for receiving and formulating experience, including psi-experience, welling up through the subconscious mind is concerned; that is, in so far as they can make themselves passive and receptive. What is, and remains, very much more mysterious is whether they can in fact be trained to use the psi-function deliberately and actively; and if so how this is done.

In our culture interest in psi, both in spontaneous cases and in experimental work, has mainly been focused upon the percipient, the person who becomes aware of telepathic or precognitive impressions. Very much less attention has been devoted to the "agent", the person who is "seen" or "heard" at a moment of crisis, or who conducts large-scale tests with drawings or cards or dice. Professor Gardner Murphy and others have argued that telepathy is closely connected with human relationships and that spontaneous instances are most likely to occur between people linked by such strong emotional ties as exist between lover and lover, husband and wife, twin and twin, mother and child (though it must be acknowledged that except in the first instance all these pairs are likely to have the associations of daily life in common, associations which, as has already been shown, are in themselves likely to facilitate telepathy). Evidence has also been adduced to show that certain kinds of personality are more successful than others as "agents" in carrying out experimental work; so much so that the scoring rate of percipients may drop significantly when Mr B takes over from Mr A, even though this fact is not disclosed to them. It does not however look as if success in this capacity demanded qualities other than those necessary for success in working with any other kind of human group—office department, factory section, youth club—where morale and efficiency have been shown by various studies in management to depend very largely upon the balance, warmth, sense, sympathy and enthusiasm of the man in charge. There is no hint of any special ability for psi transmission in itself.

Yet certain data exist from which it is permissible to deduce that psi activity—as distinct from receptivity—can deliberately be set going. Where unpremeditated telepathy is concerned, of course, the agent, ill, or wounded, or in mortal danger, may be full of longing for the percipient or even call a name aloud; but he does not deliberately focus his will upon arousing attention by means of psi. However, cases are known in which, say a husband unexpectedly stranded in a country town has succeeded in "getting it through" to his wife, then inaccessibly driving a car in the opposite direction, that she must turn, drive back and pick him up.[1] There are also one or two instances on record in which A in one place has "concentrated" on "appearing to" B in another, and in which both parties have promptly, separately and independently written down experiences which subsequent comparison has shown to tally.

The question of psycho-kinesis is especially relevant here. It will be remembered that the unaccountable movement of objects—stones, saucepan lids, furniture, crockery, shoehorns—in poltergeist hauntings has been attributed to a sort of explosion of nervous energy among adolescents and unsophisticated people in a state of severe psychological conflict; an explosion able in some unexplained way to affect the material world. These explosions often alarm those in whom they originate, and can neither be repressed nor reproduced by the normal exertion of the will; witness the fact that when the alarm wears off and the centre of the haunting begins to enjoy the excitement he is causing, and tries to organize a fresh series of phenomena, his efforts achieve no more than a collection of very obvious counterfeits. The process, whatever it may be, seems to lie as irrevocably deep beneath the level of conscious control as do those of circulation, heat-regulation and digestion.

Yet some of the traditional Yoga techniques of India are aimed at bringing just these processes under control; and it is credibly reported that those who use them do from time to time achieve some measure of success. It is not impossible that a

Rosalind Heywood, *The Infinite Hive,* London, 1964.

similar technique may serve to evoke and direct psycho-kinetic activity.

We should perhaps recall in this connexion the odd and disturbing positive results in Rhine's carefully devised and controlled experiments with "willing" the fall of dice. The curve of scoring results among the successful subjects (rising fairly rapidly to a peak and declining if the experiment were continued beyond a point at which boredom and fatigue set in) was not only very like that unexpectedly obtained in the card experiments for telepathy, clairvoyance and precognition (unexpectedly, because it might have been thought that practice would make perfect); it also tallied with all the proverbial sayings about "beginners' luck" in games of chance.

It looks, then, as if active psi, the willed transmission of telepathic impressions and even the willed evocation of psycho-kinetic phenomena, is possible, at any rate in theory. There is little definite evidence as to whether any method of doing so was ever discovered and taught among primitive human groups; and if so what it was, and in what grotesque terms it was rationalized. Perhaps the successful "rain-makers" sporadically reported by western explorers may have been acquainted with it; it is impossible to tell without a far greater knowledge of climate, weather signs and the possibilities of coincidence than is ever likely to be available. A recent European claim to be able to dispel cumulus clouds by an act of the will, a claim backed by definite records, was reduced to an appropriate nebulosity by the simple observation that such clouds tend to disperse naturally in a fairly short time.

The curious seventeenth-century English story of the Drummer of Tedworth may also possibly illustrate the workings of "active" psi, as misused by a man with a grudge; but it sheds no light upon the methods employed, except to imply that they included suggestion.

It will be remembered that a beggar playing a drum was sent to prison as a "rogue and vagabond" by the local justice of the peace, Mr Mompesson, who added insult to injury by confiscating the drum. Its owner vowed vengeance in court; and sure enough Mr Mompesson's house was haunted, over the precise period of the jail sentence by a particularly alarming and unpleasant poltergeist whose activities included drumming. The case is well-attested. It was investigated at the time, in accordance with common-sense standards and with a keen suspicion that someone must be playing tricks, by sensible and responsible people; and, unless it is felt that however able, respectable and numerous the witnesses may be such occurrences must *a priori* be rejected as impossible, it does appear to have been paranormal in some way.

There are a number of explanations besides that of deliberate fraud. One is that the Drummer possessed remarkable powers of direct suggestion, which he exerted upon Mr Mompesson in open court and which Mr Mompesson subsequently transmitted to his household, his family and his guests. Highly suggestible persons however rarely become J.P.s. Another might be that the Drummer had, and exercised, some technique of conveying suggestion telepathically, that Mr Mompesson's little girls, who were of poltergeist-prone ages, acted as recipients, and that their subsequent fear and conflict exploded in some form of psycho-kinesis. Again, it might be thought—though the idea is profoundly unacceptable—that he had some active and controllable psycho-kinetic energy of his own.

Was he a gypsy? Had he any traditional knowledge of the use of drumming in primitive rituals? Nothing is on record.

Chapter Four

ORGANIZED DIVINATION: THE ANCIENT MEDITERRANEAN CULTS

SPECIALIZATION in psi must further increase where communities abandon nomadic life and settle down to agriculture, simply because this way of making a living, with its regular routine of ploughing, sowing, reaping, storing crops and setting seed aside, demands more forethought, more planning and more closely woven patterns and ideas of time past, present and to come, and of space and distance. Many people— especially shepherds—will still have the kind of unhurried lives in which it is easy to become conscious of psi-experience; but not so many as before. The shadow of "it is later than you think" steals into sight: the domination of the seasons adumbrates the domination of the clock.

The life of urban groups chiefly dependent on trade and manufacture must necessarily speed up the process of specialization further still, even when its mechanics are no more complex than those of the handloom and the potter's wheel. It is not only that still more forethought and planning become necessary, that the mapping out of hours and miles is done in greater detail on a smaller scale. It is that a division of functions is establishing itself. Although there will still be plenty of amateurs about, the deliberate cultivation and exercise of psi will usually be delegated to the priests of the official cult, who will claim not only the privilege of serving the local gods, but also the power of discovering whether this or that project finds favour with them, and if so at what day or hour it should be begun; the power of interpreting dreams; and the ability to tell in what way a sick man has incurred the guilt for which his disease "must" be a punishment. They may also claim to be healers, as the priests of Aesculapius did. In other times and places this particular activity may be carried on by a group of what the French archaeologist Albert Champdor calls "professional magicians"[1]; though it is plain that they were benevolent rather than otherwise. He quotes from records still extant in the remains of the library of Ashurbanipal to show that in the Assyrian civilization of the seventh century before Christ, the men known as Omen-Priests were dedicated solely to the service of the temples and to the attempt to read from natural portents the will of the gods, leaving it to the magicians to treat the sick and to tell individual fortunes by gazing at the movements of drops of oil thrown into a bucket of water (a very large-scale precursor of prognostication by tea leaves, which can of course be no more than three centuries old in this country. It would be interesting to know whether any similar means of prognostication were used before that; and who began tea-leaf divining, and how. It cannot have been "the Jesuit who came from China —*Anno* 1664" and "told Mr Waller"[2] how to make tea with eggs in it; and it seems very unlikely that

> Great Anna, whom three realms obey
> who sometimes counsel takes, and sometimes tay

combined these operations).

Both in pre-conquest Mexico and in ancient Egypt, moreover, the interpretation of dreams, whose importance was felt but whose meaning was hidden in cryptic imagery, seems to have been undertaken as much by laymen with a natural talent for it as by priests; witness Joseph's interpretation of the precognitive dreams of Pharaoh's chief butler and baker, who were in the same prison as he, and his subsequent interpretation of Pharaoh's own. The butler dreamed of a vine with three branches, which budded, flowered and bore fruit as he looked at them; that he crushed a bunch of the grapes into Pharaoh's cup,

---

[1] *Babylon*, English edition (London, 1958).
[2] Oriana Haynes, *Cooking and Curing* (London, 1937).

which he was holding; that the juice turned into wine; and that he hastened into the royal palace and gave it to Pharaoh. The baker dreamed that he was walking along in the open air with three baskets on his head (like a porter at Covent Garden). In the top basket were loaves he had baked for Pharaoh's table. As he walked, the day darkened, and birds of prey came swooping down on the loaves and tore them up and ate them. Joseph had to tell him that in three days he would be taken out of prison and hanged, and the kites would pick his bones. The butler, however, would be set free and restored to favour in three days (symbolized by the vine branches for him as by the baskets for the unfortunate baker; each dreamed in the idiom of his own work). Both interpretations proved to be right; but for two years the butler forgot all about Joseph's request that he should ask Pharaoh to set him free. Then, when Pharaoh himself had his urgent dreams of wheatsheaves and cattle and, obviously unsatisfied by the explanations worked out by his official advisers, asked if anyone knew of a naturally-talented dream interpreter, Joseph was remembered and came into his own.

Dream interpreters were indeed very popular in ancient Egypt. The rich, like Pharaoh, consulted either official specialists or talented amateurs. Poorer people had to avail themselves of the written works of various experts. The Chester-Beatty papyrus III,[1] for instance, contains cut-and-dried formulae for dream interpretation drawn up by the followers of the god Horus, son of Isis and Osiris. There was once a companion collection compiled by the followers of the god Set. This, however, has been lost, and there is no way of telling whether these differed from one another as fundamentally as would in our own day the interpretations of, say, the followers of Freud and the followers of Adler. It seems probable, though, if one may judge by the fact that by the time of Herodotus there were in Egypt no less than seven centres of dream-interpretation, each with a

[1] P. Montet, *Everyday Life in Ancient Egypt*, English edition (London, 1958).

method of its own. At least one of them took cognizance of the curious punning habits of the unconscious mind. Thus, it formulated a rule that to dream of eating donkey meat meant coming greatness, as in the Egyptian language the words for "donkey" and for "great" were homonyms. It is quite possible that to minds accustomed to the use of this word, dreams of the kind may indeed once or twice have imaged the coming fulfilment of ambition; but with the laying-down of a hard-and-fast rule that such and such an image *must* automatically correspond with such and such an event, the fatal weakness of all attempts to systematize the workings of the psi-function is made manifest. It is the weakness of assuming that all minds are identical and work in identical ways; whereas every mind is different and has a different network of associations, feelings, circumstances and puns.

It is clear that in the theories and practices of priests and diviners and gifted amateurs of psi in more complex societies, the activities of the primitive shaman will be broken down into a number of different categories. It is clear too that where professionalism creeps in these activities may be conducted from a different point of view, predominantly extrovert rather than introvert, deliberate rather than ecstatic, or, to use Ruth Benedict's extension to cultures of the terms Nietzsche used to describe individuals, Apollonian rather than Dionysiac. The Apollonian, it will be remembered, "retains control over all disruptive psychological states" and even in the dance "remains what he is and retains his civic name"; while the Dionysiac attempts to "break through into another order of experience" and "values the illuminations of frenzy". At the level of tribal life, it would seem that both recognized and attempted to induce extra-sensory perception. The Dionysiac Mohave "drank *datura* in order to gain luck in gambling; they were said to be unconscious for four days, during which they received their power in a dream". The Apollonian Zuni, however, were much more business-like. Datura was indeed used to bring about a state of mind in which psi might function uninhibited

by the surface mind; but it was administered for police purposes—in order to discover who was responsible for some theft
—to one man alone, a guinea-pig as it were, by others who
retained full possession of their judgement and their senses. "The
man who is to take the drug has a small quantity put into his
mouth by the officiating priest, who then retires into the next
room, and listens for the incriminating name."[1] A more highly
developed collectivity will begin to rationalize such procedures
with an impatient zest for intellectual tidiness; a zest apt to
produce a fine coherent structure of speculation built on a basis
of insufficient data wrongly interpreted.

In most developing cultures, then, there will be sub-division.
Philosophy, the formulation of some sort of theory about the
provenance, structure and meaning of the universe; religion,
the cult, worship and service of invisible beings or Being,
through prayer, sacrifice, ritual and behaviour; magic, the
attempt ritually to constrain entities, seen or unseen, to do one's
will regardless of their own; and primitive science, organized
observation of natural phenomena, and action based on that
observation; all these gradually separate themselves out, though
never completely and never without return. The four will move
as it were in a sort of country dance, now withdrawing to step
alone, now setting to partners, now joining hands in a round.
The play of psi may have some part in all these activities or none
and must, where it is present, be discussed in whatever terms
are to be had, be formulated in accordance with the notions
of the era, the place, the traditions and the individuals
involved.

As urban civilizations increase in complexity, and reliance
upon the kind of reasoning which is of value in technical processes becomes habitual, the proportion of persons genuinely
conscious of spontaneous psi-experience seems to decline,
partly, no doubt, on the general principle previously noted that
". . . if the Beetle stops to think / of how he does it he will sink".

[1] *An Anthropologist at Work: the Writings of Ruth Benedict*, ed.
Margaret Mead (London, 1959).

The more complex a civilization is, the more are its citizens obliged to "stop and think of how" they do things; and, as Schmeidler and McConnell[1] suggest, an interest in the process involved in psi-activity tends to inhibit it.

Such a decline in psi-awareness was observed in the heyday of the Roman Empire by Plutarch (A.D. 46–120), who included in his *Moralia* a disquisition on oracles in which he attempted to find reasons why there were so few in his time, whereas earlier ages had produced so many. It should perhaps be stressed that the oracles were men or women who, after ceremonial fasting and purifications, went into a trance and spoke mysterious words supposed to be the utterance of a god. Sometimes they lived at a traditional site of inspiration, by a sacred spring or cave, by Zeus' great oak at Dodona, or at Delphi; sometimes they wandered from place to place. In neither case had they any connexion with the state-supported College of Augurs, an official establishment which had once been held in awe but was by Plutarch's time maintained chiefly out of regard for the continuity of tradition and for the feelings of the uneducated. In earlier ages its members had had to be drawn only from patrician families, probably more in accordance with the well-developed Roman sense of hierarchical organization than with any theory that an aptitude for extra-sensory perception might be inherited.

The augurs claimed the ability not only to deduce the future from the flight of wild birds—which might need a certain dreamy dissociation—but also to determine, in full possession of their faculties, whether the gods were propitious to a venture by observing whether or how a flock of sacred fowls kept for the purpose consumed a ritual feed. It is of course just possible that at a period when landed proprietors lived in close contact with their stock, one or two of them may have had flashes of precognition, or of telepathically caused anxiety, which were transmitted to the creatures in their charge and reflected in the restless, apprehensive behaviour of those creatures. Again, the creatures themselves may occasionally have shown

[1] *Op. cit.*

marked uneasiness before earthquakes and volcanic eruptions; an uneasiness which has in fact been observed to occur and which may be attributable either to genuine foreknowledge or to some exquisitely delicate sensitiveness to small preliminary earth-tremors.

As early as 300 B.C., however, the augurs lost their connexion with the land and admitted plebeians to their ranks, and by the time of Cicero, in the first century B.C., to belong to their college was to have attained a sort of magico-political dignity; rather as if the Knights of the Garter had ceremonially to feed the lions at the Zoo, and draw from their gambols political conclusions to be set forth in the leading articles of *The Times*.

Small flocks of the sacred chickens long continued to be taken on military expeditions like regimental mascots, and it is indeed recorded that one general who had duly shipped them on a sea voyage was so maddened when their ill-omened refusal of food held up his battle plans that he finally threw them all overboard, saying that if they would not eat then they must drink.

As these methods of attempting to organize precognition became stylized and repetitive, a "going through the motions" of an ancient but uninspiring ballet, public interest gradually shifted to the activities of the Etruscan diviners, the *haruspices*. When these men first came to Rome in the reign of Tarquinius Superbus, they were thought "barbarous"; but they were much sought after during the anxious times of the second Punic War and presently formed an order of their own. Whatever spontaneity they may at first have shown, they finally developed a code of omens as arbitrary and as exquisitely detailed as any English nineteenth-century housemaid's "dream book". There were natural portents to be observed: the birth of monsters, the glow of the Northern Lights, the sound of thunder. Heard on the left, these boded ill. Heard in any direction on 25 September, it foretold dissension between powerful peoples (perhaps it may be remarked in passing that harvests would have been garnered by this date, and more men would be free for better provisioned fighting). There were the changes of the moon to be considered, the movements of the stars in their courses, each identified with the shining body of some particular god, demi-god or hero, with a personal history, marked idiosyncrasies, definite feelings of attraction or hostility towards his fellow celestial beings and specific connexions with certain animate and inanimate objects on the earth, such as human temperaments, martial, saturnine, jovial, mercurial, lunatic; and animals, for instance dogs, who were inclined to foam at the mouth in the hot thirsty August weeks when Sirius the dog-star shone; and herbs; and minerals (are there still people who shamefacedly nod seven times to the new moon and turn the silver in their pockets, so that her metal may multiply with her growth ?). There were also, oddly enough, reflecting in little the majestic diagram of the night sky, the livers of sheep offered to the gods. Perhaps long ago there had been occasions in which these steaming purple-brown shapes with their regular markings and their individual warts and spots may have served as Rorschach-objects whence the awed observer might become conscious of his own underlying pre-occupations, amongst them some flash of psi.

As early as the great days of Babylon, however, it seems to have been taken for granted without question that the information sought was to be found inscribed upon the liver itself, the seat of a life suddenly cut short, in a sort of sacred crypto-graphy to be decoded by the expert. At least two bronze models of a sheep's liver have been recovered from the ruins of Baby-lonian civilization. One of them is, indeed, to be seen in the British Museum. These correspond almost exactly with others found at Piacenza and at Falerii (this dates from the second century B.C.) and are known to have been used in the training of young *haruspices*. Each is divided into compartments dedicated to various gods, and each maps out the vault of heaven, like a Victorian "celestial globe".

If the oracles had no connexion with either of the official bodies, augurs or *haruspices*, they also had nothing to do with the swarming free-lance astrologers and soothsayers who, despite repeated prohibitions, seem to have proliferated in the later empire rather as they do in our own day; except of course that they did not then enjoy the opportunities provided by universal literacy. They may or may not have believed in the efficacy of their various fact-finding techniques—which were on occasion used as vehicles for political propaganda directed towards the large numbers of people who *did* believe in them—but, like the state diviners, they seem to have carried them out in a business-like way, completely conscious of what they were about.

In the oracles, on the other hand, the methods of the shaman seem to have survived. Like him, and like the "medium" of to-day, the oracles were persons who could fairly easily abandon detailed waking awareness of their surroundings, habitual consciousness of time and space and rational sequences of thought and allow the subconscious mind to speak. They differed from shaman and trance-medium alike in that each believed herself to be selectively dedicated to *one* of the gods in the pantheon in a way difficult for those brought up in a monotheist culture to comprehend or even to imagine. Perhaps the dazzling figure of sun-radiant Apollo, or of grey-eyed Athene, ivory and gold, or of that "queen and huntress, chaste and fair" in whom shone immortal the cool heroic sexless beauty of extreme youth, played for the devotee the part of the "control", the secondary personality in whom the trance medium projects and dramatizes her activities.

These oracles frequently put their information in a curious cryptic punning way, hard to understand till after the event; a way illustrated in our own history by the warning to the Duke of Monmouth to "beware of the rhine", which turned out not to be the river, as he had thought, but a local name for the ditches draining Sedgemoor, in one of which his horse stumbled, so that he was captured; or in the prophecy that a medieval king would "die in Jerusalem", a prophecy which made him postpone a pilgrimage, but which was nevertheless fulfilled in the Jerusalem Chamber at Westminster Abbey.

It was in the oracles then that the workings of psi would most easily show themselves, most conveniently be recognized; and, as

has been seen, the supply of oracles was failing in the highly organized civilization of the Roman Empire in the second century of
our era. Though it was intellectually permissible to admit the
play of extra-sensory perception (not, of course, envisaged as
such, but seen as the message of some non-human being) in the
remarks of an oracle, it seems to have been considered credulous
and even superstitious for educated people to recognize spontaneous instances of psi, occurring so to speak in an unauthor-
ized way in dreams or premonitions or hunches experienced by
ordinary people. These could—and should—be discounted in
comparison with the safe official methods of divination, so long
established, so clearly authoritative, and so ingeniously rationalized; and even as against the techniques used by the unofficial
experts. Such a state of mind is neatly illustrated again by
Plutarch,[1] in an account of Calpurnia's dream the night before
the fatal Ides of March. "That night," he writes, "Caesar
noticed that Calpurnia . . . was saying something in her sleep
that he could not make out, and groaning. . . . In fact she was
dreaming at that time that she was holding his murdered body
in her arms . . . some say she dreamed that she saw the gable
ornament of the house torn down".

The gable ornament had been put up, at the decree of the
Senate, as a mark of supreme honour; to dream with horror and
fear of its being torn down was to perceive, in the symbolic
pictorial idiom of the subconscious, his political destruction.
In any case, when it was day, she implored him if it were possible not to go out, and begged him to postpone the meeting of
the Senate. She clinched matters by beseeching him to consult
the official diviners if he did not think her dream of any special
importance. "Caesar himself, it seems, was affected," continues
Plutarch, "for he had never before seen any womanish superstition in Calpurnia, and now he could see she was in very great
distress." It seems clear that Caesar was making a great conces-
sion in permitting himself, even in this exceptional case, to be

[1] Translated by Robert Graves in *Six Studies of the Republic* (London,
1958).

affected by a premonition which had not been brought to his cognizance through the recognized channels. He found it fatally easy to disregard.

If in a vast urbanized civilization like that of the later Roman Empire, the proportion of persons in whom spontaneous extra-sensory perception is officially acknowledged shows a marked decline and it is thought to be "womanish superstition" to admit that it may occur sporadically among "ordinary" people, a newly industrialized culture is likely to deny that it can ever occur in anyone. Not only does the necessity for thought become more acute and more general; but it is for a special kind of thought concerned with the temporal, spatial and statistical relationships of solid objects, a kind of thought within whose structure it seems increasingly difficult to establish or justify the existence of psi. Fewer people therefore allow themselves to become aware of it; and some of those upon whom such an awareness is enforced, sooner than acknowledge in themselves the play of a faculty which can neither be defended nor restrained, will deny or repress all knowledge of its existence. Otherwise they might be considered, or worse still might have to consider themselves, hysterical, stupid, maladjusted, superstitious and/or mad. In a culture of this sort—say Gradgrind's England, America in the nineteen-hundreds, some of the recently industrialized states of eastern Europe today, where the climate of opinion is hotted up by ideological pressures—it will take either a rare combination of deep self-confidence and deliberate intellectual courage, or insanity, or such a marked ignorance of contemporary habits of thinking as can only co-exist with a very low intelligence, to own a personal experience of psi. In the vast majority it must needs force its way underground to flow "through caverns measureless to man down to a sunless sea", making itself known only if some "fault" in the geological strata of personality, or some disastrous emotional earthquake, should disrupt the mind.

It is interesting to note that an Italian doctor, Roberto Assagioli, lecturing in London in the summer of 1955, indicated his belief that a refusal to acknowledge the existence and work-ings of this function of the human psyche could be as dangerous to mental health as the refusal to acknowledge those of any other of its components.

Of course, it is not only the necessity for thinking in terms of planned time, mapped space, utility cerebration which so con-ditions people of lively intelligence in industrialized cultures that they find it almost impossible to envisage the occurrence of extra-sensory perception. There is also the fact that it has come habitually to be associated with the symbols and "Ror-schach objects" through which it was once projected and made visible in exterior terms. As has been indicated, innumerable sorts of "Rorschach objects" have been used in different eras and cultures and countries. As well as those already discussed, there were the knuckle or "oracle" bones used alike in China and in Rome, the sand patterns of the Near East, the shoulder blades of sheep in ancient Britain, and the bones and tortoise-shells once employed in the province of Honan in accordance with an efficiently worked out system thus described by Sir Leonard Woolley[1]: "You had the question to which you required an answer engraved upon a bone or a tortoise-shell by a priest, who then made notches in certain places and applied heat so that the bone or shell cracked; and from the direction taken by the crack he could deduce the reply 'yes' or 'no'." He remarks, incidentally, that objects of this sort, found in Hsiao T'un, once belonged to the royal archives of the Shang Dynasty, and were engraved with questions about matters of state—politics, war and the prospects of harvest.

These attempts to capture, pin down and use the elusive psi-factor are all sadly reminiscent of the Wise Men of Gotham's effort to keep the springtime by building a fence around the cuckoo; or of the riddle about smoke, of which you can have

a houseful, a hole full
But cannot gather a bowl full.

[1] *History Unearthed* (London, 1958).

The use of all these objects, since men are rational beings, has necessarily been rationalized in terms of the dominant ideas of the epoch in which they appear were employed. There is, moreover, as briefly noted in Chapter One, one fatal idea which emerges in almost every culture from the level of the rubbing board to the level of the Stoic philosophers. It is that the objects are not means of stimulating the psi-function but things automatically significant in themselves. The perception of events remote in space and time which psi occasionally brings into consciousness through their use is taken to inhere in them and not in the mind. It is difficult, slippery, painful to attempt to consider one's own being; much easier, more convenient and, above all, more comfortable, to assume that the required information is pre-digested and recorded in these objects, in some mysterious shorthand that can be read back by those "in the know", who have been properly trained in the techniques of abracadabra and mumbo jumbo. This process is not of course peculiar to ideas about psi. The assumption that an object or concept *is* what it does no more than reflect (as if a mirror were a man) haunts all human thought as the spores of dry-rot haunt unaired timber, entering it at the slightest point of fatigue or sloth, and eating it away with monstrous fungoid growths until the whole structure may collapse.

The association between "Rorschach objects" and psi, then, commonly leads as we have seen to the idea that the former have some magical potency in themselves. This idea is then rationalized in accordance with the preconceptions of a certain culture pattern, or the arguments of a certain school of philosophy. The Azande assumes that his rubbing board "has a spirit" in it. Seneca[1] concludes that the flight of a bird, the sound of thunder, the movements of the stars can reveal human destiny to a diviner because "all has been pre-arranged in a fatal and causal series". Others, more impersonally, decide that the universe is an organism so unitary that the markings on a sacrificial sheep's

[1] Quoted in Lynn Thorndike, *A History of Magic and Experimental Science* (New York, 1923).

liver must necessarily reflect the pattern of the stars whose influences must again necessarily determine the living course of human affairs (just as sun spots in fact determine disturbances in radio reception).

Directly it becomes plain that these rationalizations are inadequate, ridiculous or totally mistaken, and that the Rorschach objects in which earlier generations sometimes contrived to mirror flashes of extra-sensory perception have no intrinsic importance, then the idea that psi occurs at all is likely to be dismissed along with them as fantastic, nonsensical, on a par with such superstitions as that thirteen is an unlucky number, that it brings good luck to kiss a sweep and that the sight of magpies, dazzling in their brilliant black and white against the soft green and brown and grey of rural landscape portends

> One for sorrow
> Two for mirth
> Three a wedding
> Four a birth
> Five for silver
> Six for gold
> Seven for a secret never to be told.

To complicate things further, secrets may still make themselves known in magpie form, so to speak, to the dreaming mind, which has little truck with reason. Perhaps I may cite an instance, literally as well as symbolically linked with magpies, in which I was myself involved. During the early nineteen-forties, I worked in the country at a house near which a group of magpies nested. Among my colleagues was a woman with whom I often chanted this rhyme, and with whom I agreed that seeing these beautiful creatures fly up so often,—at morning when we came in to work through dewy grass, during lunch-time walks at noon, and going home at night—ought to cure us of all tendency to superstition, even in war-time. When peace came, there was a general return to London and my friend got another job; we met less often, though always with pleasure in one another's talk and company. I had not seen her for some months when one night I had a vivid dream of her, walking through the sunny Oxfordshire thicket with eight magpies flying up from under her feet. I thought in my dream, how odd this was, as the rhyme only went up to seven, and awoke with the reflection "eight magpies, how silly!" and the feeling that it nevertheless made sense somehow. During the course of the morning another friend of the wartime years came into my office and said, "I've a terrific surprise for you. I saw Kathleen last night, for the first time for ages. She got married very quietly some months ago, and she's expecting a baby . . . and what's more, the doctor thinks it's twins."

Four magpies for one birth; eight magpies for two! Incidentally, both the doctor and the magpies were mistaken, and only one baby arrived, so the dream was plainly telepathic rather than precognitive. Of course, if I had not been consciously interested both in the folk-lore of magpies and the functioning of psi, I should have ignored the dream altogether. There might in fact have been no available terms in which information could easily be conveyed from one level of the mind to another, from perception to coherent formulation. Like a diplomatic telegram in war-time, psi information seems to come through much more often in cipher than *en clair*, and if no one can break down the cipher, the information is not available.

If, then, the mode in which the use of "Rorschach objects" has been rationalized is debunked in such a way as to suggest that psi activity itself does not occur, and if at the same time all the codes in which psi messages were once conveyed are ignored as "superstitious", it is plain that recognition of its existence will be fraught with intellectual difficulty and that only the most unusually vivid instances will be recognized for what they are. This is what tends to happen in highly industrialized cultures, so far as intelligent and articulate people are concerned.

There are two other intellectual attitudes towards it which should perhaps be noticed. They accompany Romanticism; both the pastoral Romanticism which led Rousseau to revere the Noble Savage, Marie Antoinette to play shepherdesses and Mr Mandragon, the millionaire, to lead the Simple Life, and the Gothic twilight kind that fed in one generation upon the mysteries of Udolpho and in another upon the terrors of Montague James's ghost stories.

Neither breed of Romantic will boggle at psi; but neither will look at it with any sort of detachment. Admirers of the Noble Savage will see in his uninhibited acceptance of it a further instance of his nobility, which will blind them to the facts that psi sensitivity is not incompatible with the kind of life stigmatized by Hobbes as "poor, nasty, brutish and short", and that it frequently co-exists with squalor, stench, pain, superstition, unimaginative cruelty and deliberate torture; witness the practices current in the South Seas when Cook first sailed there, and of the Red Indian tribes in the days of the early settlers in America. Ghost-addicts will find in certain specialized manifestations of psi a delicious shock of deliverance from normal life, and will all too often accept with willing credulity interpretations which prefer *frisson* to fact, false glamour to true wonder.

Though urban surroundings may make it hard for genuine psi experience to force itself upon the attention, and industrial societies almost automatically condition their members to ignore its existence as intellectually disreputable and emotionally subversive of the steel and concrete structures of ideas in which they live, superstition survives. Both in the non-rational strata of educated minds and in the non-rational strata of the population (a classification which has nothing to do with literacy or illiteracy, but is concerned with the will and capacity to think) lurks a belief in magic. Bang one elbow by accident and you must bang the other on purpose, if you are not to have a disappointment. Perhaps if you don't throw a pinch of that spilt salt over your shoulder something terrible really may happen; it is safer to throw it. Perhaps if you don't step on all the cracks in the pavement or touch all the posts along the path, ill luck may catch up with you. If you do not touch wood after making some statement with a flavour of *hubris* about it, events will swiftly contradict it. The raffle tickets with threes, sevens and nines in them go first. No one "believes in" lucky or unlucky days; but it would be a rare leader who planned to initiate a campaign, an unusual couple who arranged to get married, on a Friday which was the thirteenth of the month.

On the whole, these curious notions fretting away in the dark at the fabric of the mind like moths at clothes shut up in a wardrobe, are not now taken with conscious seriousness in western civilization (though there was to be sure a very odd case of recent years in which a girl actually broke off her engagement to, let us say, Mr Jones, because of the advice given in a newspaper's astrological column to those born on her birthday. She then discovered that his rival, let us say Mr Smith, had been writing that astrological column, and sued him for damages).

In other ages and in different civilizations however, such ideas have exerted a very strong influence on human behaviour. Beliefs in lucky and unlucky days, demonstrated in a papyrus calendar of 1300 B.C.,[1] survived in Tibet until the early nineteen-fifties, when resistance to the Chinese invasion was hamstrung by the fact that no important military activity could be undertaken until the experts had had leisure to carry out elaborate calculations as to when would be an auspicious time for it. In India there is still published a flourishing astrological magazine which sets forth, in closely printed detail each month, prognostications as to the fate of the groups of people born under the different signs of the Zodiac. These prognostications cover the prospects of health, commercial undertakings, family relationships, harvests, war, peace and financial speculation. They are by no means always favourable. Quarrels with in-laws tendencies to constipation and skin trouble, pecuniary losses are predicted quite often as more agreeable happenings. It is plain that where events are largely moulded by human opinion—as in Stock Exchange transactions (buying shares in the anticipation that their value will rise, or selling them in the anticipation

[1] Lynn Thorndike, *op. cit.*

that it will fall), political developments, where so much depends upon confidence and morale, and possibly even subjective feelings of health or illness, such prophecies can by perfectly natural means bring about the state of affairs they forecast. It seems probable that it was considerations such as these which led to the ferocious, fruitless and repeated prohibition of free-lance astrologers and soothsayers in the Roman Empire. Tiberius was particularly hot upon their trail. Yet even he believed in them, as was found by one terrified diviner who was arrested, sent from Naples to Capri under armed guard and made to walk up the long series of steps to the great palace with its heliograph station high, high above the sea, thinking that each hot stride brought him nearer to the moment when he would be thrown from the top of the cliff into the blue rocky clefts so far below, only to discover that he had been called in for a professional consultation.

The habit of relying on such activities, of mentally linking the trivial with the powerful (in the same way as the touch of a button can in fact switch on a powerful electric current) seems to have "come naturally" throughout all history to the human mind, intelligent enough to realize by what incalculable darting dangers our lives are threatened and how helpless we are to deal with them—sabre-toothed tiger and striking cobra, lightning and flood, fire and slaughter, plague, pestilence and famine. Prognostications, small rituals like those adopted by a timid child undressing to go to bed in a strange house (right stocking off first, then left, shoes laid on the floor at an acute angle to one another), numerical procedures and the use of innumerable tiny gestures to avert or avoid ill-luck—picking up a dropped pin, walking outside a pavement-spanning ladder, getting off an escalator right foot foremost—all these may be accumulated to make some frail shelter in which the heart can lie quivering like a hare in her forme, hoping that death's wild hunt will pass her by.

Obsessional magic has no positive relationship with genuine, spontaneous extra-sensory perception, upon which its tightly linked, fidgety repetitions probably exert an inhibiting influence, preventing its rising into consciousness in the same way as Kim's frenzied repetition of the multiplication table prevented a strong hypnotic suggestion from taking effect. It can indeed bring about an ever more abundant death, in which all available energy is devoted to carrying out protective rituals, and the shrinking "I" progressively loses the power to respond, to love, to feel anything at all but driving fear of being disturbed in weaving its ceaseless webs of defence against fear. It may well be that a preoccupation with obsessional magic arises as a natural counter-balance to attempts deliberately to cultivate both the psi function and the techniques of suggestion. These activities co-exist to a marked degree in practically all the non-Christian, non-industrial societies, primitive or complex, of which records and observations are to be found.

It is startling to find just one group in which both magic and the exploitation of psi were consistently forbidden. Genuine, unsought extra-sensory perception could be recognized, discussed and taken into account. The symbolic dreams of other groups could be interpreted. Flashes of precognition could be accepted and reckoned with. But anxiety must not be appeased by obsessional magic; and psi must not be sought, cultivated or organized for its own sake, or in any context apart from that of religion. The group, whose very language was couched in the historic present, must live in an eternal Now, attention focused first and last on God.

It is easy placidly to accept the all-too-familiar information that the Jews were the people chosen and historically conditioned to receive, preserve and transmit the direct revelation of the divine Identity. It is a very different, and almost terrifying thing to read and find out for oneself that this is true; that ultimate Being, inconceivable, a dazzling darkness of which even the thought must take one's breath away, did indeed constrain, illuminate, struggle with the wills of this stubborn, vital people, through generation after generation, from the Stone Age onwards.

Again and again they were withdrawn from the great Middle Eastern empires whose cultural level was so much higher than their own, but whose way of life distracted attention from the presence of God. Abraham left Ur of the Chaldees, with its comforts, its seething trade, its skilled craftsmen, its ziggurats, or terraced buildings whence to observe the stars. Moses led his people out of Egypt, where food was good and plentiful, economic life was well organized, and painters, sculptors and scribes recorded with beauty the exploits of their rulers. Those who had been exiled by the waters of Babylon went home without regret for the destruction of that wonderful city of hanging gardens, beautiful buildings, great libraries, efficient sanitation and a highly developed system of justice.

In these civilizations, as has been noted, divination by omens, sacrifices and oracles was practised as a matter of course, taken for granted, like ringing up for a weather report, or reading the racing tips in the paper today. If you wanted to find out something that could not be found out in any other way, and had money enough to pay a professional diviner, you consulted him. The proceeding was morally neutral and intellectually respectable. The history of the past hundred years has shown clearly that where an undeveloped society comes into daily contact with a more complex one, it tends fairly quickly to take on the ideas, values, customs and assumptions of the more powerful group. That Israel in its early wanderings was an undeveloped society can be seen from a number of the very ancient commands and prohibitions in the books of Deuteronomy and Leviticus, long orally transmitted and probably only written down during the captivity in Babylon. Among these early regulations are some closely paralleled in those of certain West African tribes at the beginning of our own century; notably the curious notions of gynaecological "cleanness" and "uncleanness", and the tabu on eating certain animals, perhaps the totems of other tribes, perhaps general symbols of mysterious power. (Attempts have been made to explain the Jewish food tabus in terms of preventive medicine, but though it may have been unhygienic in a hot climate to eat pigs which were scavengers and could transmit tapeworm infections, this does not apply to hares, which were also forbidden. It is significant that the hare[1] seems to be regarded all over the world as an irrational symbol of fertility, which goes mad in March, broods eggs at Easter and even leaps up on its long legs to oust for many observers the man in the moon).

In the one rule already noticed, however, Israel stood completely apart from other primitive communities, whether the West Africans of the nineteen-hundreds or the warring nomads and the settled rural groups which were its neighbours at one or another historical period. It was clearly, vividly and categorically forbidden to undertake any psychological procedures which could withdraw its energy from dedication to the divine Energy.

When, as an undeveloped society, it came into contact with great and complex cultures, an inner resistance preserved its integrity still. As has been seen, it was deeply involved, in different epochs, with the three powerful Mesopotamian civilizations which conquered and assimilated so many wandering tribes and peaceful villages. It learned innumerable useful arts and techniques from them and even absorbed psychological imagery from the daily sight of their noble and impressive sculptures, visualizing the mystery of God as guarded by winged monsters and numinous six-headed animals. But in the matter of attempting to use magical procedures or to tap the resources of extra-sensory perception for utility purposes, it stood, as ever, apart. The psi function, like all other human functions, was to be used only for the purposes of God.

It was with alarmed reluctance that Israel's leaders, conscious of their own inadequacy, allowed themselves to be used and empowered by an over-ruling Will. It was with an equal reluctance that the people of Israel yielded to the conviction that those leaders spoke by the direct inspiration of God. They transmitted, generation after generation, the command neither to resort to magic nor to consult clairvoyants or mediums con-

[1] John Layard, *The Lady of the Hare* (London, 1944),

trolled by secondary personalities. The question of whether the information to be had was accurate did not arise. It was forbidden "to go aside after wizards" or "ask anything of soothsayers" simply because "I am the Lord your God",[1] and beside this blazing, immediate, timeless and absorbing fact, all attempts to know what was going on in the future or the distance were irrelevant and, worse than irrelevant, distractions which might draw the mind fatally away from the only really significant experience. Again,[2] "Let there not be found among you . . . one that observeth dreams and omens," (the Authorized Version says more explicitly "one that is an observer of times", i.e. auspicious and inauspicious days or hours) "nor any wizard or charmer, nor any one that consulteth pythonic spirits or fortune tellers, nor that seeketh the truth from the dead. . . . Thou shalt be perfect and without spot before the Lord thy God".

"Let there not be found among you"; Israel was to keep itself uncorrupted by such practices and their practitioners, but it was not necessarily to condemn them amongst other peoples. Indeed, as the story of Balaam and Balak[3] shows quite clearly, it was assumed that among the Gentiles even soothsayers could on occasion be used by God. It will be remembered that Balak, who was the King of Moab, worried by the fact that the Israelites were moving into territories near his own, sent some of his senior officials "with the price of divination in their hands" to see a professional soothsayer called Balaam and ask him to come back with them and curse the invaders. (His curse was obviously supposed to have a powerful psychological effect.) Balaam, perhaps accustomed to seek inspiration in his dreams, asked them to stay the night, saying he would let them have his decision next day.

During the night, "God said to Balaam, [in what way is not recorded] Thou shalt not go with them, nor shalt thou curse the people, because it is blessed". Accordingly, in the morning he told the delegates that he could not go with them. Balak, much perturbed by the news, then sent even more important people to

[1] Levit. 19.   [2] Deut. 18.   [3] Numbers 22.

ask him again, this time offering him any reward he would like to mention. Balaam, probably reluctant to offend a powerful local ruler, prayed again, persuaded himself that he received an answer to go if he really thought it necessary, saddled his donkey and rode off. They came to a narrow place "between two walls where a vineyard was enclosed", and the donkey refused to move. Beaten, she cringed against the wall, bruising her rider's foot. Beaten again, she lay flat on the ground, as donkeys will in the last resort, braying. Balaam then perceived what had frightened her, an angel with a drawn sword standing in the way. Himself terrified, he offered to turn back, but was told to go on and meet Balak, but to say nothing except by direct inspiration. Balak took him to a number of different places whence he urged him to utter a curse on the invaders, but "the spirit of God rushed upon him" and he was constrained on three separate occasions to bless them and to prophesy not only their success, but the rising of "a star out of Jacob". Balak was not at all pleased and all that Balaam could say was, "I cannot go beyond the word of the Lord my God to utter anything out of my own head, either good or evil; but whatsoever the Lord shall say, that will I speak".

Soothsaying and divining, then, might go on uncondemned among other tribes, where the spirit of God might even use these means of communication, but not in Israel itself. Samuel, dedicated from his childhood to the service of God, might have flashes of extra-sensory perception enabling him, say, to tell a man where his strayed beasts had got to or whether they had been found already, but he did not cultivate clairvoyance as such nor make a business of it. It might happen, but only as an incidental thing. If the psi function were to work, it must do so spontaneously, even among the priests. Those of other communities might drink sacred preparations of mescalin or datura in order to dive deeply down from individual consciousness into the green subaqueous levels of collective being where telepathic currents flow free and archetypal images swim luxurious and grotesque as tropical fish, golden-winged and scarlet and velvet blue, globe-shaped, spiky, triangular, arrowy, serpentine, electric, lethal or lovely. But Aaron and his successors might not even drink wine before going into the tabernacle.[1]

In early Israelite history that rather mysterious community of men known as "the sons of the prophets" seems to have sought by corybantic methods, music and dancing and singing, for some kind of collective ecstasy in which its members might become strongly aware of the presence of God; a collective ecstasy which must have been both powerful and contagious to judge from the fact that when that very tall young man Saul met a "company of prophets coming down from the high place with a psaltery and a timbrel and a harp . . . prophesying",[2] he was drawn by a strong attraction into the group and began "prophesying" too. There is no record of what he or they said; possibly there were no words and the "prophesying" was no more than a rhythmic, awe-inspiring chant, the utterance of feeling too intense to be formulated. It has indeed been suggested that these professional prophets may have resembled the dancing dervishes of Islam who dissociate conscious from unconscious mind by spinning round and round until they are dizzy, repeating the name of Allah as they whirl, and who sometimes stimulate the functioning of psi as they do so. As Father Hastings has pointed out,[3] "the later and greater prophets" who began with Amos were "reluctant to use the name at all". This may have been, as he suggests, because "the sons of the prophets" became sexually promiscuous, as frequently tends to happen in groups where any urgent desire that survives the ritual numbing of surface consciousness and individual control is held to be divinely inspired. It is also possible that they became increasingly charged with that uncanny atmosphere of sacred madness which vibrates in "Kubla Khan":

> And all shall cry Beware, Beware,
> His flashing eyes, his floating hair

---

[1] Levit. 10.   [2] 1 Kings (1 Sam.), 10.
[3] A. Hastings, *Prophet and Witness in Jerusalem* (London, 1958).

Weave a circle round him thrice
And close your eyes in holy dread,
For he on honey dew hath fed
And drunk the milk of Paradise.

This atmosphere in itself may well have aroused a sense of profound distrust in a people repeatedly recalled to the primal necessity for relationship between living Deity and man wholly alive, giving attention and receiving grace in full, integrated being. If its priests could not be blemished in body, still less could its prophets be deliberately dissociated in consciousness.

The Jewish attitude towards the willed attempt to cultivate the psi function in itself and to exploit it for use and profit has been described at some length, partly because of its startling contrast with the views of the rest of the ancient world, partly because of its undying influence on Christian thought, and partly because it may explain why Israel does not seem to have experienced the curious situation to be discussed in Chapter Five, the situation in which the contemplative, seeking detachment from every activity which may hinder his devoting his whole attention to God, finds that this detachment in itself serves to develop a capacity for extra-sensory perception that may provide a distraction and a means of temptation even more powerful than those furnished by the senses, the desires and the imagination which he has already conquered.

Chapter Five

SAGE, CLAIRVOYANT AND MAGICIAN IN ASIA

THE growth of religious thought, like the growth of thought about every other subject, is closely connected with the use of words. Words are sometimes precision instruments, sometimes stimulants to emotional understanding. Wonder may link the two modes of using them and make possible the experience in which poetry and contemplation are rooted.

Rilke writes somewhere: "Perhaps we are simply here for *saying*" the names of things, realizing them in sound, lifting them out of the incessant stream of impressions, and so becoming aware of their full identity, *haecceitas*, inscape. By observing and brooding upon them we take their images into our own being and give them in turn the added vitality of what is loved.

The precision instrument which cuts out *a red rose* from the general awareness of light and shadow, petals and leaves and earth, the smell of rain, the sound of the blackbird singing, stills the attention for a moment upon a single object in which shape, colour, scent, cool, fragile smoothness are fused in instantaneous unity. And once the power to still attention has been gained, it can be used for many purposes.

Directly there is time and scope for wonder, wholehearted wonder untouched by anxiety about self-preservation from hunger, cold, danger or sorcery, it becomes possible to feel the impact of creation and of its Source, in joy. That God or the gods wield force and grant favours, that their existence provides an explanation of the phenomenal world and its events, is forgotten in awareness of what Is.

It is probable that most people can recollect such a state of awareness as this, usually in the metaphysical years between three and seven, when a child may wake on a summer morning and go running secretly out to the garden and dance its delight on the grass, where feet crush down the rainbow dew in dark green shapes, and in the afternoon lie looking at the sky that goes on and on and on for ever or watch the rose, unarguably *there*, and all in the breathing knowledge that these things are charged with an intense inexplicable significance. Perhaps such experiences reflect a remembrance of life before the Fall, happy to be part of creation, happy to "possess the world aright" and to "laugh and sing and rejoice in God as misers do in gold and kings in sceptres".

It has been suggested that just as the prenatal development of the body recapitulates the process of physical evolution, so the development of personality in some sense recapitulates the history of the human race. For this reason it may be interesting to consider the experience of wonder and the concomitant play of extra-sensory perception in children. They wax and wane together.

Here I must make it clear, as a warning to those who hold that the only worthwhile evidence for psi is furnished by statistical experimentation, that little work has been undertaken with young children. My reasons for believing that it exists in them are based primarily on my own observations (recorded at the time when the evidential incidents occurred); on those of other parents; on the recollections of childhood to be found in many autobiographies; and on the observations of Dr Joan Fitzherbert in this country, Dr Emilio Servadio in Italy and Dr Berthold Schwartz in the United States I am convinced that in the study of psi, which is a function of living beings, the methods of the field naturalist, the bird-watcher, the zoologist, the anthropologist, are of even more value than those of experts in the physical sciences, whose raw materials are not subject to the unpredictable fluctuations of consciousness.

In young children, then, the psi function appears to work fairly frequently, as most mothers who live in close contact with them know to their cost. It is not only that in infancy, breast-fed or bottle-fed, handled unthinkingly or handled with premeditated gentleness by someone determined to control her own irritability, each child echoes its mother's moods, cross and crying if she is tired and worried, at peace and laughing if she is happy. It also seems, at a later age, to perceive with her when she is out of its sight and hearing, and even to remember things in her mind which have sunk below the level of her own consciousness and are forgotten.

Perhaps I may cite two instances known to me. In the first, the mother of Jessica, a three-year-old, was in her own bedroom, checking through the linen that had come back from the wash. The door was open, as was the door of the room along the passage where the child was playing, but they could not see one another. As the mother sorted the handkerchiefs, she heard her little girl, who had just learned the names of colours, saying in a drawling, sing-song way "white, yellow, blue, pink . . . " and so on, and realized with a shock that each word corresponded to the colour of the handkerchief at the moment in her hands. The child continued accurately to chant the names of the colours until her mother had finished the sorting. Asked why she had done so, Jessica replied that the colours had just come into her head. In the second case, another mother, sitting with a small son on top of a bus from Swiss Cottage to Baker Street, saw walking along the opposite side of Wellington Road a woman with whom she had worked early in the war, a year or two before the boy's birth. She said, "Goodness, there's someone I used to know quite well. I wish I could talk to her again." "Quick, wind the window down and shout." "It's no good, darling, it wouldn't be manners, she'd never hear, and anyway I've forgotten her name. . . . It may be Betty, but I can't be quite sure." No more was said. The bus lumbered past St John's Wood cemetery and round the green triangle dominated by the statue of St George and the Dragon. As it came to the bridge over the Regent's Canal, the small boy remarked meditatively, "You're quite right, her name isn't Betty. It's Peggy." "Yes, of course, that's it, Peggy. Peggy Samuel," his mother replied, and then, realizing the oddity of what was going on, "but how did you know? I haven't seen or heard or thought of her since before you were born." "I just did."

This continuity of experience between mother—and other family figures—and child gradually disintegrates as the process of schooling begins, and also as the child becomes dimly aware of the possibility of choosing to retreat from the suffering to which (as well as to joy) its former openness to feeling exposed it, to shut out immediate awareness of other people's anxiety, boredom, pain, unhappiness. This ability develops in step with the ability to read, since to read means that one has learned in some degree how to control and to direct thought.

A woman of my acquaintance can still, and very vividly, recollect, with a sense of betrayal, having in her childhood deliberately concentrated herself upon a book rather than share and bear her grandmother's grief at leaving for ever a place they had both loved; the walnut trees and the secret hillside stream beyond them, the lawn with the pear tree white in spring and full of golden fruit in September when waspy windfalls buzzed in the grass, the sight of the Malverns miles and miles away, the thunderstorms rolling up the Severn valley, the walks in a June dusk pink between sunset and moonrise and shot through with the drifting smells of hay and beanflowers and traveller's joy.

After this resentful and guilty and willed withdrawal from pain, this choice to be separate, the little girl gradually realized that childhood was gone and Paradise lost in "the light of common day".

Such a chosen isolation may well be necessary in our world as a measure of self-defence, a means of weaving a sort of psychological cocoon within which personality may develop; it may be an inevitable concomitant of growing up. It need not of course hinge upon a single incident such as this, which may indeed only have been remembered as a symbol or summary of innumerable, small, piecemeal happenings. But once it has finally been chosen, there is no going back. With the rejection of the capacity to experience the feelings of the family group as one's own, a capacity closely involved with psi, vanishes that innocence wholly absorbed in the wonder of living and knowing for which so many poets have been homesick.

It is, however, after this point of no return that the impulse springs up to look for God, not as Providence arranging for peace, prosperity and good harvests as the reward of conscious virtue, not as the First Cause of all things, but as the Presence which gave meaning to the morning dew, the infinite sky, the momentary, perfect rose.

Directly contemplation—that attempt to gaze at God whose fulfilment lies in the Beatific Vision—becomes a conceivable pursuit, men will set themselves apart from the world to follow it. They will be concerned with two things. First, to consider what they are about, to clarify their ideas and formulate their aims; and here there will be a diversity of concepts as wide as the traditions and rationalizations of experience which they inherit. Second, to find and to use means of focusing their gaze.

In order to do this it is necessary to shut out those stimuli which compete to distract the attention. The child unthinkingly mirrors all experience, rejoicing in "the orient and immortal wheat that never should be reaped nor ever was sown", "the sounding cataract", the "jewels more rich than Ormuz shows" within the cut pomegranate, as things reflecting and echoing and smelling and tasting not only of themselves but of communicated glory. The would-be contemplative, full grown and fatally aware of his own desire to catch and grasp and hold down these joys which die in his possession, must renounce them for the sake of the very glory which they communicate, disregard the "dome of many-coloured glass" for "the white radiance of eternity".

After leaving behind the bustle of everyday existence, preoccupied with worry, money, competition, ambition, personal relationships, display, he must then struggle with all the forces that even in his isolation—either individual or in a community of like-minded persons—still hold him back from his heart's desire; greed, lust, sloth, hatred, obsessive love, boredom, and three more complex compulsions. One draws him inwards towards that preoccupation with his own merits, struggles and achievements which taints asceticism and the exercise of the will. One pushes him outwards towards absorption in the visions projected by his own mind, visions which may mediate truth for a time but which will tend, like other symbols, to become opaque, as it were, instead of transparent, and to solidify until they come to be regarded as ends in themselves rather than as means to the knowledge of God. One draws him down into inertia, towards what (as has been noted) medieval thinkers called the "animal soul"; the force through which the body understands untaught how to live and survive, breathing, sweating, pumping the blood around, assimilating food, and so on, a force whose sphere of influence widens to cover the learnt activities of habit, in routines and rituals once established and followed with energy and purpose but finally reiterated as part of a behaviour pattern which the somnambulist organism cannot cease to repeat.

In this *fainéant* state the inclination is to cut out spontaneous conscious activity as far as possible, to relegate everything to the realm of that automatism with which instinct is amplified and all too often to achieve not life, but death more abundant, since humans cannot of their nature return to the collective unconscious of a non-human species and must, if they attempt to do so, become not living but clockwork animals. (It is, incidentally, interesting to note how many traditional ghost stories are marked by this repetitive, clockwork character, and concern a figure "perceived" to perform the same series of actions over and over again, without regard for changed surroundings.)

The psi function will play a considerable part in the life of the contemplative. It may well be argued indeed that in our species its true use and fulfilment are only to be found in prayer and that its primary purpose for man is to enable him to become increasingly aware of God. In any case, quiet, solitude and a diminution of exterior activity are precisely the conditions needed to make its workings, and the impressions transmitted by them, well up into the conscious mind.

Clearly, it will be involved in the three compulsions just discussed. It will link a man with the animal soul active within its own limits, in him as in the other living creatures. It will link him with the collective unconscious of his species. Most clearly of all, it will provide exciting material for pride and preoccupation with his own achievements. He may well develop powers of telepathy, clairvoyance, precognition or psycho-kinesis, or variations and combinations of all four. He may become aware of the unspoken thoughts, desires or mental imagery of other people. He may have veridical hallucinations of what is happening at a distance. His body may so dramatize his longing for God that he may find himself—as did Richard Rolle, St Catherine of Genoa and St Philip Neri, for instance—generating an intense physical heat perceptible and even painful to those near him, and affecting material objects; or, like St Joseph of Cupertino and others, he may be levitated.

Although I am attempting to discuss the connexion between contemplation and psychical phenomena in non-Christian religions, I have used illustrative instances involving Christian contemplatives because they are better known in our civilization, and because the evidence for them has been examined with scrupulous care. A detailed discussion of such phenomena in the western world, and of secular parallels to them, where such parallels can be shown to exist, will be found in the late Father Herbert Thurston's cautious, scholarly and fascinating volume *The Physical Phenomena of Mysticism*.[1]

The longing for God, the attempt to concentrate attention on His Presence, some of the methods adopted (the use of rosaries and of particular musical formulae, for instance) and all the psycho-physical mechanisms at work, are common to all mankind. The differences lie in what is held to be the truth about His Being, Its relationships with man and with the universe, and the significance and potential sanctity of created things.

If the whole process of creation is visualized as "a Fall into

[1] Ed. J. Crehan, S.J. (London, 1952).

matter", as the Gnostics taught, and as Aldous Huxley[1] believed Buddhism and Hinduism to affirm (but has not some Indian seer written of the continuous creation of everything, from the ladybird to the Milky Way, as *lila*, the sacred play of Brahma ?), then the contemplative must withdraw himself physically, imaginatively and intellectually from all concern with it, and live to die. If, on the other hand, the dancing universe, stars and suns and patterned energies, seas and flowers and men, is held to be the expression of God, and its evil and suffering are thought consequent upon its highest quality, the gift of free will, which could not be free without the capacity of choice between right and wrong; then the contemplative, still withdrawing from that universe because its multiplicity distracts his wavering attention, withdraws in love, prays for his fellow beings, dies to live.

In practice the distinction may not be as clear as it is in theory. At least one school of Buddhism reverences holy men who pledge themselves not to enter the passionless peace of Nirvana until all sentient creatures in the long, long cycle of rebirth can enter too. But it seems fairly clear, for instance, that someone who believed that God could only be known by men who withdrew from being involved in the process of creation, would demur, say, at St Thomas More's decision that because he did not feel able to maintain lifelong chastity, he was intended not to become a Carthusian, but to marry and bring up a family in love, and live Christian in the world. It also seems probable that neither Buddhist nor Hindu nor Taoist could agree with Father Victor White's[2] remark in connexion with a saying of St Thomas Aquinas, that "unsublimated sexuality and extravert activity, the two main obstacles to spiritual insight, may, if at the service of charity, be of more eternal worth than the spiritual perceptions which they hinder".

It is plain in any case that the development of psychical powers may, unless very carefully handled, prove to be a strong

[1] *The Perennial Philosophy* (London, 1946).
[2] *God and the Unconscious* (London, 1952).

and constant distraction to the would-be contemplative, whatever his concepts. A man in whom the pull towards preoccupation with his own will-power and his own achievements is marked may gradually become so much absorbed in psi-phenomena, and in his own glory as a wonder worker, as to lose real interest in his ultimate goal, relaxing instead into the enjoyment of admiration, the exertion of power, and the deep satisfaction of being his wonderful self. The pride which has deflected him from his original purpose and made him from a contemplative into a clairvoyant may stop here, leaving him blinded with self-satisfaction, or may consume him completely, so that like a drug addict he is always craving for more, more recognition, more power, savouring the pleasure of ordering other people's lives until he comes to regard them as puppets (the more reluctant, the more satisfying), relishing the awe which he inspires until he has to pepper it with fear, and developing a fierce malevolence against those who do not yield him their tribute of admiration and obedience. It is not difficult to see where the figure of the black magician originated or to understand the horror it aroused.

The danger of this most terrifying corruption of the contemplative life is probably known wherever the latter is attempted. It is a corruption which can plainly be seen both to prevent the contemplative from following his chosen path and to have a profoundly evil effect upon the world at large.

The case is maybe somewhat different in those Eastern cultures where bodily techniques of manipulating consciousness are deliberately undertaken, as in the yoga exercises, the systems of regulating the breath, and all the other methods of inducing trance states taught to aspirants after contemplation in the traditional schools of Buddhism and Hinduism, and by the early Taoist hermits. Here, though it seems to be taken for granted that psi activities will be set going, it is not always easy to discover any consistent teaching as to what is to be done about them.

On the whole, western writers seem to assume that they are all regarded as something to be ignored as irrelevant (going further, in this instance, than Christian tradition, in which attention would be yielded to them in so far as they brought home to the heart the need to act or pray for someone in distress). Thus Aldous Huxley writes[1] that "the masters of Hindu spirituality urge their disciples to pay no attention to the *siddhis* or psychic powers which may come to them unsought. . . . A similar attitude is taken by the best Buddhist teachers"; and a contemporary convert to Buddhism, John Blofeld,[2] noting that Thailand "abounds" in "those lesser 'spiritual' phenomena. . . fortune telling, the summoning of spirits . . . and similar matters of small importance", comments that "the world's greatest religious teachers, including the Lord Buddha, have warned us that they are more often harmful than beneficial, and never of the slightest use towards general spiritual purposes."

There seem to be grounds, however, for thinking that these generalizations are rather too sweeping. The contemplative lamas described by Alexandra David Neel,[3] for instance, do not seem to have ignored or rejected their abilities to produce supernormal phenomena. On the contrary, it looks as if they had taken a gentle but profound satisfaction—like that of a gardener whose vegetable marrows have won prizes time and again at the village show—in their reputed powers deliberately to levitate, to use second sight and to generate by some unexplained psycho-somatic technique (obviously akin to the mechanism spontaneously and symbolically at work in the case of St Philip Neri) such an inner heat as could keep them cosy in a snow-drift and an east wind.

Again, Edward Conze,[4] in his anthology of Buddhist Scriptures, cites a passage on the Five Miraculous Powers which shows quite clearly that the possibility of developing them was

[1] *Op. cit.*
[2] *The Wheel of Life—Autobiography of a Western Buddhist* (London, 1959).
[3] *With Mystics and Magicians in Tibet* (London, 1931).
[4] *Buddhist Scriptures* (London, 1959).

not only discouraged or regarded as unimportant, but held out by certain authorities as a positive inducement to enter the life of a Buddhist monk: "*The Lord . . . wishes to show . . . the advantages*" [my italics] "and the increasingly sublime *dharmas* which flow from meditational development. With this in mind he has described the Five Mundane Superknowledges, which include the various magical powers, cognition by the heavenly ear, and the knowledge of other people's thoughts."

The methods recommended to develop the functioning of psi in these ways are set out in a repetitive and ritual detail which in itself implies the technique of auto-suggestion. Briefly, if the meditator wishes to make either himself or someone else visible to those who could not normally see him, either because they are too far away or because walls or hills cut off their line of vision, he must go into the fourth stage of a trance (achieved by concentration upon some image or idea). Emerging from it, he should prepare the miracle by intently thinking, "'May this object, now covered up, be uncovered' . . . and sustain this thought with a firm resolution". Then, when he has formed the resolution, it is realized; others can see the object, even from a remote distance. Various techniques of self-suggestion are described; there is one for becoming invisible, for instance, and another for floating crosslegged through the air. To do this, a man "determines his mind to accord with his body" and "a sensation of lightness and ease comes over him". He keeps at bay states hostile to trance, such as discursive thinking. "His physical body becomes as light as a tuft of cotton down", and off he goes. The desire to move along is the last decisive factor. He is also given instructions on how to "conjure up a mind-made body", a sort of double or fetch, by imagining that there is another body within his own, and pulling it out, as a snake pulls itself out from its skin; and he is taught, as well, how to give up his normal appearance and appear in the guise of "another man, a dragon, a god, an animal". There is one warning, however. "He should never resolve, 'May I become an elephant', but always, 'Let there be an elephant,'" though nothing is said of what happens if the wrong resolve is used; does he become an eastern version of Apuleius' Golden Ass?

Whether any or all of these techniques produce objective as well as subjective results cannot be known without observation or experiment with those who claim to use them. If spontaneous psycho-kinesis occurs in poltergeist outbreaks on the one hand and in levitation on the other, and if experiments with dice provide evidence that it can sometimes be produced at will, the possibility of "floating crosslegged through the air" (a curiously unstreamlined method of transport) cannot be denied out of hand. If "crisis apparitions" can in fact be shown to happen, and if there are reliable cases in which an agent has experiment-ally succeeded in "appearing" unexpectedly to a percipient, it is not impossible that a "mind-made body" could be caused to impinge upon the attention of distant persons, even though in our time and surroundings they might find it hard to accept as veridical the hallucination of a dragon's presence (even the benevolent dragon of China, who guards people against evil spirits), and might take that of an elephant as evidence for the necessity of temperance rather than of psychical research.

That these techniques for developing and exercising the psi-function in modes not directly concerned with contemplation should be detailed in a collection of religious writings, does seem to show that certain Buddhist groups[1] at any rate did not regard such attempts either as a waste of time and energy on irrelevan-cies, or as dangerous temptations to distraction. Such an idea as this is in fact nowhere to be found in Mr Conze's comprehen-sive anthology.

Is it just possible that the belief that this idea is inherent in *all* serious contemplative traditions can arise from preconcep-tions so deeply rooted in the minds of western translators of ancient eastern documents and of European exponents of Asian religions, as to be unrecognized?

---

[1] The same point is made about Hindu mysticism on pp. 110–112 of *The Lotus and the Robot*, by Arthur Koestler (London, 1960).

Translation even from one European tongue to another linked with it by long centuries of history, philosophy, tradition and constant interchange, is a very tricky exercise. Anyone who undertakes it becomes quickly, sharply conscious that words have not even the rough equivalence of currency, which in itself is rough enough. You can buy a given number of francs for a pound, but the francs will not necessarily buy the same kind or quantity of objects in France as the pound will buy in England. With verbal currencies the matter is much more complex, and this complexity is increased beyond measure where translation is not only from one language, but from one ancient cultural idiom into another. The names of the simplest objects—dogs, cats, houses—and of humans in basic relationship—mother, child, husband, wife—may be surrounded by circling planetary systems of associated ideas which are totally different in different civilizations. Dogs, loved in one place for their warm, silent, affectionate fidelity, may be despised in another as unclean scavengers ("Deliver my darling from the power of the dog," the Psalmist prayed). Cats, purring, cosy emblems of the British domestic hearth are in Siam lean, temperamental, blue-eyed, exotic, their streamlined bodies coloured chocolate and cream like very expensive motor cars. Houses may be blue pagodas or copper-green domes or igloos made of snow. The mothers who live in them may be veiled, idle, deprived of their sons when the boys are seven years old. The husbands may be polygamous, or regard even a single wife only as a means of breeding and live all their intellectual life with men or *hetairae*, as in ancient Greece. Where imagery is used symbolically,[1] where abstract terms are involved and where the discussion of ideas and beliefs is in question, it is surely harder than ever to be quite certain

[1] Charles Williams, the poet and critic, once gave me a startling instance of the extreme difficulty of transplanting traditional imagery from one ambience to another. A group of Fundamentalist missionaries, to whom the letter of Holy Scripture was intrinsically as sacred as the spirit and significance it could transmit, found themselves upon an island where sheep were completely unknown, and were obliged, with extreme discomfort to themselves, to explain that a lamb was the equivalent of a small, woolly pig.

what is meant and almost impossible to grasp what is taken for granted.

This problem of the different assumptions of the translator and of the original writer is sympathetically indicated and discussed in a recent fascinating study of Chinese mystical theory and practice by Holmes Welch.[1] Incidentally, he quotes Arthur Waley as noting in *The Way and Its Power*[2] that the contemporaries of Lao Tzu believed that that great traditional work, the Tao Tê Ching, was "written by a practitioner of *tso-wang*, the early Chinese equivalent of yoga . . . (and was) . . . intended to show how to use the Power given by trance states induced by breathing exercises over the material world, *and also* [my italics] how such trance states could be the basis of a metaphysic". This seems to suggest that the stimulation and use of the psi-function had been the primary object of the training undertaken and that mystical experience, and the metaphysical systems built upon it, came as an unsought secondary development.

These activities issued from time to time into a potentiality for reflecting the Presence of God, still, clear and silent as a mountain lake that mirrors the sky, and into a belief that "Reality . . . is an 'aesthetic continuum' whose differentiations provide the transitory objects of the external world" and that "the Taoist can perceive this aesthetic continuum without differentiation. For him the aesthetic object and the aesthetic self become one" and "being one with this timeless continuum he is immortal"; since

> Tao is for ever, and he who possesses it
> Though his body ceases, is not destroyed.[3]

Such an awareness could, however, appeal only to those of a

[1] *The Parting of the Way: Lao Tzu and the Taoist Movement* (London 1959).
[2] *The Way and Its Power* (London, 1934).
[3] Holmes Welch, *op. cit.*, discussing *inter alia* F. C. S. Northrup, *The Meeting of East and West*.

specialized temperament already capable of understanding what was meant by it, and endowed with a perseverance that could carry them through the long hard solitary discipline necessary to its achievement. People of other temperaments might take it on trust that something of the kind was possible, just as composing an opera is possible, but that it was not for them. They might then either turn away to some other activity or re-examine the doctrine to see if it contained anything really interesting and practical (for surely these hermits and solitaries could not in fact be solely concerned with getting themselves into a curious state of mind; there *must* be something more to it than that). As far as can be seen from the recent English studies of Taoism which have come my way, there are no specific warnings against the dangers of distraction by psi. It would be rather surprising, in any case, to find them in a cult which seems originally to have been based on a deliberate cultivation of this faculty. Moreover, specific warnings of any kind are hardly compatible with Lao Tzu's maxim that no one can achieve his aim by direct action (which stirs up direct opposition), but only through *wu-wei*, that yielding which might (rather unfairly) be called a sort of jujitsu of the spirit, in which the activity of the opponent, exterior or interior, defeats its own ends.

Whether for such reasons as these or for others, the insights of the Chinese sages, and even of Lao Tzu himself, could not prevent Taoism from degringolating from an experience into "a mythology . . . a recipe for physical immortality, and a quest for magical islands",[1] in fact abandoning the secondary desire and effort to be absorbed in wonder, and returning to the primary preoccupation with psi as a useful means of exerting "power over the material world" (a means whose efficiency and accuracy in no way approach those achieved by radio, television, aircraft and central heating).

It looks, then, as if in two of the great Oriental religious traditions, that of Taoism and that of Buddhism, there was no

---

[1] H. Welch, *op. cit.*

universal teaching that to pay undue attention to psi phenomena hinders contemplation. (Indeed, if it be true that the choice of a new Dalai Lama is made from among small boys who claim to have personal "remembrances" of his last incarnation, an active psi-function capable of retro-cognition, and of the telepathic garnering of data from the subconscious minds of older persons is very highly valued in Tibetan Buddhism at least.)

It may be worth while to put on record that when I planned this chapter I took it for granted myself that all great religious traditions, Christian and non-Christian, Eastern and Western, specifically taught that a human being whose supreme desire was to be absorbed in realizing the Presence of God (no matter how this desire was formulated) must be prepared to resist the distractions conveyed not only by the senses, the imagination, and the discursive reason, but also by the psi-function; whether those distractions lay in its data as food for speculation, or in itself, as food for self-occupation or spiritual pride. I assumed that it was made plain in every contemplative discipline that the will must struggle to control, integrate and use all these scattered and discursive activities in dedication to its single, profound and fundamental aim. The search for documentary evidence to support this assumption has made me realize that it is immensely over-simplified; that it certainly does not hold good *en bloc;* that only a lifetime of research by a student at ease in oriental languages, steeped in the atmosphere and history of each individual cult and trained and exercised in each culture-pattern's methods of thought, could hope to indicate the groups of whose practice it is true and the degree of its truth there; and that to attempt to generalize about it is just about as useful as going fishing for minnows with a salmon net.

It is probably justifiable to say that as far as the written word goes there do not seem to be, among the ancient eastern religions, any definite, universally applicable and generally recognized warnings against the possibility that a man may be drawn away, by yielding his attention to the play of sporadic and uncoordinated psi phenomena, from fulfilling the purpose for which he exists: "to know, love and serve God". Though there doubtless were, and are, living, strong, oral traditions to this effect handed on from teacher to disciple in small groups and communites set apart from the bustle of the world, it seems doubtful whether they are universally accepted even among such men as these. Thus, though both Hindus and Mahayana Buddhists desired deliverance from the endless cycle of rebirths upon the wheel of life in which they believed, into the "existence, consciousness, bliss" of Brahman, the Godhead, or into Nirvana, and though they sought this end by different austere and demanding disciplines, from fierce asceticism to meditation, from psycho-somatic techniques to the "rooting out of greed, hatred, and delusion", nevertheless, says a contributor to the *Concise Encyclopaedia of Living Faiths*,[1] both Brahmins and Mahayana Buddhists practised "magic". Another contributor, writing on Buddhism in China, remarks that certain of its followers like certain followers of Taoism "are concerned with magic powers, miracles, and spells for the fulfilment of mundane wishes".

It is plainly commonsense to refuse to be distracted from a final aim by any lesser activities; but what if that final aim be not always very clearly envisaged? If even specialists wavered from it, what happened to the ordinary man, peasant or soldier or trader, writer or painter or singer; had he any means of distinguishing between the ascetic vowed to contemplation and the ascetic corrupted by pride, or between either of them and the man absorbed in the fascination of the strange world of the collective unconscious? Could he differentiate even to the degree that Thomas the Rhymer was taught to differentiate after he had "left the living land behind" and "heard the roaring of the sea"? (It is interesting to remember his first thought was that the beautiful strange speaker was Our Lady, and that it was she herself who told him her real identity.)

---

[1] Edited by R. C. Zaehner (London, 1959).

O see ye not yon narrow road
So thick beset with thorns and briars?
That is the Path of Righteousness,
Though after it but few inquires.

And see ye not yon braid braid road
That lies across the lily leven?
That is the Path of Wickedness
Though some call it the road to Heaven.

And see ye not yon bonnie road
That winds about the fernie brae?
That is the road to fair Elfland
Where thou and I this night maun gae.

... green Elfland, the ancient wood, where the bird sings and the monk listens and a thousand years go by in "the lost traveller's dream under the hill".

This chapter has no claim to be a study of comparative religion. It is no more than a brief and scrappy attempt to elucidate what is thought, taught and done about psi-activity in various religious contexts, of which only the relevant aspects have been examined. Such a procedure must inevitably and of its nature throw out of focus the religions to which it is applied, and may even perhaps seem to present a distorted picture of them. If this has happened, the result should not be attributed to any lack of respect for the lights and insights to be found in the beliefs under discussion, or to any implicit denial that their followers may find in them the reflection of God glittering like sunshine on wind-patterned water. Indeed, I believe that some of these lights can, because of their very unfamiliarity, stimulate a fresh realization of truths so long and so well known to us that we hardly notice them. Thus, of the splendour of God, by which the Conqueror swore, consider these lines from Isa Upanishad 8:

He encircles all things, radiant and bodiless
Unharmed and untouched by evil.
All seeing, all wise, all present, self-existent,
He has made all things well for ever and ever.

And, of detachment and duty, these from the Bhagavad-Gita,[1]
spoken by Krishna, avatar of Deity:

Do the work you are ordained to do
always without attachment,
for the man who works without attachment
reaches the supreme. . . .
Cast all your acts on me
With your mind upon the highest Soul.
Have done with craving and selfhood. . . .

And, of the creative Spirit, from the Tao Tê Ching:[2]

The Tao that can be expressed is not the eternal Tao,
The name that can be defined is not the unchanging
name. . . .

[The thing] which existed before heaven and earth
Motionless and fathomless,
It stands alone and never changes;
It pervades everywhere and is never exhausted.
It may be regarded as the mother of the universe.

As a tailpiece, I should like to cite three eastern sayings specifically about psi-phenomena. One, quoted by Aldous Huxley,[3]
is "the Buddha's own characteristically dry comment on a
prodigious feat of levitation performed by one of his disciples:
'This', he said, 'will not conduce to the conversion of the un-
converted, nor to the advantage of the converted.' Then he went
back to talking about deliverance." Chu Hsi, a follower of the

---

[1] Both quoted in the *Concise Encyclopaedia of Living Faiths.*
[2] *The Tao Tê Ching*, translated by Ch'u Ta Kao (London, 1959).
[3] *Op. cit.*

genial, brilliant, agnostic social philosopher Confucius, remarked, to explain the occurrence of apparitions of the dead, that "if a man is killed before his life span is completed, his vital spirit is not yet exhausted and may survive for a while as a ghost". The third saying, also Chinese, is a practical and traditional recipe for making a haunted house normal and liveable; "let it, at a low rent, to a large cheerful family".

Chapter Six

PSI AND MIRACLE

IT might well be thought inadvisable to touch upon the relationship between psi and miracle, both in the life of our Lord and in the development of the early Church. It would certainly be very much easier not to do so. But as the general recognition of the fact that psi exists becomes more widespread, so does the tendency to "explain" all apparent miracles in terms of it. A hundred years ago it was maintained that, since "the laws of nature were immutable" (that is, since a series of constant observations and tests of the behaviour of natural objects yielded results from which statistically useful generalizations could be made), Christianity must be false, because the miracles recorded in its living tradition as in its earliest documents *could* not possibly have taken place; Q.E.D. Now, the pendulum of opinion is swinging back to something like its position in the first centuries of our era, when Christians had to explain again and again that they were not benevolent if terrifying magicians adept in occult wonder-working techniques, but very ordinary men through whom God exerted His infinite power.

The occurrence of "miracles" is coming to be accepted, sometimes with a gluttonous and ostrich-digestioned credulity which refuses to envisage any normal explanation of an event that may satisfy its appetite for the marvellous, sometimes with a refusal to accept that anything which has taken place can in fact have gone beyond what the individual thinker believes to be explicable, in terms, say, of suggestion, of psycho-somatic activity or of psi, at work either singly or combined in various proportions.

It should of course be stressed that this attitude is not only adopted towards the paranormal phenomena associated with religion. It is constantly to be observed in psychical research. It is very difficult indeed for an observer to accept that something has happened which cannot be explained in terms of what he has already tested, weighed, thought out and assimilated into his mind. If he swallows as fact what is actually a misinterpretation, it may both vitiate the results of his past hard thinking and falsify his future conclusions. If it is fact indeed, it must painfully purge a mental digestion previously in a state of happy, healthy equilibrium. It is not surprising that there are some investigators who will consider the possibility of extra-sensory perception but not that of precognition; or of extra-sensory perception and precognition, but not of psycho-kinesis; or of all three separately, but not as occurring spontaneously and together in "haunted houses". It may be useful to give an example of this interesting refusal of credence.

A house in north Oxford has produced during the long years of its occupation by a family I know to be scrupulously, even painfully truthful, the following phenomena: rumbling and knocking "like furniture being moved about" in various rooms where nothing was subsequently found to have been shifted; the rattling, at four o'clock on a clear summer morning, of a necklace left on a mantelpiece "as if it were being picked up and dropped again"; the actual movement "as if it were being thrown" of a shoehorn across a room; the repeated rattling and turning of door handles (observed not only by the family, but by various guests staying in the house, one of them a young man absorbed in thinking not about psychical phenomena, but about his Viva next day); the repeated opening of shut doors (on one occasion during a Mozart concert on the wireless, to which everyone present, including this same young man, was listening with rapt attention); the turning-on of lights in every room in the house when all the occupants were out and the place was locked up, and also after everyone had gone to bed (again observed not only by the family on various occasions, but also by a young couple who had been lent the house and were staying there alone); a sudden unexpected sense of a presence which made the mother of the family almost automatically move to one side as she ran upstairs, to make room for "someone" coming down to pass her; and an occasion when the elder daughter, then aged twenty-four, was relaxing in a hot bath, and saw first with incredulity and then with alarm a petticoat which she had left on the back of a chair turn right over.

The agnostic family itself put forward tentative theories to account for the phenomena. They were attributed at one time to the desire of a forceful grandfather, lately dead, to attract attention, and at another to the possibility of adolescent psychological conflicts in one or other of the children; but the trouble recurred long after the grandfather's death (and long after special Masses for the repose of his soul had been said at the request of a Catholic member of his family) and long after the children were fully mature. They had not, in any case, been of the dull and inarticulate kind with whom poltergeist outbreaks are so often associated, but were both extremely conscientious and of a high intellectual calibre.

Some of the rumbling and knocking might perhaps be accounted for by Mr Lambert's useful and ingenious hypothesis as to the noise caused by structural disturbance in houses shaken by the movements of tidal or flood water very far underground.[1] The turning-on of the lights could perhaps be attributed to faulty electrical fittings; though these were of course overhauled from time to time. The rattling and turning of the door handles could be ascribed either to an imagination inflamed by the other odd occurrences (but would not the imagination produce something more picturesque?) or to a sensory hallucination brought about by some extra-sensory stimulus in the way already outlined. A "sense of presence" can, I believe, be produced both by the administration of mescalin or by the body's manufacture of a similar chemical substance. No such drug had been swallowed in this instance and the experient is, was and remains quite sane, which is not the case with those who suffer from this particular disturbance of their bio-chemistry. (Incidentally, the thesis that

---

[1] For a very illuminating discussion of an instance of this kind, see E. Dingwall and T. Hall, *Four Modern Ghosts* (London, 1958).

such intuitions of presence must *always* be illusory because they *sometimes* arise from physical stimuli originating either outside or inside the body is surely no more reasonable than the argument that the normal working of the senses can never be trusted because drunkenness, or a high temperature, can produce hallucinations.)

Now, all the phenomena reported in this house rest upon the same kind of evidence: the observations of guests and of three members out of a family of four, or four members of a family of five, if the evidence of the terror shown from time to time by the household dog be admitted. There is also the local tradition, known to a young man who had lived in the same road as a child, but unknown to the family (and their guests) during the first five years during which they lived there, that there was "something very odd about that house". Few psychical research workers, however, seem willing to admit that all the phenomena did in fact occur. They will accept some with ease but reject others as things which "could not" have happened as described. The two most commonly refused credence are first, the spontaneous opening of the doors and, second, the movement of the petticoat. The first is "explained" either by the idea that the doors were not properly shut or that the locks were defective (which was not the case) or by the theory that the whole affair was an hallucination (which ignores the fact that those doors had to be shut again, a fact recollected with vivid annoyance by those who had to get up and do so when trying to listen to the concert). The turning over of the petticoat is said to be purely an optical illusion; though it seems possible that the static electricity with which nylon garments become charged might provide a normal explanation. If they can produce a shower of sparks when pulled off on a frosty night, is it not possible that in certain conditions they might move?

More than enough has been said to illustrate the contemporary propensity to reject as impossible those occurrences which cannot be fitted into an intellectual frame of reference either provided by some scientific discipline or worked out over years of thought and experiment. Perhaps in honesty I should add that my own tendency is to reject in just this way clairvoyance occurring in a purely secular context; clairvoyance being defined as the paranormal knowledge of a fact not already in some individual or collective mind, conscious or unconscious. Yet the remarkable evidence of success in map-dowsing seems to demonstrate that clairvoyance of this kind does indeed occur, like it or not.

Non-Christian thought, aware of the existence of the psi-factor, and willing to recognize its activities up to this point or that, will take up just such an attitude as has been outlined towards the recorded miracles of our Lord and His followers over the centuries, interpreting them in accordance with what it accepts. It is therefore vitally important that informed Catholic thought should take parapsychology into account and be ready to acknowledge what can and what cannot be attributed to the paranormal rather than to the directly supernatural in those miracles. It is of course extremely difficult to do this, as man is not divided into neat pigeon-holes, here biological drive, here reasoning power, here intuition, but is a being in whom all these things fuse, a psycho-somatic unity (single though not harmonious, in that the limited energy at his disposal seems to flow almost independently of the controlling will now into this channel and now into that, and efforts to direct it from one to another may in themselves exhaust it).

"Grace builds on nature" but does not alter its unitary being and may release, strengthen, illuminate and transform any normal ability to an almost unrecognizable extent. Psi, existing in insects, birds and animals as well as in man, is one of those normal abilities; and psi, whose ordinary workings may link man both with his fellow men and with the original sin tainting the morph of his species, can also so link him with the Mystical Body of Christ that in his daily activities it will be almost impossible to distinguish which power, the dedicated natural one or the inflowing supernatural, is at work in the telepathic knowledge, the psycho-somatic healing, the intuitive common suffering experienced, exerted and endured in the service of God. Among ourselves, then, we can rest and be happy with awe in the presence of sanctity, where love, joy, peace are irradiated with the Divine Power; but for the sake of the world for which the Church exists it is necessary to attempt some rough distinction between psi-activity and the Pure Act of Deity. It cannot possibly be more than a rough distinction for, as has been seen, in the lives of dedicated men the two unite as indissolubly as light with water, "gilding pale streams with heavenly alchemy".

The following example, set in a slightly different context, may serve to show more vividly than any argument why it is urgently necessary that such difficult and delicate subjects should be discussed, and how false reverence may corrupt the presentation of truth. It is well known, as has been indicated in earlier chapters, that human emotions can express themselves symbolically in various skin conditions. It is also known that long brooding upon the Passion may bring about in some cognate, little understood, genuine and natural way, what is called stigmatization; the reproduction, especially in the hands and feet, of the wounds made in Christ's Body by the crucifixion. (May I stress *genuine* as well as *natural*? I do not mean to suggest that conscious or unconscious deception or self-mutilation by way of penance, or for purposes of attracting attention are necessarily at work in such cases, but simply that there are persons in whom body and brooding imagination are so closely interwoven that the operations of the latter stamp themselves upon the visible flesh.) These facts are familiar to most intelligent people; who are not impressed when they hear—as I have heard—zealots adduce the stigmata as proof of the supernatural.

It is plainly undesirable that the world at large should assume that our faith is founded upon the erroneous interpretation of facts whose true significance is now being discovered by scientific investigation. It is equally undesirable that any Catholic should entangle his faith with such erroneous interpretations.

If it is extraordinarily difficult even in the lives of holy men to separate the operations of psi, as released by sanctity, from the direct exertion of God's will, it is harder still to do so in the life of our Lord as the Gospels report it. Our own nature, taken for granted as we sleep and wake, work and play, is profoundly mysterious when it is examined; the collective unconscious joining us to our fellow men throughout history and pre-history, the "animal soul", keeping the body going with a swimmer's unformulated knowledge and ease, the individual subconscious with its specific habits and memories and associations and feelings, the mind aware of sensation and movement and time and place and circumstance, judging situations, linking facts, reasoning, deciding, planning, acting; and the strange, frightening capacity that co-exists with all these and that can realize in dark flashes "I am I", and sometimes and in some persons (like St Francis of Assisi, who murmured it, overwhelmed in wonder, a whole night long) "My God, and All! What art Thou, and what am I?" Yet with all these diversities at work in him, and with the spotlight of attention illuminating now one and now another, each human knows himself to be a single person.

In the Person of Christ, complex humanity was one with God. I cannot write of that. All I shall try to do is to consider His human nature in relation to His miracles, and to indicate some of those which go far beyond even the powers of perfect Man, Man born without the disruption of desire and will arising from the collective taint of our species, and without the continual nagging attraction towards actual wrongdoing— ill-will, pride, anger, lust, avarice, self-importance—which makes so much of our existence like trying to ride an old bicycle whose steering veers continually to one side. His faculties were integrated, psi among them. The Gospels reiterate like a chime of bells the many instances in which He showed Himself aware of what was going on in other men's minds and answered questions which they dared not ask.

He inherited the Jewish tradition that though spontaneous psi-activity might be accepted, it must never be sought or cultivated or used for its own sake, or for any other purpose than the service of God. It is interesting to consider the great temptations in the light of this tradition. After His baptism by His strange, gaunt, ascetic cousin, six months His senior, in the little river Jordan—some of whose reaches look like a Cotswold troutstream, a stretch of the Windrush—He had gone away to be alone for six weeks in the utter silence of the desert, quiet then as perhaps nowhere in the habitable world can be quiet now; no cars, no jet-engines, no helicopters, only day following night, and sometimes birds flying across the unimaginable stillness. He was hungry. He was physically exhausted. He was clearly aware that His every man's life of growth, development and breadwinning was over and that the years of struggle were beginning. The temptations matched the conditions. They were to use His abilities to satisfy His own urgent hunger; to demonstrate and advertise His importance instantly and conclusively by a spectacular feat of levitation; and to employ evil means to gain power that might be used at once for good ends. One in fact was concerned with instinct, one with psi and one with reason. All were rejected, moreover, in a curiously anonymous way, not with personal refusal or with reasoned argument, but with words from the living tradition of His ancestors, that tradition which He later declared Himself to have come "not to destroy, but to fulfil".

It may be useful to consider in relation to this episode a twentieth-century instance in which a most remarkable man yielded to temptations that had something in common with these: the instance of Rasputin, a Russian peasant who became a monk and a man of prayer and who was endowed with that gift of "paranormal healing" which frequently co-exists with intense physical vitality and with the natural power of exerting strong suggestion. He seems at first to have dedicated this gift, this "wild talent", wholly to good ends. Presently the Tsarina heard of him and called on him to help her haemophiliac only son, a fragile child for whose recurrent bouts of illness the ordinary medicine of the time could do very little. In the beginning, this awe-inspiring primitive prayed and exerted his healing capacity for the small Tsarevitch with simplicity, and succeeded again and again in alleviating his symptoms, a boon which must not be underestimated since to someone suffering from pain and fever, and to those who have to watch him suffer, the first consideration is that he should *feel* better, refreshed, peaceful, hopeful. Then Rasputin began to enjoy the money, the rewards, the prestige he was acquiring, and to publicize and exploit this last so as to satisfy his inordinate greed and lust, his growing and insatiable pride in his own capacities, his simultaneous desire to exert political power for its own sake. His assassination, whose difficulty demonstrated his terrific physical strength, came too late to prevent the corruption he had engendered from helping to bring down a dynasty and a civilization that might otherwise have been saved by peaceful change.[1]

It was when our Lord, His human nature tested, and His temptations clearly formulated and rejected, returned from the desert to preach and to gather disciples, that the concurrent stream of miracles began, but not for His own sake. The first, most human in its ambience and least in its power, seems to have been done almost reluctantly. Humanly speaking, a young man absorbed in the consciousness of an immense task does not at once realize the intense embarrassment of the host and hostess at a wedding celebration where the wine is running short. If he does realize it, he does not want to interfere with their arrangements, to manage their affairs for them, possibly to hurt their feelings by showing he has noticed something has gone wrong. "It is nothing to do with us really . . . "and then, at the plea of someone who has had household affairs to cope with and knows exactly how the party givers will be shamed if a guest asks for another drink and there is none left, it is done, but very quietly and unobtrusively. The waiters are the only people who know much about it and the toastmaster, who notices the goodness of

---

[1] This view of the situation will of course commend itself only to those who consider that historical events depend as much—or more— on personal decisions, choices and relationships as on the economic trends contemporaneous with them.

the new supply, has no idea where it comes from. Nor has the host.

Many of the miracles of healing are not demonstrations of authority as such, but flow from His compassion. The blind, the deaf, the lame, the leprous, the insane, are cured not as guinea pigs or object lessons, but because they or their friends plead for help. Sometimes He holds back for a moment, to bring out a motive, saying, "Unless you see signs and wonders you will not believe", and acts when it has become clear to the bystanders that the request has not been put simply so that He may be induced to demonstrate His power, but from overwhelming need: "Master, come quickly, before my child dies".

Only to the puzzled, disheartened followers of His cousin John, now in the prison where he was finally to be beheaded, did Christ speak of these happenings as primarily evidential. It was with genuine bewilderment that they came to Him asking if He were indeed the One Whom they awaited, or whether they ought to "look for another"; and even when He answered them, telling them to draw their own conclusions from the happy healings that had accompanied His journeys, He ended the list of reasons why they should recognize Him for what He was with the culminating point, more significant than all the rest, "and the poor have the gospel preached to them"; the poor, the unlearned, the unimportant, for whom none cares but God.

He gave a different reply to the repeated request for a really telling and conclusive "sign" made by the Pharisees, who already "knew all the answers", and whose teaching had dried up the service of God from a living and spontaneous activity into an elaborate, self-regarding, anxiety-ridden ritual within whose minutely regulated and detailed repetitions they could feel almost safe and quite superior, dramatizing their fasts, "putting the expression into" long prayers, washing their crockery with a housepride reinforced with overtly religious ardour, weighing dried mint and seeds as small as caraways on tiny scales and setting aside a tenth part for the temple. To them He said that the only sign they would be given would be the sign of Jonas.

This must have been extraordinarily baffling and frustrating; that is, if it were not dismissed at once as nonsensical. Even to hindsight the symbolism, though plain enough, has a certain dreamlike oddity about it. Who could have foreseen that the legend of that warning prophet, better known in England as Jonah—Jonah who has given his name to the innocently unlucky, the scapegoats, the accident-prone who involve others, Jonah thrown overboard in a storm by sailors who thought that he brought them misfortune and that it was better that one man should die than the whole ship's company, Jonah swallowed by a fish-eating monster from the depths of the sea, Jonah cast ashore still alive after three nights in the fabulous darkness of its belly—was a foreshadowing of that other innocent Scapegoat, that other putting to death of one Man for the sake of the people, that other swallowing up in the darkness of the tomb and the company of the unnumbered unremembered dead, and of the Resurrection itself? The very strangeness, the very grotesqueness of the Jonah/Jonas story is in point of fact typical of the way in which spontaneous precognition tends to crystallize out. Its fulfilment is as recognizable as it is unexpected.

It is extremely difficult to differentiate between those cases in which Christ healed the sick by suggestion or by some paranormal energy, and those in which they were cured by His divine Power. One might perhaps put in the former category those of the people to whom He said, "thy faith hath made thee whole"; especially that of the woman who had had a haemorrhage for twelve years and touched the hem of His cloak in the jostling crowd, thinking that He could not possibly know who had done it or why. He is said in this instance to have felt that "power had gone out of Him". There also may have been some hysterically blind or deaf or paralysed among them, and some reputed to be lepers who were in fact suffering from psycho-somatic skin disorders; but there is no reason to suppose that there were no true lepers, and none blinded by the fly-borne ophthalmia even now prevalent in the Near East. The man with a withered arm could not have been cured by suggestion, however powerful; nor the maimed; nor could the dead child, over whom the mourners were already keening with an intolerable noise, have been revived, nor the widow's son whose body was being carried to the cemetery at Naim; nor Lazarus, who had been dead and buried for days,[1] in a hot climate, with results bluntly indicated by his sister.

There are three things to be noted about the miracles of healing, to whichever of our Lord's powers they may be ascribed. One is how often in the early days the patients were asked to keep what had happened reasonably quiet, not to go about telling all and sundry who would repeat it as gossip—"I've heard of *such* a marvellous man, he is supposed to have cleared up so-and-so's trouble that she's had for years"—and so set a gaggle of self-regarding hypochondriacs to dog His footsteps.

The second is that lepers were told to conform to the sanitary regulations of their time and place by reporting themselves to the priests so that they might be fully examined and given a clean bill of health, thus simultaneously fulfilling the law, preventing others who might have had a temporary remission of symptoms from taking for granted, without inspection, that all was well with them as it was with these, and bringing to the Temple the knowledge of what was going on.

The third is that the healings were most often done in such a way as to imply something fundamental to those willing to reflect upon what had happened, rather than merely marvelling and forgetting, as people today marvel at and forget the headlines about cancer-cures or flying saucers from outer space in

---

[1] A suggestion, more ingenious than plausible, was made about 1938, (I think by Mr Gerald Heard, or some other member of the group of Vedantists then in California), that our Lord had taught Lazarus the technique of suspended animation and breathing which certain Indian yogis claim to practise, in order that he should deliberately go into a trance whence Christ would later resuscitate him as a demonstration of His miraculous powers. This suggestion does not take into account the facts already noted—that the whole Jewish tradition was against the deliberate development and cultivation of psi, or of any paranormal technique; and that our Lord continually refused to produce "signs and wonders" simply as a stimulus to faith.

the more sensational Sunday papers. In that age wonders were more easily accepted than they are in our own. The good roads of the Roman Empire, of which Palestine was a part, were used not only as military highways and commercial routes, but by itinerant pedlars, troupes of acrobats and jugglers, fortune-tellers like the two men described in the Acts of the Apostles who travelled about with a girl clairvoyant, conjurers and astrologers, wandering quacks with a stock-in-trade of mixed medicine and magic, amulets and herbs and potions and love philtres and words of power, and wonder-workers of all sorts. There would be no particularly cogent reasons for disbelieving in an inexplicable cure, because there were so few explanations even of normal ones.

If, however, those cures were effected by a prophet who was a Jew, and He repeatedly used His powers of healing on the day when His people were strictly forbidden to do any work; if He cured publicly and argumentatively on the sabbath a deformed man, and again a woman with some disease of the bones (osteomalacia? arthritis? she had been hunched together for thirteen years, unable to lift herself up and stand straight) and again a man with the dropsy, then the implications of what He was doing might begin to stand out. He was making the point that the sabbath was not an institution sacred in itself, of itself and by itself, to be observed with the timid, rigid ardour of a minor official maintaining a major regulation; that "the sabbath was made for man, not man for the sabbath".

But who was He, to make this point?

There was a wide range of answers: that He was an impudent young man, flouting sacred ordinances; that He could disentangle ends from means; that, though He cured people, His powers were evil, and "He cast out devils through the power of Beelzebub, Prince of devils"; or that He had authority to override traditional ordinances.

This problem must have been hard enough to solve. It must have been almost impossible to shelve. Suspension of judgement could not have come easily to a vital and intelligent community

of men whose minds were sharpened by argument and disputa-
tion, and whose chief intellectual discipline was that of law (as
ours is that of the physical sciences).

The problem which followed it was more arresting still and
challenged judgement even more urgently. It hinged precisely
upon that mysterious connexion between personality and bodily
process, psyche and soma, emotional guilt and physical disease
on which so much contemporary interest is focused. It linked
the healing of the body with that of the psyche, not by declaring
the whole concept of guilt to be unreal, but by recognizing that
it could be based on fact, could spring from having deliberately
done something known to be wrong, and needed to be
acknowledged and forgiven for what it was. Chapter nine of
St Matthew's Gospel, the earliest of the four to be written down,
contains a stripped account of an event implying this problem.
I quote from Mgr Knox's translation:

> They brought before him a man who was palsied and
> bedridden; whereupon Jesus, seeing their faith, said to the
> palsied man, Son, take courage, thy sins are forgiven. And at
> this some of the scribes said to themselves, He is talking
> blasphemously. Jesus read their minds and said, Why do you
> cherish wicked thoughts in your hearts? Tell me, which
> command is more lightly given, to say to a man, Thy sins are
> forgiven or to say, Rise up and walk. And now, to convince
> you that the Son of Man has authority to forgive sins while
> he is on earth (here he spoke to the palsied man), Rise up,
> take thy bed with thee, and go home.

A footnote points out that Jesus' remarks to the scribes made
it plain that though an impostor might have said "Thy sins are
forgiven" without being detected (since it would not have been
possible for anyone to check up on the inner result of the saying),
the effect of forgiveness was made plain by the fact that the man
who had till then been physically helpless did indeed get up and
take away with him the stretcher on which he had been carried
by his friends.

This exertion of power followed the pattern of faith-healing, flowed along psycho-somatic channels, exemplified in yet another context the poet's line "the soul is form and doth the body make"; but to anyone brought up in accordance with Jewish teaching it was clear as a landscape lit by lightning that the personality whose impact freed that power came from beyond the ordinary world. That impact carried, for the paralysed man who received and was reintegrated by it, an almost incredible implication, a seismic shock of joy and terror. For the Jews held that only God could forgive sins.

There are two ways of dealing with an event which shakes the foundations of that inner sphere of assumption, habit, conviction, intellectual structure and religious belief in accordance with which every man interprets what happens to him. One is to re-orientate that world, certainly in bewilderment, possibly in distress; "I can hardly believe it; but I must recognize it. I cannot reject or deny what I know has taken place. And that it has taken place must mean this, and this and this . . .". The other is to defend the *status quo*, to preserve that inner sphere inviolate in subjective confidence, as an articulate caterpillar might defend the enclosing surface of its self-woven cocoon: "I cannot believe it. It cannot be true. What has apparently taken place must be explicable in such and such terms already familiar to me".

It was thus that, in the Judaic climate of thought, some who realized that Christ both claimed the power to forgive sins and concurrently restored to fullness of life the maimed, the blind, the insane, the paralysed, reached the profoundly shocking and terrifying conclusion that He came from God; while others rationalized the course of events in accordance with another, ready-made, pattern of assumptions and decided that, as His claim to forgive sins must *ipso facto* be blasphemous, the things He did, though good in themselves, could only be accomplished by some supernaturally evil force.

It is clear, then, that it is possible to interpret some of the miracles of healing in terms of suggestion and of psi, variously combined. It is also clear that in those flowing from the assurance that sin was forgiven the Jews who were cured—and the vast majority were Jews—must have been aware of the impact of an immense authority before they could accept such a statement with its consequences for themselves and its implications about the healer.

Some form of psycho-kinesis may be adduced to explain the stories of our Lord's walking on the water. It may also just possibly be linked with those of His calming the storm, since both in primitive and in developed societies there are just enough instances of what does seem to be a curious synchronistic correspondence between weather and personality to make one hesitate to dismiss the whole idea as fantastic until repeated observation and, if possible, experimental investigation have shown it to be so. Among such instances may be cited Geoffrey Gorer's accounts[1] of deliberate attempts at "rain-making"; the different traditions of "Queen's weather" associated in our changeable and unpredictable climate with the ceremonial appearances of Queen Victoria and of Queen Elizabeth II; and the odd fact noted by St Thérèse of Lisieux in her autobiographical writings that wind and rain, sunshine or sparkling snow seemed to come as a reflection of her own inner mood. I say "as a reflection", since the mood is recorded as having preceded the weather and not (as in general experience) the weather the mood. It is of course perfectly possible to explain this in terms of precognition.

It is definitely out of the question, however, to associate the workings of the psi-function to whatever degree it may be developed, with the restoration of the dead to life[2]; with the cure of the mutilated; with the miracle of Cana; or with the repeated multiplication of food—the bread brought by the disciples for themselves, the five rolls and the cold fish packed by some careful mother for her son's picnic—to satisfy the

[1] *Op. cit.*
[2] A lucid and objective discussion of miracles in connexion with faith-healing and suggestion is to be found in Dr C. S. Lewis' fascinating volume—*Miracles* (London, 1947).

hunger of the crowds, thousands strong, which had followed Christ into the lonely uplands without stopping to think how far they were going and how impossible it would be to find anything to eat there.

That the Church lives still in the continuity of the divine life appears in the recurrence of such miracles, nearly sixty generations afterwards, in the lives of two nineteenth-century saints, close enough to us in time to have been known by the grandparents, say, of anyone over fifty. The French St John Vianney and the Italian St John Bosco, praying at a time of the utmost need, were answered in this way; the former with flour, when there was none left to make bread for the children in his orphanage at Ars, the latter with rolls. Perhaps I may be allowed to quote from my article in *The Month* for December 1957:

At the Turin college for three hundred students [for the priesthood, a college founded by St John Bosco without endowments] there were only twenty stale rolls in the house, and the baker, whose bill they had not been able to pay, would supply no more. Don Bosco, asked what was to be done about breakfast, said he would distribute whatever was there. A young man ... went and stood behind him to see what would happen as he gave out the rolls to the students who came up for them. He observed that the basket had no more than twenty rolls in it, that each student was given a roll, and that when the distribution was over there were still the same number of rolls in it as there had been at the beginning. ... This happened in 1860. The young man, Francis Dalmazzo, who gave this evidence on oath in the beatification process, had meant to leave the training college, whose life he found very hard; but was so much impressed that he stayed on.

It remains briefly to consider in connexion with psi the four cardinal experiences upon which the first Christians fed their faith: the Transfiguration, with three witnesses, Peter, who had to try to work off his feelings by building cairns of rock, James, and John absorbed in wonder, "breathless with adoration"; the Resurrection, and the subsequent appearances of Christ; the Ascension; and the coming of the Holy Spirit.

Normal awareness of objects outside oneself is brought about by a kind of image-making carried on through the body-mind. First, as has already been noted, the senses, stimulated by electrical waves of differing frequencies, bring to their owner what he transforms into experience of light, colour, sound. He then interprets these experiences in accordance with patterns of significance gradually built up from earliest infancy, when he began to select from the welter of successive sensations a repeated coincidence of warmth, smell, taste, sounds of a particular pitch, colours of a particular sort, which came to be recognized as his mother. These twin processes in which stimulus is transformed into sensory experience, and sensory—and, I believe, extra-sensory—experience into significant imagery, are among the most mysterious modes of interaction between the exterior and the interior world, event and consciousness.

By the time maturity is reached the process of interpretation often seems to have gone too far, and to have become an automatic sorting, packaging and labelling mechanism. Each set of images, once recognized, is simply classified, ticketed and set aside for possible use in theoretical argument or practical work; if no such use is found, it is ignored. This facilitates technological thought but inhibits wonder. The living purple foxglove becomes a botanical specimen with a Latin name and medicinal properties. The child-enchanting puddle, reflecting sky and face, coloured in London streets with the metallic rainbows of spilt petrol, and capable everywhere of being transformed, at the stamping of a Wellington boot, into arc after arc of flying crystal drops is, as generations of aunts and nurses have remarked, "nasty, dirty water".

It must of course be acknowledged that this utilitarian process of choice and exclusion, of ticketing this item of experience for use, ignoring that as irrelevant, rejecting the other as harmful, is necessary to everyday life. The question is one of degree. In every full-grown person, sensory experience and the pattern of images and associations built up from it come to be taken more or less for granted as an habitual background to the necessity of staying alive and looking after one's dependants. The painter, the writer, the musician, the naturalist will do this to a lesser extent than the administrator, the engineer, the efficiency expert, the bustling matron; but the process will—must—go on in them all. Among groups of images not recognized as being of practical importance, attention will only be yielded to those already associated with profound emotion; and profound emotion newly apprehended may make itself known in terms of those groups of images. There are, moreover, moments at which it is impossible to differentiate between an image, what it already symbolizes and the fresh emotion with which it is being charged, witness those many well-authenticated instances in which the figure of someone deeply loved is "seen" at the instant of that person's death.

All this should be remembered in considering the Transfiguration of our Lord. Peter, James and John had joined Him early in His preaching, had tramped the roads and tracks of Palestine with Him, sailed with Him, talked and argued with Him. The pattern of sensory experiences which each of them had built up into an image of Him was familiar; the voice, the noble face of which we may have some reflection in the Holy Shroud, the hands moving in explanation or blessing, or breaking long loaves at suppertime, the clothes of the day, woven of natural wool like their own, the well-trodden sandals, the hard dusty feet. *He* was always God and Man, but *they* had become habituated to His human presence which was to be changed, battered and wounded and disfigured, killed, and buried. It was profoundly necessary for them to realize that He was more than their taken-for-granted sensory image of Him.

Every human being is, of course, much more than any other human being's image of him, and this fact is realized, on occasion, by quite ordinary people who love one another. It is possible to sit at peace, listening to music perhaps, and to become unexpectedly aware of the person beside one not as a dear physical presence, but as a living consciousness, as it were an immediate flame.

Peter and James and John, however, had to become aware of an identity divine as well as human. They were taken away from the roads, the crowds, the familiar towns and villages and from their usual companions to the height and stillness of a mountain slope. Here, stripped of their habitual activities and associations, and free from the stimulus-and-response of every day, they could become aware of things in themselves without relating them to their own purposes or necessities or desires.

It was there that suddenly and unexpectedly they saw Jesus radiant with light. Their words eddy from awe to commonplace, freeze into paradox. He shone like the sun. His clothes looked whiter than any laundry could possibly make them. They were all "overshadowed" by a cloud which was yet "dazzling". They were aware of Moses and Elias talking to Him, two historical persons who were also heroic figures, representing the two great traditions of their people; Moses, through whom the divine Law had been formulated, and Elias through whom the divine inspiration of prophecy had flowed. From the dazzling darkness of the cloud the words distilled: "This is my beloved Son, in Whom I am well pleased". They could bear no more; they fell on their faces, shielding their eyes with their arms against the intolerable and sweet and terrifying splendour. As they breathed on, the timeless moment faded. The terror and joy were gone. They looked up, and "there was Jesus only", telling them to remember what had happened, but not to speak of it until after His death, perhaps so that it should remain clear and vivid in their minds (without evaporating in talk and discussion and rationalization) until the time came when it should be needed.

In this event, image and symbol and vision shine fused. It is impossible to know whether the minds of the three men, made suddenly, overwhelmingly conscious of Christ's Divinity, projected this knowledge in terms of light[1] (supreme symbol of given joy, exterior and interior, of given understanding, clarity, glory, spring's renewal, dawn's peace after night-time fear and anxiety, the sun in splendour) or whether that consciousness was mediated to them by some physically generated radiance impinging upon their senses; whether their profound, simple, unitary cognition that He was both that God and that Neighbour upon whose love "hang all the Law and the Prophets", imaged itself in the figures of Moses and Elias "conversing with Him", or whether those presences were perceived not only as symbols but as self-aware identities. It is clear though that the psi-function was being used, in that, as God is a spirit, the voice heard could have nothing to do with the senses, but resulted from some direct, irresistible stimulus to the psyche to clothe in words an intuition of truth.

Something comparable was to happen at Pentecost, which shows the same sort of fusion of image, symbol and sense. As the word "light" was—and still is—doubly charged to mean the illumination of both sight and mind, so in the Jewish parlance of the time the word "wind" or breath was doubly charged to mean both the movement of the air and the movement of the Spirit. Thus, the "rushing, mighty wind" that was heard could have been either a projection in auditory imagery of some over-whelming awareness of the Spirit's active presence, or a physical means of bringing the knowledge home by way of the senses. The same thing holds good, in visual terms, of the "tongues of fire". It is with the voices again that it becomes clear that the psi-function was involved. The influx of the Spirit of God suddenly and unexpectedly fused the disciples into a unity so complete that a new collective unconscious came into being, a new group-mind was formed, the mind of the Church, with more abundant life replacing the animated automatism of habit; freedom irradiating

---

[1] Fr Joseph Crehan, S.J., who has most kindly read this chapter, points out that the association of light with Deity (found in many religions) was especially familiar to the Jews, who believed that "God approached them by means of the *Shekinah*, which is generally des-cribed as the light of God".

law; and grace—another doubly charged word, grace the given, unstudied rightness of movement in the soul as in the body—welling up from the depths of the new morph, integrating and transforming the ancient conflicting impulses of nature.

The disciples had not had an English conditioning as to being inconspicuous or using understatement. They had no inhibitions about showing their feelings or about making a noise. They shouted and sang for joy, and a large crowd assembled to see what was going on; there were Jews up for the festival from all over the Middle East and Africa, Mesopotamia, Crete, Egypt, Libya, Persia, Iraq and even Asia. Many of them were drawn into this new collective mind, even though they remained detached enough to register amazement at realizing that, though those who spoke were Galileans, they could understand all that was said. They comprehended one another, in fact, at a level of such depth that each individual, each small group with its different origins and memories and dialects and languages, clothed the impulse received through psi in the verbal imagery which was most familiar and so "heard", each in the appropriate words, the disciples rejoicing in the wonderful activity of God.

One may contrast with this the ancient legend of the babble of Babel, where each tribe came to be so rigidly enclosed in its own separate history, conditioning, associations and interests that it literally could not understand a word that anyone else was saying, rather as if one group of ardent Marxists, one of logical positivists, one of Empire Loyalists and one of liberal humanists should sit down together to work out a policy for world unity.

An important and interesting attempt[1] to interpret the Resurrection appearances of our Lord wholly in terms of psi has been made by a young Anglican writer, the Rev. Michael Perry. His motive is to present the facts in a mode comprehensible to the average intelligent contemporary mind, conditioned sometimes by the discipline of a physical science and always by the technological assumptions of our age. His assembly of the scriptural and non-scriptural documentary evidence that these

[1] *The Easter Enigma* (London, 1959).

appearances occurred, and his examination and assessment of this evidence and of the theories advanced at different times over the last two thousand years to explain them, are alike admirably clear, scholarly and detached. His own theory is that our Lord's human body perished and that, immortal and bodiless, He succeeded in convincing His followers and friends of His victory over death by inducing in them veridical hallucinations of His physical presence. Veridical hallucinations are, it will be remembered, sensory images in which extra-sensory perception is projected and then reflected back to the percipient's mind.

There is no reason to rule out the possibility that our Lord may sometimes have made Himself known in this way, notably in the case of St Paul, and possibly too on that occasion when the disciples recognized Him "in the breaking of bread", the gesture associated with so many wayside meals together, as well as with the Last Supper. (It is interesting to remember that, after the bread was broken, they ceased to perceive His human presence, perhaps as a reminder that that presence was henceforward to be known in the Blessed Sacrament.)

There is, however, every reason to reject the attempt to apply such an interpretation to *all* the appearances. It leaves unexplained the finding of the empty tomb. It implies that, for lack of language to explain the true state of affairs, Christ was perpetrating a pious fraud upon His disciples when He said that He was not an apparition. It ignores the incident in which, after fishing rather disconsolately all night, they found Him waiting on the shore for them beside a driftwood fire on which they grilled and ate with Him some of the catch, finishing the meal with a honeycomb.

One of Mr Perry's difficulties seems to lie in his horror of any Fundamentalist interpretation of the phrases "the resurrection of the flesh" or "the resurrection of the body", a horror which reference to contemporary documents does not quite justify. St Paul deliberately contrasts the body, as we now experience it, with the resurrected body, and says that those who are physically alive when our Lord returns will be "changed".

The association of consciousness, which is non-spatial, with matter, which can be weighed, measured and handled, has always in itself been very odd, profoundly mysterious. It is no less odd and mysterious now that matter is known to be an aggregation of differing patterns of electrical energy. It is still strange moreover to reflect that, when these patterns of energy cohere in living beings, they are able to take up and assimilate into that conscious coherence other energy patterns in the form of food.

At the Incarnation, the Identity of the Second Person of the Blessed Trinity was united with a human identity expressing itself in a body, such a coherence of energy patterns as our own bodies are. This body died on the cross of shock, agony, bleeding, thirst and exhaustion, and was taken down, wrapped in grave-clothes and put in a rock tomb until the sabbath should be over and it could be prepared for formal burial. Is it not possible to hazard that, before its coherence could disintegrate, the patterns of electrical energy which constituted it were taken up into a new coherence, that of the glorified Body; like the old one, in that it could (if only on occasion) be seen, touched, heard, recognized and could even assimilate those other patterns of energy of which fish and honeycomb are constituted; unlike it in that it was not conditioned by space, by time, or by appearance and that its Identity could be united with the collective being of the Church as with the tiny planetary systems of atoms that form the Host.

Traditore traduttore: the translator is a traitor. Both physicist and theologian may well disown such an attempt as this to consider in terms of their concepts (wrenched from the matrix of thought in which their meaning matured) those three familiar things whose strangeness I have just stressed, and may perhaps be allowed to reiterate. First, the shattering oddity (patent even to a child when it first begins to reflect at the age of five or six upon the nature of things as it finds them), the shattering oddity of the union between ponderable matter and imponderable consciousness; of the knowledge that an "I", invisible but aware of itself, inhabits and can to some degree command a visible body, willing it, say, to lift one finger and put it down again or to exclude the world by shutting its eyes. Second, the peculiarity of the fact that this composite being can change other forms of matter into its own, a peculiarity which is the sole theme of Walter de la Mare's poem chanting that "Whatever Miss T. eats/Turns into Miss T". These are known to all human beings. The third is the Incarnation, fulfilled in the Resurrection and continued in the Blessed Sacrament, with its implications as to the hallowing and transformation and renewal of the body, the intense significance with which its activities are charged, and the eternal value of temporal and material things.

But one cannot so much as attempt to think without using concepts, images and analogies of some sort; and it is very hard to find any adequate way to express even the relationship of conscious, continuing self-aware identity that can experience and think and choose, with patterns of energy susceptible of alterations in form without destruction of being, alterations such as those exemplified in the whole cycle of change celebrated in the lugubrious song about the man who went to Ilkley Moor without his hat, caught cold, died and was buried in the earth, where worms changed the energy patterns that had formed his body into theirs and yielded theirs in turn to be changed into ducks, which served in the end to feed other men.

These concepts and analogies that I have used, then, have been employed less as verbal currency exactly weighed and stamped than as means of attempting to bring the profound strangeness of familiar events home to the understanding.

It may be useful to bear them in mind in considering the Ascension, the last symbolic bodily gesture made by Christ, on the last occasion that those who had worked and travelled and lived with Him were to perceive His Presence with their senses. They had had a meal with Him and were talking to Him in the open air. He had said they were not to leave Jerusalem but to wait there for an event He called the baptism of the Holy Spirit. They had asked, even at this juncture, whether political power were going to be restored to their nation and had been told it was enough for them to know that the Holy Spirit was to come upon them, giving them strength and energy, and that they were to bear witness to Jesus "to the ends of the earth". Directly He said this, "they saw Him lifted up, and a cloud caught Him away from their sight", a cloud which must have soared away into the depths of the sky, since they stood straining "their eyes towards heaven" till they could see it no longer.

In the Acts of the Apostles, as in the Gospels themselves, there are a number of miracles which could be interpreted in terms either of psi-activity or of suggestion, or of a combination of both; and a number of others which are not susceptible of any such explanation.

Of the first kind may be the healing of some of the sick who were brought into the hot, bright streets so that St Peter's shadow might fall on them as he went along, and some of those cured by contact with pieces of linen, handkerchiefs and aprons that St Paul had touched; as may the two flashes of precognition shown by Agabus, who foresaw, when he was at Antioch, the famine which was to happen in the reign of the Emperor Claudius (thus enabling his hearers to organize a relief scheme in time to forestall the need) and who, at Caesarea, seems to have projected first in muscular movements and only afterwards in words a realization of something else to come. He tied up his own wrists and ankles with a girdle belonging to St Paul and said that in just this way would the Jews at Jerusalem bind the girdle's owner before handing him over to the Gentiles, the occupying Power of Rome. This did not deter St Paul from going to Jerusalem, where the prediction was in fact fulfilled.

Of the second kind are St Peter's revival at Joppa of Tabitha, whose dead body had already been washed and laid out ready for burial by fellow members of the widows' sewing group, and St Paul's healing at Lystra of a man born with a deformity that had lamed him all his life.

Two of the most interesting and startling cases recorded in the Acts are, however, of a mixed provenance. In each an outside stimulus from "a power not themselves" activated, co-ordinated and used a vivid telepathic interchange between two men who had never met, an interchange which had results that neither could have foreseen.

The first instance was that of St Paul who asked our Lord after the bewildering dazzling shock of vision and conversion what He wanted him to do, and was told to go on to Damascus, in accordance with his original plan, and wait for someone who would be sent to help him. Blinded, fumbling in his movements, holding the hand of another traveller, he obeyed and went to his lodgings in Straight Street. Praying there, he visualized someone he did not know, called Ananias, coming to him. At the same time Ananias, made suddenly aware of the Divine Presence, asked what he was to do and was told to go to those lodgings in Straight Street, and enquire for a man called Saul of Tarsus, whose blindness he was to cure. Ananias, taken aback, did not think he could have understood properly and said so, pointing out that it was well-known that this Saul had come precisely in order to arrest and imprison Christians and was indeed empowered by the Jewish authorities to do so. Overruled and convinced of what must have seemed a most unlikely development, he took his courage in his hands, went to the house and gave sight and baptism to the helpless man from whose preaching, arguing, journeying and suffering so much was to grow.

The second instance concerns St Peter, who was staying at the time with a tanner called Simon, who had a little house by the sea at Joppa. He went up to the flat roof of the house to be alone and to pray in peace and quiet, while waiting for lunch. He was hungry, and it is fascinating to note how his unconscious mind dramatized in terms of that hunger the intuition that was being given to him. Three times over, he had a very vivid waking dream in which he saw, being let down from the sky as he used to let down his net into the sea, a big container[1] full of creatures that Jews were forbidden to eat—pigs perhaps, and

[1] "Sheet" in the Knox translation, "vessel" in others. It has been suggested that in St Peter's mind the image was associated with remembrances of the story of Noah and the Ark which rescued animals of *all* kinds from the flood.

hares, and lobsters: a voice told him to eat; he refused with horror, saying he had never eaten any forbidden food, and the voice said, "It is not for you to call profane what God has made clean".

Odd and grotesque as this dream was, it carried a sense of significance; and Peter was puzzling over what in the world it could mean when three men came to the door and he knew that he was being told to go down and meet them and do as they asked.

When he got downstairs he found two servants and a soldier who had been sent over from Caesarea, a day's journey away, by Cornelius a centurion in the Italian Cohort of the Roman Army who was stationed there. They brought a message from him asking Peter to go back with them and see him. Jews did not usually go about with men of other races, and these were neither Jews nor proselytes, nor was Cornelius. However, part of the meaning of Peter's thrice-repeated dream was flashed upon him and next morning he and one or two others duly went off to Caesarea with them. Cornelius, his family and some of his friends were waiting; and Cornelius, who had long been drawn to the adoration of the One God, explained that four days before, when at prayer, he had perceived a shining figure who had said he was to send men to a specified address in Joppa, with instructions to ask someone called Peter who was staying there to come over and tell him what to do.

Peter preached to them all, and to the amazement of the Jewish Christians who had come with him the occurrences of Pentecost were repeated and they heard these strangers rejoicing in God as their own people had done. Peter, by now aware of the full meaning of his dream, baptized them, arguing then, as later at Jerusalem, that as they too had been given the gift of the Holy Spirit, it was clear that they too were to be received into the Church, which was meant for men of all nations.

The Acts of the Apostles can indeed be read as a chronicle of the new group-mind which had come into being, and of the way in which the individual and collective psi-function of its members was released, activated and used by the Holy Spirit, so that grace was to the new human morph what instinct is to the morph of animal species. Many who saw what was going on believed either that the apostles were angels or gods in themselves—an impression instantly, strenuously and repeatedly denied—or that they were extremely powerful, benevolent and accomplished magicians. Even after his conversion by Philip, Simon Magus, who had himself been a widely publicized magician and took a professional interest in "signs and wonders", understood so little about the source of the apostles' power that he offered to pay Peter and John to transmit it to him and had to be rebuked and told to pray for forgiveness.

It was St Paul, however, in whose experience the psi-factor had played so large a part, St Paul the visionary and the intellectual, who saw things in their right relationship and proportion, distinguished means from ends: "Though I speak with the tongues of men and of angels, and have not charity, I am become as sounding brass or a tinkling cymbal. And though I have the gift of prophecy and understand all mysteries and all knowledge; and though I have all faith, so that I could remove mountains, and have not charity, I am nothing".

Telepathic transmission of thought and ideas; precognition, learning; psycho-kinetic powers; none had any value in itself, none was of any importance beside what could exist without any of them, the love of God and man.

Chapter Seven

PHILOSOPHICAL ASSESSMENTS: FROM THE WORLD SOUL TO PROPHECY

UP till the sack of Rome, and perhaps even a little later, there was some philosophical speculation as to the nature of psi-phenomena as such.

Cicero[1] had already made a distinction—all too quickly forgotten—between spontaneous and artificially induced extrasensory perception; he called them intuitive and deductive divination respectively.

Plutarch, who has been observed trying to account for the decline in the number of oracles in his time, hazarded that "divination"—in which he included both telepathy and precognition—was a natural power, waning in the autumn. This is, incidentally, a very interesting suggestion if it is considered in the light of the traditional connexion—empirical as much as moral[2]—between the maintenance of chastity and the capacity for psi-experience; a connexion recorded in our time in Ronald Edwin's autobiography.[3] It looks as if the same energy could be used either for extra-sensory perception or for reproductive activity, though very seldom for both at once—a hypothesis which would be much strengthened if the capacity for psi-experience were shown to increase with the impetus towards reproduction in the spring and to wane as it declines in urgency as the year goes on. Plutarch maintained also that this innate faculty for divination could serve as "a state of receptivity through which the soul becomes the instrument of God, just as the body is the instrument of the soul".[4] He was moreover

[1] *De Divinatione.*
[2] Cp. p. 115, above.　　　　[3] *Op. cit.*
[4] *Chambers' Encyclopaedia*, "Divination".

deeply interested in the way in which Socrates' "daemon" (perhaps a secondary personality projected by that profoundly rational man so that knowledge received by way of psi could reach his conscious attention in an acceptable form) made itself understood. He concluded that it worked neither by the usual interior psycho-somatic code of sneezing, nor by the exterior one of omens, nor by veridical hallucinations of sight or sound, vision or voice, but by exerting a direct impression on the mind.

Pliny, working in A.D. 77, distinguished in his natural history between magic, which was bad by intention, and marvels, which could, he thought be brought about, given proper training, by virgins or those observing a rule of chastity, provided that they were naked and fasting at the time. He maintained that "magical force" could act at a distance and held that certain persons—he instanced one named Pyrrhus—were gifted with a "healing touch". The same distinction between magic and marvel was made by Apuleius of Madaura in the second century; that same Apuleius who wrote the *Metamorphoses* in which the stories of the Golden Ass and of Cupid and Psyche are to be found. Black magic, *magica malefica*, was, he claimed, completely different from that art or discipline by which it was said that people could divine the future and know what was being talked about in their absence. It is worth mentioning that he was accused of the former; perhaps he did not want to disclaim the use of the latter. Galen, the great doctor born in Asia Minor in A.D. 129, believed in the occurrence of precognition, and held that on occasion he learned from his dreams how to diagnose and treat disease. His own career, indeed, had been determined by a dream, when he was seventeen years old and studying philosophy, that his dead father, an architect, was telling him to turn to medicine. He had, incidentally, a number of Christian admirers, despite the fact that he held a salaried appointment as doctor to a team of gladiators.

A hundred years or so later Hippolytus, a hearty sceptic, examining phenomena observed at the *séances* of his day, concluded that they were entirely bogus and gave some entertaining accounts of the methods used to produce them. If not technically so far advanced as those of the American mediums who conceal tiny wireless sets in their imposing coiffures,[1] they show ingenuity of the same sort. He describes darkened rooms in which a woman lies upon a sofa in a trance, while her awe-stricken clients gape at "apparitions" contrived by the help of mirrors, tremble at the sound of thunder off-stage, and are dumbfounded when their questions are answered by a male voice, that of a confederate the other side of a partition, speaking through a hidden tube made out of the windpipe of a crane.

It was from the ancient University of Alexandria, however, that the most interesting ideas about extra-sensory perception seem to have sprung. Here the philosophy of Plato and the theories of Pythagoras (who was, as well as a mathematical genius, a believer in the transmigration of souls) were taught and discussed and elaborated in various forms for well over eight hundred years, from 323 B.C. to A.D. 529, when it was closed by an edict of the Emperor Justinian because its teaching had become specifically gnostic and anti-Christian. In its earlier days, however, it had taught a theory (revived in medieval Christendom in the contention that universals are more real than particulars) that abstract ideas are not generalizations made by man from his observations of the natural world, but truths pre-existing in the mind of God. The soul of man was half-way between these eternal truths and the intrinsically imperfect matter in which they were expressed; and it had three parts, reason, spirit and appetite (as we might say, intellect, emotion and instinct), of which reason alone was immortal. Plainly, then, man should cultivate only the reasonable part of his soul; Plato himself had logically excluded from his ideal community anyone "inspired" and not intellectually in full control of himself. In theory, this was admirable. In practice, when men attempted to withdraw attention from the realm of sense, feeling and instinct, they became increasingly aware of the collective unconscious—

[1] Réginald-Omez, O.P., *Psychical Phenomena* (London, 1959).

with which the "world soul" may plausibly be equated—of archetypal figures interpreted as those of the gods, and of psi-phenomena.

Writing at Alexandria as early as the first century A.D., Philo Judaeus used this concept of the world soul-collective unconscious in his classification of significant dreams. He put them under three headings. There were those which came direct from God, and were self-explanatory. There were those in which the dreamer's mind was "united with the world soul" and which were neither quite clear nor very puzzling. And there were those in which the dreamer's mind was "moved by some frenzy of its own",[1] (that is, apparently, used its own private system of symbols) and which had to be interpreted. Philo puts into this category the dreams of Pharaoh's butler and baker[2]; but it is equally well exemplified by a precognitive dream of Bishop Nonnus recorded without any particular surprise by one James the Deacon in the *Lives of the Desert Fathers*.[3]

Nonnus one day saw the notorious courtesan Pelagia pass by in great beauty and elegance and was struck with sadness by the thought that he did not give nearly as much time and pains to preparing his soul for God as she devoted to making her young body attractive to her lovers. That evening he dreamt that he saw a black, foul-smelling dove standing by the altar. After the prayer for the catechumens it flew away until after the congregation had gone; then it returned and kept fluttering round him until he caught it and plunged it in the holy water stoup. It "rose up out of the water as white as snow, and flying upwards was borne into the high air and vanished out of sight". On waking, Nonnus went to church, where he was due to preach a sermon. Pelagia, going along the road outside, was suddenly moved to enter the church and listen to him. When the congregation had gone, she asked whether she might confess her sins and receive baptism, and, these things having been done,

[1] Thorndike, *op. cit.*
[2] See Chapter Four.
[3] *The Desert Fathers*, translated and edited by Helen Waddell (London, 1936).

went off to the deserts to live and die a solitary contemplative. It is, incidentally, fascinating to note how in Nonnus' dreaming mind the image of the traditional, gentle, amorous dove of Venus seems to have become fused with that of the dove as symbol of the Holy Spirit, so that the same creature, now black, now cleansed, but the same, is the type first of profane and then of sacred love.

Plotinus, educated at Alexandria two hundred years after Philo's time, still used the same kinds of concept. He held that sorcery did indeed occur and visualized it as a stimulus to psycho-somatic experience working, as drugs did, through man's bodily and irrational side, and he maintained that charms and incantations were effective because of a "sympathy" existing throughout nature in virtue of the indwelling world soul. This view commended itself in the fourth century to the Emperor Julian who reverenced the observation of omens, the practice of astrology, and the knowledge to be gained from dreams, as revelations of "the spirit behind the elements".

Synesius, later a Christian bishop, was in his youth a pupil of Hypatia at Alexandria, and regarded divination as one of the noblest of human pursuits. He is said to have had precognitive dreams, one of which indeed saved his life.

Christian thinkers were on the whole, however, less concerned with the nature and implications of psi as a natural phenomenon than with the necessity to differentiate between organized magic on the one hand and miracles on the other. Thus, when Celsus accused both Jews and Christians of magical practices Origen replied that "there would indeed be a resemblance between miracles and magic if Jesus, like the magicians, had performed His works only for show; but . . . there is not a single juggler who by means of his proceedings invites his spectators to reform their ways, or trains in the fear of God those who are amazed by what they see". St Augustine again—though he distinguished between *goetia*, sorcery, what Charles Williams called "the twisted malice of goetry" and *magia* or magic—insisted that Christians have nothing to do with any such activities and that their miracles "are wrought by simple confidence and devout faith in God, not by incantations and spells". What is more, those who concentrate upon producing marvels, sometimes by the agency of demons who "construct phantom images"(suggest hallucinations ?) "to delude human souls", may well achieve more spectacular results than Christians, whose whole concern is to serve God in love and humility, accepting the exercise of His power in whatever way He may show it.

As has already been noted in Chapter Four, a succession of Roman emperors who were by no means Christian had long been trying to prohibit the activities of astrologers and soothsayers, partly, no doubt, for political reasons, since what is prophesied with sufficient conviction and vigour tends to make itself come true, simply because men think it useless to struggle against "what *is* to be" and turn their energies instead to discovering in what direction the Great Bear is going to jump, or climbing on the bandwagon of King Charles's Wain. It was also in all probability in the interest of public order, since (despite the repeated distinctions made, as has been seen, between black magic and induced psi-phenomena) those who attempted to cultivate and use extra-sensory perception in whatever form and by whatever means, whether as precognition or as telepathy, whether by using the stars as "K objects"[1] or by practising techniques of psychological dissociation, were frequently lumped together, both in the public mind and for administrative purposes, with sorcerers, wizards and all who attempted to exert mysterious powers for evil ends, supplementing them with material devices if need arose, helping along ill-wishing with poison, reinforcing love-charms with aphrodisiacs and brewing abortifacients to kill what love had created.

There was already, then, a strong general distrust and suspicion of everything that could be associated with psi.

The great persecutions sharpened individual fear amongst the Christians, and the repeated barbarian invasions shook and

[1] Carington, *op. cit.*

finally shattered the whole collective secular background to their lives and the lives of the inhabitants of the great Roman Empire. The *Pax Romana* had prevailed for so many hundreds of years that it had come to be taken for granted as part of the nature of things that law and order, justice and reason, should continue. It began to be clear that this was not so. There was more and more necessity for self-defence, less and less leisure and inclination for detached thought; never, in any case, so congenial to the Roman pattern of culture as it had been to that of the Greeks. Popular ideas as to the nature of the cosmos, such as that demons with "subtle bodies" made of solidified air lived in the mid-regions of the sky and stirred up storms, came to be taken for granted, as did the equally popular assumption that *all* precognition, except that respectably rationalized in terms of astrology,[1] and *all* telepathic phenomena, must be attributed to the activity of spirits.

It was, then, impossible to regard extra-sensory perception as a natural, morally neutral power. It was good if produced by God or by a good spirit; bad if produced by a bad spirit. By the time that St Isidore of Seville (560–636) wrote his *Etymologiae*—a sort of dictionary-encyclopaedia of which the nearest modern equivalent is perhaps the invaluable French *Petit Larousse*—all distinction between witchcraft, divination, "white" magic, and spontaneous non-Christian precognition and telepathy seems to have been obliterated. He gives, incidentally, a most interesting list of methods of divination in current use; they include modes of using earth, air, fire, water, sacred knots, incantations and the involuntary muscular movements of arms and legs. This method of projecting in a code of semi-automatic physical activity information received by way of the psi-function is plainly essentially the same as that employed by the Eskimo shamans

---

[1] Though astrology was "respectable" in the general view, it was of course deprecated by Christians because of its implicit contradiction of the teaching that the human will was free, at any rate in its more detailed applications. In later epochs, however, many of them continued to consult astrologers rather as we now consult weather prediction authorities or those who compile demographical statistics.

who have already been discussed. Those who used it in St Isidore's time were called *salisatores*.

The urgent, pressing, ever-increasing need of that twilight of civilization which deepened into the Dark Ages was for self-preservation, self-defence, whether against the exterior wild unreason of the invading tribes, the unpredictable Huns and Goths and Vandals for whom anarchic force was the only law, or against interior corruption and evil. There was no time, no energy, no motive, for looking at created things in themselves. The Old Testament writers had rejoiced in day and night, fire and frost, conies and ants, lions roaring after their prey, whales and all that move in the waters and had declared that all created things in their strangeness and magnificence glorified and reflected God by being themselves. "O all ye works of the Lord, bless ye the Lord, praise Him and magnify Him for ever." Herodotus and Pliny had written their natural histories with wonder, pleasure and thought (not unmixed with credulity!). Now, as men clung in desperate, helpless insecurity to God they began to think of Him not so much in His self-existent, creative splendour as solely in relationship to themselves, their own necessities, emotions, guilts and longings, and they assumed increasingly that the rest of creation, where it was of no obvious use to them, could only have been designed "to point a moral and adorn a tale". The line of thought they followed ran clear from Aesop's fables to the medieval bestiaries, now illustrating the virtue of perseverance by the Tortoise's defeat of the Hare, now warning women against the dangers of vanity by citing the story that those who wished to capture tiger cubs could do so safely by hanging mirrors along their homeward path, mirrors at which the tigress would stop so long to admire her striped reflection that she would never catch up with those who had stolen her children. It was as if nature no longer existed and

> Tyger, Tyger, burning bright
> In the forests of the night. . . .

could be faced and tolerated only as an allegory. It is not surprising that in much of what had once been the Roman Empire all idea of psi as a natural phenomenon was forgotten for some seven hundred years, until St Thomas Aquinas began to ask himself whether it was not possible that certain animals possessed a natural, non-rational gift of prophecy.

The intellectual clarity of the ancient world was clouded over, the traditional disciplines of thought atrophied, the mental grasp of generation after generation grew weaker; except in the monasteries where, though learning and argument continued, the prime necessity was to grapple with the new dimension of being granted by grace.

In general, the emotional emphasis shifted as ever in time of stress from the maxim that "He who is not against us is with us" to the contrasting "He who is not with us is against us". Religions combining academic and spiritual snobbery and exalting the attainment of gnosis by persons of high intellectual calibre and acute aesthetic sensibility, in whom the attitude of the philosopher kings shaded imperceptibly into that of Auntie knows best: religions urging emotional identification with some sacred animal symbol of force and fertility, in mysteries such as that of the Mithraic Bull; or cruelty and domination, as in the wild worship of Thor and Odin; or the achievement of some especial state of consciousness, whether by yogic techniques or by the exploitation of sexual energy; or the militant fatalism of Islam; all these were a living, a mortal danger, and it was therefore necessary to know and to proclaim in the words of *The Song of Roland* that "*païens ont tort*". It was difficult, if not impossible, to reflect with detachment that there might be some aspects of good in these beliefs, that invincible ignorance might yet find in them some sparks of the "light that lighteth every man coming into the world", and that psi-phenomena occurring in their adherents were not *ipso facto* diabolical; as difficult as it would have been in the darkest days of World War II to realize that the loyalty, courage and self-sacrifice to be found among adherents of Nazism were good in themselves though exploited for an overall evil purpose.

In the territories conquered by the Arab armies of Islam, however, a settled peace ended anxiety, and brought confidence and leisure and detachment for thought. Despite the Mohammedan doctrine that there were no such things as secondary causes, and that every event, great or small, arose from the direct will of Allah (a doctrine which Moslem thinkers today believe to be vindicated by contemporary atomic theory), and despite the idea that extra-sensory perception occurring among mystics of the Sufi school was a self-evident sign of sanctity; already in the ninth century the philosopher Alkindi was speculating as to the nature of psi activity, some varieties of which he was inclined to attribute, in a modern but not necessarily accurate manner, to "rays emitted by the human mind and voice".[1] These rays, he thought, "become more efficacious in moving matter if the speaker has fixed his mind upon, or names, God or some powerful angel". It should be noted that this process does not look like prayer; the speaker was not asking for help, he was using a psychological technique, focusing his attention, mentally and vocally, upon one dazzling concept or another so that the psi-function could be set free to work unhampered by conscious observation.

In a treatise translated into Latin under the title of *De somno et visione* by Gerard of Cremona some three hundred years afterwards, Alkindi discussed clairvoyance and divination by dreams, both of which he accepted as valid. He was particularly interested to know "why we see things before they happen; why we see other things which need interpretation before they reveal the future; *and why at other times we foresee the contrary of what is to be*"[2] (italics mine). The first two categories resemble those sketched by Philo, as does the explanation that the soul has an innate natural knowledge of these things; and indeed Alkindi may well have known something of Philo's theories, since Moslem thinkers began very early on to translate philosophical works into Arabic. That he should have noted the third category, however, shows him to have been an objective and accurate

[1] Thorndike, *op. cit.*   [2] *Ibid.*

observer on his own account. That "we foresee the contrary of what is to be"—a phenomenon recognized in English tradition in such proverbs as "Dreams go by contraries" and "Dream of a funeral, hear of a birth"—is, of course, significant in the same way as are those long runs of scoring markedly *below* chance expectation in experimental card tests recorded by Rhine and his colleagues and discussed by Schmeidler and McConnell.[1] Though the climate of thought in Islam was not, like our own, apt to inhibit by its basic intellectual assumptions the conscious recognition and acceptance of psi-phenomena, it is plain that in any swiftly expanding military empire there will be a large number of those personality types whose main drive is "towards dominating both their own impulses and the outside world", and who tend unconsciously to compensate for that repressed extra-sensory perception which they feel to be weakening, distracting and potentially dangerous, not simply by denying all knowledge of it to themselves and to everyone else, but by formulating it, so to speak, in reverse.

It would be interesting to know whether the same person could have precognitive dreams now, so to speak, in code, and now *en clair*, according to his outlook at one or another part of his life, or his mood, or the state of his health, or according to the degree of inner censorship exercised over the dream's emotional content. There seems to be little published evidence available. J. W. Dunne was writing down his dreams before Rhine had noted the significance of negative scores, and was in any case fully occupied with those in which the future seemed definitely recognizable. The results of some unpublished research carried out between 1955 and 1960 by the late Mr Justice Geoffrey Jobling[2] may well prove relevant here.

He worked with a team of dreamers who concentrated on trying to obtain precognitive knowledge of the winners of certain races, a target which had the advantages of arousing lively in-

---

[1] *E.S.P.* and Personality Patterns (London, 1958). Cf. also Chapter Three.

[2] Personal communication.

terest and providing incontrovertibly accurate results. One of the things most clearly shown by this enterprising and painstaking experiment is the way in which the emergence of extrasensory perception tends to be inhibited by focused attention. Though a dreamer may at first have a series of successes in which he "sees" the name of the actual winner in a paper, or "hears" someone shouting it, the more he becomes interested in his dreams the more his subconscious mind seems to withdraw and to express itself in symbols incomprehensible at the time, though often maddeningly obvious after the event, or even to show a "scatter" effect, bringing to consciousness the horses that are to run second and third or to win other races on the same day.

Alkindi's further remarks are also valuable, not to say stimulating. He maintains that the working of the senses, which acts so as to draw attention to the outer world, inhibits awareness of knowledge gained by means of the psi-function (a knowledge which he held to be innate and natural to the soul). This knowledge "comes through" in dreams because when a man is asleep the imaginative powers of the mind are more active than the senses. Such knowledge can also be received, as a vision, when a man is awake but is paying no heed to the senses, having withdrawn into concentrated thought.

Whatever is felt about "the imaginative powers of the mind", no field-naturalist observer of spontaneous psi-phenomena can deny that Alkindi was right in noting the fact that extra-sensory perception does seem to come through most clearly either when the percipient is in that drowsy, relaxed state between sleeping and waking in which vivid dreams occur, or when he is thinking hard about something quite different—a chess problem, a piece of close reasoning, a mathematical demonstration. Nowadays, perhaps, though the dream may still be vivid, the vision may well be replaced by a "hunch" or wordless conviction, for reasons noted in Chapter One.

By the eleventh century, western civilization in its new feudal pattern was beginning again to have some sense of rooted continuity, some breathing space for thought.

That Gerard of Cremona who translated Alkindi's treatise was one of the many scholars, including our own Adelard of Bath, who made their way to Toledo during the half-century after its capture from the Moors in 1085, to learn Arabic and to study Moorish mathematics, medicine and metaphysics. Among the many works done into Latin were those of Averroes and of Avicenna. The former seems to have anticipated Jung in his "theory of a common human mind or soul, one psychic stock as it were, sprouting out into various branches or personalities something like an aquatic plant with many heads showing above water, and these distinct, but all meeting in one root under water".[1] He seems to have believed that after death the individual soul was reabsorbed into this communal one.

Avicenna made a number of remarks of interest to psychical research workers. One concerns the basis of investigation: "no science can prove the existence of its own subject" before looking into it. It must take that existence temporarily for granted.

Another, the convenient, schizophrenic and fatal doctrine of the Two Truths, signposts the path to an intellectual wilderness never very far away from those who cannot bear to reserve judgement. It teaches that philosophy and theology (compare science and theology; or reason and intuition; or thought and feeling; or the experience of spontaneous psi-phenomena and the discipline of statistical experiment) *can* never be reconciled in unity. Each must rule in its own separate realm, heedless of the other.

A third relates to the use of suggestion. St Thomas Aquinas, who found Avicenna a supremely interesting and stimulating intellectual antagonist, quotes him as saying that "if the soul is pure, not subject to bodily passions, and strong in its suggestive power, not only its own body but other bodies will obey its suggestions, *even to the healing of the sick*" (my italics). He seems, moreover, to have connected suggestion not only with

[1] Footnote by Fr Joseph Rickaby, S.J., to his translation of *God and His Creatures* from the *Summa contra Gentiles* of St Thomas Aquinas (London, 1905).

the relief of illness but also with the phenomenon of the "evil eye", saying that "any soul having a strong tendency to male-volence is capable of making a noxious effect on another, par-ticularly a child"; he means, presumably, a being especially open to direct or telepathic suggestion because its reasoning powers were not yet developed. It may be worth remembering that in England, almost to within living memory, animals—cows, hens, sheep—were also thought particularly susceptible to "ill-wishing" or "over-looking" by people with a grudge against their owners, and that carthorses still wear the elaborately patterned brasses whose original purpose was to repel those malign glances. Whether Avicenna intended his remarks to apply not only to *malocchio*, which is conscious and deliberate, but also to *jettatura* is not clear; the latter has not necessarily any connexion with "malevolence", or even with irritability, but seems, as shown in the Appendix, to be more like a sort of accident-proneness projected by the sufferer upon those near him.

Where prophecy was concerned, Avicenna seems to have worked from preconception rather than observation. He maintained that "though the qualities of a prophet are entirely human" (in our diction this might be paraphrased as "though the psi-function, which is strongly developed in him, is perfectly natural"), "the intense purity of his soul, and his firm link with the Active Intelligences [angelic beings] makes him ablaze with intuition".[1]

St Thomas himself took a more down-to-earth and objective view. He did not think that prophecy depended on intense purity of soul. He recognized precognitive psi as a morally neutral function, and termed it "natural prophecy". This, he held, existed in non-human creatures—notably in ants—as well as in humans. It was, in fact, sub-rational and it could be act-ivated in man not only by natural stimuli but by God, by angels, by demons or by those spirits believed, in the science of the day, to guide and animate the stars in their courses, a belief

[1] S. M. Afnan, *Avicenna, his Life and Works* (London, 1958).

still current when Shakespeare set Lorenzo murmuring to Jessica:

> . . . look how the floor of heaven
> Is thick inlaid with patines of bright gold:
> There's not the smallest orb that thou behold'st
> But in his motion like an angel sings
> Still quiring to the young-eyed cherubins.

Where the psi-function was used by God to inspire a man, it was not simply to foresee the future, but to understand and to make vivid to his fellow-men some revelation of the Divine will and purpose. Inspiration of this sort would be given independently, for the most part of his own will, and could not be achieved by his own efforts, though St Thomas notes the Biblical statement that Eliseus used music, with its rhythmic relaxation of consciousness, to revive the spirit of prophecy when he felt it to be fading within him.

Prophetic revelation, moreover, could come through men who had neither sanctity, nor charity, nor a good moral character (*De veritate*). "If sexual excess and worldly preoccupations are inimical to prophetic insight," writes Fr Victor White. O.P.,[1] commenting on this, "it is only because they withdraw attention from the interior image to the external world," as they do with writers and painters and composers and mediums. With all of these a change of mood, an alteration of focus, may swing the man who has been absorbed in prophetic or poetic or aesthetic experience away into an equally vivid experience of raging anger, or ecstatic sexual attraction; or the thought of profit, or of financial anxiety, may temporarily inhibit insight or creative work of any kind. This is perhaps more widely realized today in connexion with what is called "the artistic temperament" than in the context of religion or of psychical phenomena; but it is true in them all. Poets and seers are not far apart in their make-up.

Prophets, wrote St Thomas, may not always understand what they are seeing or saying, may not always know which part of

[1] *Op. cit.*

their message comes from God and which from their own sub-conscious. A man may even be used for prophetic purposes without realizing that his words bear a more fundamental meaning than he assigns to them, as happened to Caiaphas when, thinking only of the political situation as he imagined it, he said, "It is expedient that one man should die for the people."

There are, St Thomas thinks, two ways in which the prophet's mind may be instructed. One is by an express revelation, crisp, clear, and without ambiguity. The other is by a mysterious intuition of whose workings he may not be fully aware. Sometimes, however, he is given discrimination so that he can determine for himself which among the images thronging in upon him is significant, and reference is made to St Monica's experience, recorded by her son,[1] that she could, through a certain feeling which she could not express in words, distinguish between Divine revelations and the dreams of her own soul. (This sense of discrimination which cannot be formulated is not, of course, confined to saints who wish to differentiate between revelation and personal fantasy: it is familiar on a purely natural plane to people who occasionally have telepathic or precognitive dreams and instantly "know" the difference between these and the ordinary, jumbled documentary films of sleep, though they cannot tell how.)

He quotes the *Etymologiae* of St Isidore as saying that revelation can be given through dreams, through visions and through ecstasy, and as making the further distinction that there are three kinds of vision, by the eyes of the body, by the eyes of the mind and by the soul's imagination. The second and third kinds of vision probably refer to veridical hallucinations and to the sudden "coming into one's head" of some vivid picture; both, of course, are familiar as modes in which natural extra-sensory perception makes itself known.

The list of "degrees of prophecy" has some marked correspondences with the list of methods of divination. It seems clear that the different means of expression natural to different tem-

[1] *Confessions of St Augustine*, VI, 13.

peraments were being used, spontaneously in the case of the prophet and deliberately by the diviner. Thus, for example, the form of prophecy in which a man is "moved by an inward impulse to some [symbolic] outward action" clearly has much in common both with the symbolic leg-jerkings of the *salisatores* and with what happened to the precognitive somnambulist described in Chapter One, whose muscles carried him again and again to wake with horror looking out of that window whence he was later to see a body dropping to the ground. It may be fruitful to compare this curious expression of knowledge by movement with Jung's contention that the *mandala*, the pattern in which the human psyche can project and reflect back to itself its experience of balanced fulfilment, does not necessarily need line or colour or imagery, but can be *danced*. This form of prophecy shades into mime and thence into drama, as in the case of Agabus, whom we have observed acting out with St Paul's girdle what he foresaw would happen to its owner.

Again, the process spontaneously working itself out in the prophet who "sees visions" and in the sensitive who suddenly becomes aware of extra-sensory perception in external form is plainly the same as that deliberately employed by the diviner who looks into a pool of ink or a ball of crystal to obtain significant imagery. It is unnecessary to work out all the parallels; they are plain to be seen.

The age had a passion for hierarchy and, accordingly, St Thomas graded the types of prophecy he described from the lowest to the highest, though he noted that a prophet might receive and formulate his apprehension in accordance now with one type and now with another. He regarded as the lowest that unexplained impulse to movement which does indeed occur at the most primitive levels, which sends ants swarming and bees dancing and swallows into migrant flight, and goes on, as has been seen, in primitive shaman and somnambulist gesture. The vivid confusion of the dream came next, and then conscious vision, and highest of all, a direct intellectual impression, without image, voice or word.

Today prophecy means two things, the foretelling of events to come and—often combined with it—an inspiration as to God's will. It sometimes looks as if for St Thomas the word must have had a third, concurrent meaning, and have involved contemplation. He writes,[1] plainly enough, that "the end of prophecy is to show forth a truth beyond man's normal capacity. That in which a supernatural truth is seen by intellectual vision is more excellent than that in which this truth is shown in the form of imagery." It may in itself be "more excellent", but it is also infinitely more difficult to communicate to other men. Imagery is clear, moving, self-explanatory, instantly understood. Intellectual Vision demands—if it is to be transmitted distinctly—a slow, agonizingly difficult formulation in words which will in any case only be understood by those who already have some inkling of their theme; and words can carry, at best, but a very low voltage of meaning, as St Thomas himself realized after that last, blazing intuition which made him score through his exact, hard-thought, hard-wrought sentences and think them "no better than straw" (as Pascal, half a millennium later, forgot hard argument and mathematical logic and symbolism in *"joie, joie, pleurs de joie"*).

But in fact the distinction between prophecy and contemplation is not always easy. If prophecy is given to a man for the sake of his fellows and if he must communicate it as best he can to their conscious minds, by movement or mime or sound or imagery or verbal explanation, still the contemplative carries into the Presence of God not only his own self but all those united with him, living and dead, in the collective unconscious of mankind, and grace overflows through him to them. The one communicates truth by words, the other by his very being.

In St Thomas's synthesis of philosophy, of theology and of the science of his time, medieval thought found its culmination. As the later, lesser scholastics elaborated and refined upon his work they focused attention ever more sharply upon perfecting the

[1] *Summa Theologica*, II[a]–II[ae], translated by the Fathers of the English Dominican Province (London, 1935).

tools of thinking rather than considering the objects of thought, and a situation grew up curiously like that created by logical positivism today: that is, one in which philosophers deny reality to any idea that cannot be caged within the intellectual concepts, the verbal formulae, which they have fashioned with a goldsmith's minute care. The statement in which an attempt has been made to embody such an idea is rejected as "not meaningful", and the idea itself is ignored, the possibility of its validity is repressed into the unconscious. (To give a contemporary example: "the question of personal immortality" is dismissed out of hand as a meaningless phrase because "person" has been arbitrarily defined as an object perceptible to the senses, and the fact of its associated consciousness of itself is blandly burked.)

Later scholasticism, in fact, shows the recurrent human tendency to revert to mechanism as an escape from living, mechanism, which is the intellect's clockwork substitute for instinct. Raw experience, terror and love and awe, real responsibility and choice, are exacting. It is much more orderly, much less demanding, to live in a world of robot concepts, setting them in motion when information is needed, like those figures of the great fifteenth-century clocks, king, priest, knight, lady clicking their way round and round to strike the hour. It is so reassuring to assume that if one does this, or says that, a prescribed number of times, one is safe, and everything works as a machine works if treated in the proper way.

But it is intellectually dangerous to deny that something exists because it cannot be fitted into a ready-made conceptual framework, however ingeniously this may have been devised. It is emotionally dangerous to repress unwelcome knowledge from the conscious mind and drive it underground, unseen and unassimilated. Repression breeds black fear, and fear breeds suspicion, rumour, hatred, cruelty, injustice and violence, each reinforcing the other in a vicious circle. The refusal of the later schoolmen to envisage the inadequacy of their intellectual system was not unconnected with the explosive panic which initiated the witch hunts that clouded Europe for over two hundred years with a phantasmagoria of smoke, stink, fire, terror, blasphemy and obscenity. It certainly had much to do with Luther's denunciation of "the harlot Reason" (substitute ratiocination) who seemed to him as venal as the power of statistics seems to many today. It is no coincidence that witch-hunting, like Jew-baiting, was at its worst in the German-speaking countries where there has always been a tradition—still, alas, extant—of *a priori* argument from abstract ideas assumed to have an existence independent of those who conceived them.

Witchcraft in itself was nothing new; the idea of black magic seems to be current all over the world and its incidence has already been discussed. In the ninth century, the Council of Corcyra had laid down that though the wills of witches were by definition evil, a large proportion of what they thought they did was imaginary; much the same point of view was advanced by Selden the seventeenth-century English jurist who had no doubt either that a man who believed himself able to murder someone by "turning his hat thrice around and crying Buz!" and did so, was morally guilty, or that his proceedings would have little effect.

The fourteenth-century was already prepared for panic by two visitations of the Black Death and the consequent breakdown of the feudal system, which had worked reasonably well for many generations. Panic needs someone to blame, some objects on which to concentrate. The notion of a fifth column, of a cult concealed within the body politic working for its destruction, comes almost as a relief. Jews have served this purpose time and again. So have Catholics. So, for over two hundred years, did "witches". It is not even known for certain whether they had any collective existence before the myth of fear created a pattern into which such neurotics as now confess to imaginary crimes could fit themselves and such lunatics as take their delusions from the notions current among their neighbours could be fitted. It is difficult to stretch Margaret Murray's theory,[1] that the witch cult was the survival of some ancient

[1] *The Witch Cult in Western Europe* (London, 1921).

fertility religion driven underground when Christianity became the official faith of Europe, to cover all the facts. For one thing, in those primitive regions where fertility rites have survived until within living memory, the belief in evil witchcraft has also survived, survives even now. For another, the actual crimes of which they were accused, and of which they sometimes boasted with a defiant pride, were connected with *destroying* fertility; raising hail-storms to ruin the crops; ploughing good ground with toad-teams harnessed by couch grass to a ram's horn, so that only thorns and thistles should grow there; rendering men impotent and women sterile; killing babies by roasting wax images of them before a slow fire; casting sickness and death on humans and animals alike. The extraordinary sexual phantasies both confessed by witches and imputed and suggested to them by their examiners concerned not fruitfulness, but the stimulation and satisfaction of pathological forms of lust, particularly sadism.

The atmosphere of the business seems to have had little in common with that of the ancient cyclic sacrifice by "the priest who slew the slayer and shall himself be slain", but much with that of the young gangsters of American cities, whose lives are a series of unrelated moments each of which must be filled with the strongest possible sensation, whether by aimless destructiveness, wanton cruelty, murder for its own sake, desire not as love but as a cocktail improved by violence and drug taking. There are also startling parallels to be drawn with certain hippie groups "turned on" by heroin or lsd or organised promiscuity to a numinous experience of evil which finds expression in such humanly pointless crimes as the Manson murders.

Where gangsters and hippies use up-to-date laboratory preparations, the witch drank infusions of henbane and rubbed in hallucinogenic ointments compounded of fat mixed with deadly nightshade, wolfsbane and other herbs. It is not surprising that such gangs were feared. It is not surprising that angry and helpless persons who had no other weapon should have threatened those who injured them with witchcraft reprisals. What is surprising is the growth of that legend of a pact with the devil which is typified in the story of Faust. Its exact origin and development seem to be unknown, but once it was there it became—perhaps— a pattern for gang-leaders who wished to initiate new members, and certainly the reason why the edicts of the Council of Corcyra were ignored. For the witch hunters now felt and argued that they were not simply trying to stamp out black magic, but an infernal, powerful and terrifying adoration of living evil. It was this that gave a cutting edge to panic, this that twisted the instruments of torture, this that underlay the frenzied questioning of those on the rack to name their associates, this that brought about the maiming and burning of thousands who steadfastly denied all knowledge of witchcraft, this that fed the fires of mass hysteria. There is no doubt that evil was at work, though not quite in the way that was envisaged.

These persecutions are of interest in connexion with psychical research for two reasons. One is that their long-drawn-out horror so sickened the kind-hearted, the level-headed, the reasonable, that it made them unwilling even to admit the existence of psi-phenomena, which they associated with superstition, injustice, fear, torture and death.

The other is the near-extermination, in those areas of Europe where the persecution was at its height, of families in whom the psi-function was strongly developed. For the ability for "white magic"—telepathy, precognition, healing by suggestion—was considered as much a sign of witchcraft as was the exercise of "black magic", or as the possession of "familiars" (pet black cats, dogs, hares), or the presence of warts, moles, extra nipples or anaesthetic areas on the body. It may be because of this that psi-phenomena today seem to be observed more frequently in England than in some other parts of Europe, for, except for a brief period during the seventeenth century, there was comparatively little persecution here. The whole idea of witchcraft was taken more calmly, the penalties were less severe and unless, like Mother Demdike and the Lancashire group, witches got themselves involved with political activities, such as melting wax images of persons of the blood royal, they were not burned. A village might indeed duck a malevolent old woman—if she floated, she was a witch, but not if she sank—but it might equally well take a pride in an eccentric local figure with unusual powers. Mother Redcap still has a pub named after her in urban Kentish Town, and the hideous, illegitimate, precognitive Mother Shipton, born in 1488 during the first fury of the witch persecutions abroad, lived cheerfully in Yorkshire till her death in 1561. She is said to have forecast the execution of Charles I, the Interregnum under Cromwell, the Plague of 1665 and the Great Fire of London, not to mention the wonders of modern science:

> Chariots without horses shall go
> And accidents fill the world with woe.
> Around the world thoughts shall fly
> In the twinkling of an eye. . . .

As Mother Shipton's quatrains did not find their way into print until the seventeenth century, one may doubt the precognitive quality of the earlier 'prophecies'; but cars and telecommunications still lay two hundred and fifty years ahead.

Chapter Eight

THE ENLIGHTENMENT: "WHAT I DON'T KNOW ISN'T KNOWLEDGE"

IN his masterpiece *The Allegory of Love*, Dr C. S. Lewis traces over a thousand years in the field of literature, the process through which human beings first projected their emotions in the names and shapes of living gods and goddesses, Venus, Cupid, Mars, Diana, and then retained these named shapes long after Christianity had been fully accepted, as poetic symbols strongly charged with feeling, poetic symbols presently joined by such grave figures as those of the cardinal virtues. He shows how this method of forming and dealing with concepts came in the end to strike people as unreal, artificial, even repellent, and how the personifications of Beauty, Passion, Aggression, Prudence, Justice, Temperance and Fortitude, and so on, were ultimately recognized as images made by the psyche itself so that it might become objectively conscious of the feelings and of the abstract ideas which they represented.

An analogous process is to be observed in the development of thought about the psi-function. Evidence has been adduced to show that this function seems to occur in all living species, and that in man, who is self-aware, its activities flash into consciousness. In peoples living a very primitive nomadic existence it may be taken for granted, though even here some of the information it brings in is often attributed to the activities of a numinous totem animal. But once a certain kind and level of culture is achieved, all sorts of elaborate projections of psi are made. There is an extreme reluctance to realize that though the stimulus to extra-sensory perception may come from outside a man's individual being, it draws strength from the love or hatred or self-identification that link him with other beings. There is an even greater reluctance to recognize that the means of registering this stimulus, clothing it in appropriate associative imagery and bringing it to the attention of the conscious mind, is part of his own make-up. He rationalizes the whole sequences of events in animistic terms, attributing all that goes on to the action of "spirits"; as if a man should say, in the context of emotion, "passionate love has nothing to do with me, it is not an energy of my own being. It is *nothing but* an inflammation set up by a wound from Cupid's arrow."

So long as this method of projecting and handling ideas was still found psychologically indispensable, or even valid, it was consciously or unconsciously necessary for those interested in psi-phenomena to affirm the existence of invisible entities who, though dangerous (as a powerful electric current is dangerous) to the ignorant, were morally neither good nor bad. If the occurrence of secular telepathy, clairvoyance, precognition, hunches as to the whereabouts of buried treasure or underground water, could only be taken to originate in this or that image (whence in fact it might simply rebound as an echo does) then, unless all such occurrences were to be thought either holy or evil, these images had to be conceived as neutral.

For the world of Islam the djinns may sometimes have served this purpose. In Renaissance Italy the spirits believed to inhabit the sun and stars, and that *spiritus mundi* whose modern equivalent seems to lie somewhere between the collective unconscious and the idea of creative evolution, played the same part. Ficino, who claimed to practise a good, "natural" healing magic, using the *spiritus mundi* in order to influence the human *spiritus* ("a corporal vapour centred in the brain and flowing through the nervous system . . . an instrument for sense-perception, imagination and motor activity, the link between body and soul"[1]), insisted that everyone who used his methods must concentrate his attention on a planetary angel seen, perhaps, as an animated version of the Heaviside layer reflecting wireless

[1] D. P. Walker, *Spiritual and Demonic Magic from Ficino to Campanella* (London, 1958).

waves from transmitter down again to receiver. This is reminiscent of Alkindi's technique.

Lazarelli, writing in 1494, some five years after the appearance of Ficino's *De Triplici Vita*, maintained that "man's mind by means of words could create immortal progeny . . . created gods [that give] prophetic dreams". Music and singing were also used in the process. In view of Mr Walker's remarks that both Bruno and Campanella thought it possible to employ similar powers for social and political ends, it is tempting to draw a parallel with such temporarily successful twentieth-century attempts to produce "immortal progeny" as engendered Nazi, Fascist and Communist totalitarian groups, brought into being by verbal incantations and revitalized at regular intervals by the repeating of such incantations and by rhythmic song. Such collective minds as these would certainly be capable of giving rise to telepathic dreams, and like those Egyptian statues "wrought by magic art" of which Ficino wrote, might well "attract demons" into themselves.

As early as 1510, however, Agrippa formulated in his *De Occulta Philosophia* (published twenty-three years later) the idea that psi did not always, or necessarily, depend on the activity of non-human creatures. He said it was possible "naturally . . . and through the mediation of no other spirit, for a man to convey his thoughts to someone else in a very short time, however far apart they may be. I know how to do this, and have often done it. Abbot Trithemius did too".[1]

Another twenty-three years, and Pomponazzi was explaining in his *De Naturalium Effectuum Causis* that the words used in incantations had no intrinsic power of their own, but stimulated the imaginative energy (*vis imaginativa*) of enchanter and enchanted alike; and by 1600 a Jesuit, Martin del Rio, writing on magic at Louvain, denied both that there was a special potency or sacredness in any language as such, even Hebrew, and that the heavenly bodies were animated. He affirmed, however, that

[1] *Ibid.*

there was such a thing as a good *prisca magica*, as did Francis Bacon in England.

Bacon, who died of a chill caught while investigating the principles of food-refrigeration by stuffing a chicken with snow to see if it would keep better, was perhaps the first man ever to envisage the application of experimental methods to psi. The *Sylva Sylvarum* contains sketches for experiments in extra-sensory perception, as well as the following ingenious exercise in healing by suggestion: "If you want to cure a sick gentleman by faith, pick out one of his servants who is naturally credulous. While the gentleman is asleep, hand the servant some harmless concoction, and tell him it will cure his master within a certain time. . . . The spirits[1] of the servant, made receptive by his complete faith in your medical powers, will be powerfully stamped by the image of this future cure; they will flow out and similarly stamp the spirits of his master, also in a state of receptivity because he is asleep." And, presumably, the cure will take place with the timed precision of a post-hypnotic suggestion.

The experiment is fascinating both in what is taken for granted and in its very ingenious combination of vicarious suggestion and telepathic activity.

It is taken for granted that the gentleman, having received some education and training in thought, is less likely to be suggestible in the waking state than is the credulous servant.

It is taken for granted that the healer cannot cause his own "spirits" to overflow into the spirits of the sleeping patient. He gives an exterior command, a verbal stimulus to believe in a cure. The overflowing is the interior transmission of belief itself.

It is taken for granted that the servant will be what is called *en rapport* with his sick employer; rightly, in view of the close, almost familiar relationship obtaining then and for many centuries between master and man. This relationship is illustrated

---

[1] The word "spirits" here indicates the energies of the psyche; compare Ficino's *spiritus*, the expression "in high spirits" and the Victorian description of a lively child as having "plenty of animal spirits".

on a comic level by Mr Pickwick and Sam Weller, by Bertie Wooster and Jeeves. Perhaps the nearest modern workaday parallel is that between officer and batman. This sort of mundane sharing of life's indispensable daily detail sets up just such a network of common associations as facilitates telepathy. It would be interesting to know whether medical men using hypnotic therapy to treat functional or psycho-somatic disorders have ever made experiments with this kind of vicarious suggestion, using as the telepathic agent who gives the "harmless concoction" or placebo the wife or close relation of a patient. Though literacy may now be universal, such an education as precludes implicit faith in the doctor as wonder-worker is not.

The Civil Wars and the Cromwellian Interregnum shook for a time in England the process of scientific enquiry, experiment and reflection, partly because this is the temporary effect of all political upheavals and partly because the Puritans were inclined to attribute to the powers of evil all that they could not understand. Thus, Prince Rupert's big white poodle "Boy" was supposed to be a diabolical "familiar", apparitions of the living, the unknown or the dead were devils in disguise, and so on. One curious result of this attitude was that the early Quakers, in whose silent collective unity of purpose and of prayer flowered many instances of extra-sensory perception, kept very quiet about such phenomena, concerning which indeed nothing was published until our own time, lest the Society of Friends should be accused of "working superstitious miracles like the Papists".

The foundation of the Royal Society, after the Restoration, made scientific curiosity fashionable. Charles II gave its members a characteristic impetus towards the experimental verification of hypotheses by asking them why, if goldfish were put into a bowl already full of water, not a drop was spilled. (Some of them composed learned arguments to explain why this should be so. Others put goldfish into brimming bowls and found that it was not.) The climate was set fair for empirical investigations of all kinds. The engaging Aubrey collected data not only about his fellow men, but about apparitions, especially of course, that of "anno 1670 at Cirencester" which, "being demanded whether a good spirit or a bad?—returned no answer, but disappeared with a curious perfume and a most melodious twang. Mr W. Lilly believes it was a fairy". He noted that "Horse and Hattock" was the traditional expression used by fairies (and, it may be added, witches) when they wished to take off from the ground into flight and remarked, perhaps a little sadly, that "it is said they seldome appear to any persons who go to seeke for them"; it is an observation that the experience of psychical research workers shows to be only too true of all sorts of apparition.

The fairies, indeed, seem to have played in a small way in the gentle English landscape of blue and white skies and green grass and grey stone, the part of the djinns in the deserts of Arabia, the planetary spirits in the Italian night, acting as neutral images whence telepathy, precognition, the psycho-kinetic disturbances of poltergeist haunting, the somnambulist benevolence of Lob-lie-by-the-fire, could be reflected back to the psyche.

Robert Kirk, Presbyterian minister at Aberfoyle towards the end of the century, was convinced of their existence and activity, arguing in his "Secret Commonwealth of Elves, Faunes and Fairies"[1] that they were of "a Middle Nature between Man and Angel, of intelligent studious Spirits, and light changeable Bodies [of solidified air] which they can make appear or disappear at Pleasure". He wrote also that they lived in fairy hills, feared cold iron, and were often seen by Highlanders with second sight, sometimes feasting or dancing together, and sometimes, on quarter days, moving house. This looks as if some possibly well-founded tradition[2] of a Stone Age people, conquered by those who had learned to use iron (which is why cold iron was feared among them) and driven literally underground to live in mountain caverns, had become fused with other beliefs

[1] Quoted by K. M. Briggs, *The Anatomy of Puck* (London, 1959).
[2] Cf. John Buchan's really gruesome story of this theme in *The Watcher on the Threshold*.

and perpetuated by that curious psychological process which inclines people to think they see, or have seen, what they long[1] or expect or fear to see. Many persons are familiar with something like it in the form of hallucinated memory, the certainty that one has perceived something which was not in fact there. This can, like other sorts of hallucination, be either illusory or veridical. An example of the illusory kind is to be found in the case of a woman who opened an envelope, read a letter referring to a cheque enclosed with it, and spent hours hunting in bags and wastepaper baskets and pockets and down the sides of chairs for that cheque, which she "knew" she had seen and mislaid somewhere, if only she could remember where; and which the writer had forgotten to enclose and forwarded by the next post. This kind of experience is particularly common among people such as housewives who have to deal with a multiplicity of problems all at once (the milk boiling over, the baby crying, the dog getting underfoot, the telephone ringing and the laundryman standing waiting at the door, without any change, for his bill to be paid). They tend to relegate as many of them as possible to the care of that usually reliable part of the mind which works by learnt habit, automatically setting familiar skills in motion, but not automatically recording in remembrance what has or has not been done. It may be hazarded that some of the moving of objects attributed to poltergeists may occur in this way; not of course those observed to fly in the curious characteristically curved trajectory across rooms or gardens, but those which unaccountably disappear from one place to reappear safely hidden in another.

The veridical kind of hallucinated memory is illustrated by the incident on record in the archives of the Society for Psych-

---

[1] *The Times* for 4 September, 1959, reporting the Proceedings of the British Association, noted a paper read by two members of the Queen's University of Belfast, dealing with a number of experiments in what they called "wishful seeing" or "autism", in which individuals asked to bet on which of a number of symbols would be shown, tended to "see" those which they had backed even when they did not in fact appear.

ical Research, in which someone "knew" she had just read in a letter received that morning, of the serious illness of an old lady who had been her Nanny, and later discovered that though Nanny had been, indeed, very ill, the letter had said nothing about it, for the very good reason that the illness had come on suddenly *after* the post had gone.

Needless to say, it is hardly likely that the experiences of Mr Kirk's second-sighted Highlanders were of this latter sort. People with the knack of projecting information received by way of psi in visual imagery are likely to project their own ideas in the same way, especially unsophisticated people, who are unconscious that hallucinations may smell of insanity and who find seeing visions as little extraordinary as dreaming dreams. The Highlanders probably "saw" just what they expected or dreaded to see if they went on long lonely journeys "up the airy mountain, down the rushy glen" in dark December, or during the equinoctial gales of Michaelmas and Lady Day, or on St John's Eve when Beltane fires were lit.

As has already been noted, those who remembered with abhorrence the hysterical cruelties and phantasies and injustices of the witch persecutions were correspondingly reluctant to admit to themselves even the possibility that the psi-phenomena they associated with them might occur. Others began to build up clear and useful working hypotheses as to the nature and structure of the universe, into which such phenomena (especially as formulated in the intellectual idiom of the day) could not possibly be fitted. Both groups attempted to ignore, to dismiss or to ridicule the evidence that such phenomena happened, whatever interpretation might be put upon them.

Protests were made against this all or nothing attitude. It was pointed out both in this country and abroad that there was Biblical and ecclesiastical authority for the occurrence of "marvels" and the existence of diviners and of non-human good and evil spirits, even though, as Malebranche[1] noted, contact with the latter by way of witchcraft was probably very rare. It was

[1] *Recherche de la Vérité.*

also pointed out (on a basis of such empirical commonsense as underlies the rules of evidence) by that same Joseph Glanvill, F.R.S., who put on record the well-authenticated story of the Drummer of Tedworth, that "matters of fact well proved ought not to be denied because we cannot conceive how they can be performed. Nor is it a reasonable mode of inference first to presume the thing impossible and thence to conclude that the fact cannot be proved. On the contrary, we should judge of the action by the evidence, and not of the evidence by the measures of our fancies about the action".[1] This axiom is based upon such plain commonsense as underlies the rules of legal evidence. In this connexion it is interesting to note that a German lawyer, taking the facts as he found them, submitted as a thesis for his doctorate at the University of Halle in 1700 a *Disputatio Juridica de Jure Spectorum*[2] or *Juridical Argument upon the Law regarding Spectres*. In this, after enumerating different classes of spectre (including "those who overturn all in the house, throw tables downstairs and shout"—Halle plainly bred robust poltergeists), he discussed the following very practical questions.

Can a man divorce his wife because she has a poltergeist? Answer, No; though a tutor can give notice if his pupil is afflicted in this way.

May a purchaser who finds the house he has bought is haunted demand that the contract of sale should be rescinded? Yes, so long as it can be proved that the house was haunted before the sale took place, and that he was ignorant of the fact.

If an apparition accuses someone of a crime, can this be brought forward as evidence in a court of law? Not unless there is additional evidence of another kind.

Can death be presumed from the apparition of someone known to be inaccessibly far away? Yes, for many purposes; but the apparition of one spouse would not in itself be enough to warrant the remarriage of the other.

The writer does not seem to have thought these cases far-

[1] *Sadducismus Triumphatus.*
[2] H. C. Lea, *Materials towards a History of Witchcraft*, ed. by A. C. Howland (New York, 1958).

fetched or fantastic; he treats them as ordinary problems which a lawyer might well have to handle. "Matters of fact well proved ought not to be denied because we cannot conceive how they can be performed. . . ." In sum, as T. H. Huxley remarked a century and a half later, a man concerned with the discovery of truth must be ready to "sit down before the facts like a little child", observing what they are without any distorting, pre-conceived conviction of what they ought to be, and prepared, while working out an interpretation that *may* explain them all, to face the scientist's tragedy, that of "a hypothesis killed by a fact"; "a fact", one small, awkward, undeniable occurrence that cannot be integrated into the useful pattern of theory into which all the rest so easily fall.

Such humble, sober and objective statements were no more acceptable to the Age of Enlightenment than to our own, when such a distinguished philosopher as Bertrand Russell could re-mark that even if it could be proved beyond all reasonable doubt that psi-phenomena did in fact occur, they were so rare and so sporadic that it was impossible either to make general state-ments about their behaviour or to fit them into the framework of natural law, that they could therefore have no particular significance and that thus they were not worth scientific con-sideration.

Glanvill's contentions were by-passed by much the same route. If Biblical and ecclesiastical authority affirmed the exist-ence of non-human spirits and the occurrence of marvels under the Old Dispensation and of miracles under the New, so much the worse for Biblical and ecclesiastical authority. Though Anglican thought encapsulated such events in piety, its more intellectual exponents took for granted that they were of an especial, exceptional kind which had happened a very long time ago and were most unlikely to recur before the Last Judgement. To suggest that they might, still worse, that they did recur, savoured of Popish superstition on the one hand and Non-conformist enthusiasm on the other; it was subversive of the whole established order of things.

Deist philosophy made no exceptions at all. The existence of God was not denied, but His relationship to the physical universe was envisaged as that of a Divine artificer to a watch. He had contrived its mechanism with infinite care. He had wound it up and set it in motion at the beginning of time, and He was certainly not going to make any arbitrary interference with its workings or, to use another metaphor, to cut even one of the links of that network of causation whose nature was beginning to be observed and tested with ever increasing accuracy.

Thus Hume, defining a miracle as "a violation of the laws of nature . . . laws established upon a firm and unalterable experience" (which looks remarkably like such a greatest witness of the greatest number as might in the tropics deny the possibility of snow), proclaimed that such an occurrence was "impossible", and that "the proof against a miracle from the very nature of the fact is as entire as any argument from experience that can possibly be imagined". It might be thought that "experience" in this context meant unsupported individual experience, subjective to fluctuations of memory, and to the exaggerations brought about by a desire to attract attention. But no. The experience of a group, so long as it was a minority group, could also be ignored in the interests of maintaining the ordered respectability of a well-conducted cosmos.

Many observers saw and vouched for the extraordinary phenomena that took place in the early 1730's at the tomb of an austere Jansenist deacon in the cemetery of Saint-Médard; cures of paralysis, trances, babblings, an inexplicable rigidity of the muscles, and convulsions so violent that after a time the dressmakers of Paris produced a new fashion in the *robe de convulsionnaire* (a sort of gym tunic, as Mgr Knox suggested in his fascinating study, *Enthusiasm*). Charcot's work lay far in the future and Hume, perfectly certain that he knew what the laws of nature were and supremely confident in his axiom that these laws could not be "broken", commented simply that one could only "oppose to such a cloud of witnesses . . . the absolute impossibility or miraculous nature of the events which they relate".

It was easier to believe that those witnesses were all liars or that they were singly and collectively deluded day after day than that what they said was true. These things could not have happened because such things did not happen. Q.E.D.

Such a refusal to examine evidence, such a reluctance to consider the possibility that current hypotheses as to the workings of the physical universe might not necessarily apply to living, conscious creatures, were perhaps natural in men engrossed in making and testing and discussing all the fascinating new discoveries based upon those hypotheses. There were very few who resembled Newton in being as deeply interested in theology as in astronomy, physics and mathematics. The spheres of scientific and religious thought withdrew from one another, moved ever farther apart, much to their mutual impoverishment. The subject matter of each was assumed to be irrelevant to the other, and attempts to demonstrate that it was of interest to both parties, or to integrate their conclusions, were regarded as intellectually disreputable, the equivalent of poaching on another man's preserves, not only a crime but an ungentlemanly crime, an attitude which persists to this very day in certain quarters.

This tacit arrangement allowed at first of an uneasy "Don't look now" sort of peace between those concerned, in which each party could get on with its own work undisturbed by any need to stop and explain itself in terms familiar to the other, any dread of interference with its invaluable working models of thought. It meant, however, that in those instances where common ground might have been considered to exist each side claimed it for its own and notably where psi-phenomena or even healing by suggestion were concerned. The scientific philosophers postulated, as has been seen, that since neither "miracles" nor meddling by "spirits" with the normal workings of nature *could* occur, all evidence for such phenomena must be dismissed, however well authenticated it might seem to be. Theologians, especially in Britain, scientifically and industrially the most advanced of all eighteenth-century nations, clung to such evidence as evidence not that the phenomena had occurred, but that discarnate spirits existed and acted. In this conflict of interpretations both missed valuable data as to the nature of man, in whom matter and consciousness are in constant interaction, data relevant as much to the field of science as to that of religion.

Wesley's remark in this connexion is very illuminating. "The English in general," he said, "and indeed most of the men of learning in Europe, have given up all accounts of witches and apparitions as mere old wives' fables. They know well that if but one account of the intercourse of men with separate spirits be admitted their whole castle in the air (Deism, Atheism, Materialism) will fall to the ground." He himself seems to have attributed all psi-phenomena to the activity of such spirits, though Robert Southey, his biographer, writing of that very odd poltergeist haunting which disturbed Wesley's parents and sisters at Epworth Rectory in 1715-16 and was recorded in the family letters of the time, remarked sensibly that "such things may be preternatural and yet not miraculous; they may not be in the ordinary course of nature and yet imply no alteration of its laws".

It is worth while to examine in some little detail both this episode and the explanations which were, or could be, put forward to account for it. Two curious incidents, in both of which Mrs Wesley was concerned before the outbreak, should be borne in mind. In one whose date is unknown she was sitting in her own bedroom (having perhaps a little peace from the society of any of those twenty children each of whom she taught to "cry quietly" before it was a year old), when of a sudden "the doors and windows rang and jarred very hard, and presently several distinct strokes, three by three, were struck"; all this at the moment when one of the boys was in fact having a bitter quarrel with his sister Susannah well out of earshot below. This might possibly be taken in connexion with later events, to indicate that Mrs Wesley was both telepathically in touch with her children (which is not uncommon in mothers) and inclined to project her emotions in some telekinetic way. The other incident occurred in

St Joseph of Cupertino in flight

Photograph lent by Dr E. J. Dingwall

Prosper Lambertini, Pope Benedict XIV, 1675–1759

After the painting by Cars

1701, when, as a staunch supporter of the Stuart cause, she had refused to join in prayers for William of Orange, saying she did not think him the rightful king. At this, her husband had left her, vowing he would not return until she consented to pray for that monarch, but after a twelvemonth's estrangement family life was resumed in 1702, the year of Queen Anne's accession to the throne.

The main trouble began in December 1715 when a maid heard "several dismal groans" in the dining room. Regular knockings followed, heard at first by everyone but old Mr Wesley; which alarmed his family, as they thought this must portend his death. There were also rumblings, "footsteps" heard going up and down stairs, noises of "dancing" in locked empty rooms, and so on. On being informed, Mr Wesley very practically attributed everything to mischief on the part of the children, or sounds made by his daughter's suitors; but after having himself been awoken one night by three knocks three times repeated, investigating, and finding nothing, he was not so sure, especially when his mastiff showed signs of extreme terror. Mrs Wesley then had the bright idea that rats might be responsible and had a hunting horn blown all over the house, as a neighbour had got rid of some in that way. This only exacerbated matters, and the knockings began to invade the day-time *and were especially disturbing at family prayers during the petitions for King George I and the Prince of Wales*.

The knocking ceased when, as an experiment, Mr Wesley omitted these petitions. But it continued at other times and seemed to echo or mock raps made by the family themselves.

There were other phenomena. Latches were lifted up, and doors seemed to open and shut of their own accord. A bed on which Nancy Wesley was sitting was twice lifted from the floor. A door was pushed against Emilia Wesley "when there was no person on the other side". Mr Wesley was himself "thrice pushed with considerable force" by something he could not see and his wooden trencher "danced" one day on the table. The children, even when the noises all around did not awaken them, were seen to "sweat and tremble" in their sleep. Then, after six weeks, all ended but for a brief recrudescence in March, when a door was again seen to open and shut by itself and a sound "like the rubbing of a beast against the wall" was heard.

The phenomena were clearly not caused by rats. They did not bode evil either to Mr Wesley or to the brothers away at school. Conscious trickery by the children could be ruled out, as the disturbances continued while they were seen asleep; and, as Southey commented on the suggestion made by Dr Priestley (who first edited the letters dealing with the affair) that the servants or the neighbours were responsible, "many of the circumstances could not be explained by such a supposition, or by any legerdemain, nor by any secret acoustics". Emilia, who had no doubt that the cause of the disturbances was alive and invisible, nicknamed it old Jeffery and thought it had been sent by local wizards, in revenge for a sermon her father had preached against "cunning men" as they were called at that place and time. He himself wondered whether he were being punished for breaking his solemn vow never to live with his wife again until she would pray for a non-Stuart royal family.

Mr G. W. Lambert's idea that many, if not all, poltergeist hauntings are in fact miniature earthquakes caused by the movements of underground water might, if the lie of the land were favourable, explain the rumblings, the noises in the locked room and perhaps the "footsteps", but not the initiating "groans", the invisible "pushings", the movements of the trencher, the lifting of the bed, or the knockings, either the spaced, spontaneous ones or those which echoed raps made by the family.

It has been suggested that one of the children was in a state of adolescent turmoil, and unconsciously set going some sort of psycho-kinetic process. It has also been suggested that Mrs Wesley herself may equally unconsciously have had something to do with it, either directly or indirectly.

That there is often a connexion between a poltergeist outbreak and the presence of someone suffering the emotional conflicts sometimes associated with early puberty seems to be pretty well established. There is a certain amount of evidence indicating a similar connexion between such phenomena and the emotional conflicts sometimes associated with the menopause, though I do not know whether this has ever been methodically assessed or discussed.

On the other hand, the possibility that Mrs Wesley's tension may have expressed itself indirectly through one of her children is not so fantastic as it may sound, in view of the following quotation from an article[1] in the *Journal of Analytical Psychology*.

In 1927, the American child-psychologist Frances Wickes described cases of children who showed symptoms which disappeared after the problems of the parents had been successfully treated. (*The Inner World of Childhood*, Appleton: New York, 1927). ... Mrs Wickes has recently (1955) published three case histories from her own experience, the last of which should satisfy the most exacting criteria regarding the inconceivability of a mechanical transmission. ... [It] concerns a mother-son projection of which both were unconscious, and the main point is that the cessation of the sender's projection under analysis had well attested synchronous . . . effects on the carrier [i.e. the son] although he did not know about the treatment *and was* 3,000 *miles away at the time* [my italics].

If a telepathic link between two people separated by such a distance and such an ignorance of one another's activities can be so vividly demonstrated, it is easy to understand the intensity of one constantly being reinforced by the daily renewed associations of family life.

Moreover, the strength of Mrs Wesley's feelings about the Stuarts should not be underestimated. Monarchy today is only one of several current methods of government. Where it does exist, it is as much an emotional symbol as a political force. But even now, loyalty to the living person who embodies that

[1] C. A. Meier, "Projection, Transference and the Subject-Object Relation in Psychology", *Journ. Analyt. Psychol.*, IV, 1 (1959). I am indebted to Mrs Heywood for this, as for many other references.

symbol is in the majority of his or her subjects instant, powerful and unreasoning as family affection. In 1715, with the belief in the divine right of kings still lingeringly strong, the monarch was perceived as more than ruler, champion, father-figure of his people; for some of them he was still hedged with divinity, hallowed and dedicated to a sacred function first by inheritance of the blood-royal, and only later by coronation. A usurper was still seen not only as tyrant, exploiter, stepfather, but also as a figure tainted with blasphemy. With such feelings as these, and with an equally strong consciousness of her marriage vow of obedience, Mrs Wesley was, after the crushing of the Stuart rebellion of the 'Fifteen, in a cleft stick, involved in an evil she could neither accept nor abjure. It would not be surprising if her helpless mounting inner tension had indeed dumbly communicated itself to one of her children, through whom a series of psycho-kinetic explosions was so to speak set going.

Such a process would have certain resemblances to that which may be traced in the life of St John Vianney two hundred years later. It will be remembered during his early years in his parish he was subject to very alarming poltergeist manifestations[1]: banging, shouting, trampling, hammering, muttering and the inexplicable movements of physical objects perceived, on various occasions by different witnesses, including the village blacksmith, as well as by himself. These manifestations frequently coincided with periods of violent interior temptation and probably arose from the unconscious projection of his interior conflicts in a psycho-kinetic form. It will also be remembered that there is overwhelming evidence of his telepathic powers, for instance in answering the unspoken questions and in divining the hidden problems of penitents who came to his confessional from all over France and of whom he knew nothing. As he grew older, these poltergeist outbreaks—which happened

[1] I have ignored those which, as Lancelot Sheppard points out in his fascinating recent biography of the saint, may possibly be attributable to the Curé's own activities in a dissociated, somnambulist state of which he himself had neither cognizance nor recollection.

when he was away preaching as well as in his house at Ars— were observed to occur almost as a signal that some notorious evil-doer was about to repent and come to confession. Fr Vianney indeed commented upon it himself to a group of priests at St Trivier-les-Moignons, who, roused from their sleep by an explosion of hammering and rumbling, rushed into his room to find him lying quietly in his bed, which had been shifted into the middle of the floor. Telling them not to be alarmed, he said that the *grappin*, the devil, always did this before "a big fish came into the net", and sure enough a local magnate of evil reputation arrived unexpectedly next day, and was reconciled to the Church. It looks as if the Curé's prayers, fastings, penitential practices offered to God on behalf of those firmly and habitually "tied and bound by the chain of their own sins" had established some sort of telepathic *rapport* with them, serving not only to stimulate them to some new struggle but also to transfer that struggle to be enacted within himself, and to be expressed and endured, as his own early struggles had been expressed and endured, in noise, movement and terror.

Where St John Vianney, who had voluntarily dedicated his whole self and all its energies, conscious and unconscious, to God to be used for his fellow men, found himself both passively and actively involved in the exhausting drama of their conflicts, it seems not unreasonable to surmise that on a lower, a nonvoluntary and uncomprehending level, one of the Wesley children may in the same way have endured and projected her mother's tension.[1]

In passing I may note how interesting it would be to have a map showing in detail the distribution of poltergeist hauntings, and indicating not only the geological structure upon which the "haunted" buildings are erected but also the use to which those buildings are put. This would serve to check both the contention that such phenomena are in many instances linked

---

[1] Compare the case of Agabus, already discussed, acting out, though in a rather more conscious way, what would happen to the owner of the girdle with which he bound himself.

with the ebb and flow of underground water, and my own strong impression that they are significantly frequent in the rectory, the parsonage, the presbytery, the manse. These are places inhabited by people sometimes absorbed in intercession and always aware with particular sharpness of their own shortcomings, struggling with particular energy against temptation and conscious, with a particularly high tension, of their own guilt (not necessarily that subjective, ill-founded, self-loathing which it is the task of the psychiatrist to dispel, though this can plainly be involved to some degree, but the objective realization not only that "the evil which I will not, that I do" but that the will itself yields again and again; to the delicious relief of rage, for instance, or to the fascinating discussion of scandal, or to lying rather than facing a reproof, or, worst of all, to self-justification).

Need it be pointed out that there is no real discrepancy between the Curé d'Ars' ascription of his own poltergeist hauntings to the activity of the devil and the hypothesis put forward here? Temptations to evil are just as real whether they are experienced wholly within the psyche or projected outside it.

To return to the eighteenth-century scene: Wesley was of course mistaken in his belief that "most of the learned men in Europe have given up all accounts of apparitions as old wives' fables". No Catholic man of learning did so, or could have done so. One in particular devoted a great part of his time and energy to examining and checking such accounts and attempting to assess the nature, temperament and character of the persons involved. This was a brilliant and delightful Italian, in whom wit, warmth, gusto and immense erudition were combined with an overruling passion for accuracy and for truth. Prosper Lambertini, born in 1675, showed even in his childhood an avidity for knowledge, a zest for understanding, which continued throughout his life. His writings quote aptly and vividly not only from the classics, not only from the early Fathers, not only from religious authors of every age, but also from such contemporaries of his own as Boyle and Spinoza. His abilities were early recognized. He was educated by the Dominicans in Rome, became an ecclesiastical lawyer, and was many times entrusted with the duties of *Promotor Fidei*, or "Devil's Advocate". Perhaps these should briefly be sketched.

If the long, tedious, painstaking researches made into the lives of people suspected of sanctity bring in enough evidence as to their heroic virtue, and as to the possibility that miracles have occurred as a result of their intercession, then this evidence is adduced in something resembling a legal trial, the process for beatification (for determining whether an individual should be recognized as especially blessed by God). This is sometimes, though not invariably, followed by a similar process for canonization, recognition as a saint. In such processes it is the duty of the *Promotor Fidei* to examine the evidence with the greatest care, to present every imaginable argument that could be put forward to disprove the holiness of the man or woman under discussion and, where miracles are involved, to point out every possibility, however remote, that normal events have been misinterpreted, that incidents have been exaggerated and that inaccuracy, self-deception, or even deliberate fraud can be detected. It is not difficult to see how the *Promotor Fidei* came by his nickname.

Lambertini was made Cardinal in 1728 and elected Pope twelve years later, taking the name of Benedict XIV. He was loved and revered by many besides his fellow Catholics. Such unexpected characters as the trenchant, mocking Voltaire who hated all pretence, and the gentler but no less clear-eyed and teasing Horace Walpole, held him in affectionate admiration. The former wrote him an elegant Latin epigram[1] during his life, the latter an elegant English epitaph after his death. Englishmen, wrote his biographer, the Marchese Carracioli,[2] were especially

---

[1] "Lambertinus hic est Romae decus et Pater orbis
Qui mundum scriptis docuit, virtutibus ornat,"
which may roughly be translated as:

"Here is Lambertini, fitting Father of Rome and of the globe,
Who teaches the world by his writings, and makes it lovely by his virtues."

[2] *La Vie du Pape Benoît XIV*. Paris, 1783.

drawn to him. The human feeling and good sense, shown in his condemnation of the *autos da fé*, still occasionally mounted in Spain at that time (those who conducted them, he said, would "destroy religion in the hope of honouring it"); his truth and honesty, displayed, among other ways, in a vigorous insistence that no relics should be distributed unless their full history were known and their genuineness could be guaranteed; his warmth and intelligence, all were combined with that quiet, leg-pulling sort of gaiety which has always endeared its possessors to our countrymen. It is well exemplified in his showing to two sympathetic but non-Catholic Englishmen the notes of an entire canonization process, notes which convinced them of the sanctity of the person concerned, only to tell them at the end, with subdued enjoyment, that the Congregation of Rites had in fact declared it non-proven. Of the thirteen volumes he published, eight dealt with problems arising in processes for beatification and canonization. Here and elsewhere (I quote, translating eighteenth-century French into twentieth-century English, from the edition of his biography already cited—I cannot trace any Italian original), "he formulated sure principles to discern what came from man and what from God. Physicians, learned men, theologians, he made them all recognize what a variety of phenomena could spring from nature and from the imagination".

The Catholic procedure adopted for investigating reports of religious apparitions is still based upon his work:

> To carry out this procedure [if I may cite an article of mine in *The Month*][1] the Bishop of the diocese concerned generally nominates a diocesan commission composed of theologians, doctors of medicine, and experts in the taking and assessment of evidence, who conduct the enquiry. They visit the place where the apparition is said to have been seen and attempt to exclude the possibility that it could have been produced by natural causes, fraud, imagination and so on, or by an evil spirit.

[1] "Psychical Research, the Catholic Contribution", December 1957.

The person or people claiming to have seen it have both a medical and a moral examination, and any trace of psychopathological tendencies on the one hand or of lack of genuine humility on the other will lead to a negative judgement at once. The question of whether the apparition, though genuinely independent of the percipient, was projected by an evil spirit, will be settled fairly easily by the test of whether it suggested anything "contrary to faith or morals". Thus if an apparition (not explicable by natural causes) of the patron saint of Germany Saint Boniface had been reported in the Rhineland of the 1930's, adjuring people to murder Jews in the national interest, or to worship the Führer, it would not have been difficult to guess its provenance.

Perhaps it should be added that even if the commission of enquiry gives what is called "a favourable decision" this means only that Catholics may believe in the authenticity of the apparition, not that they must.

Though the immense developments in neurology and psychiatry that have taken place over recent years have widened and complicated the range of subjects to which Benedict XIV's criteria for the judgement of miracles of healing are applicable, the underlying principles remain the same as they were when he decreed that cures of epilepsy must never be regarded as supernatural since it might recur at any time; that in all cases a specialist in the disease involved must be consulted; and that the patient cured must be re-examined, after an interval, to see whether there were symptoms either of a relapse, or of any other form of disease. I do not know why this was originally done, but it fits in well with the fact, recognized in our own century, that if one physical manifestation of psychological *malaise* is cleared up, it may later express itself in another.

Lambertini's survey of healing miracles is extraordinarily thorough within the limits of the science of his time. He discusses the symptoms and cures, natural, unaccountable, and possibly miraculous of lameness, gout, diseases of the bone, paralysis, hernia, dropsy, dysentery (the "bloody flux" that decimated armies until after the Boer War), wounds, gangrene, cancer, leprosy, various fevers, pleurisy and apoplexy. Hysterical disorders (including sensations of choking and inability to swallow) he classifies with epilepsy.

His discussions of holiness in itself and in its manifestations are based on a quotation from St Gregory (*Moralia*, 20 c.7): "The test of sanctity is not to perform miracles but to love everyone as oneself, to have true thoughts of God."[1] He distinguishes two ways in which grace, the activity of God in relation to the human psyche, can be perceived to work. The first, *gratia gratum faciens*, stimulates, feeds, transforms the very being of a man, enabling him ever more fully to know, love, serve and rejoice in God, a process described in Stephen Langton's vivid Latin poem "The Golden Sequence" (*Veni Sancte Spiritus*) read in churches at Whitsuntide.[2]

The second way in which grace shows itself, *gratia gratis data*, is when it is given to a man for the sake of other people, issuing in prophecy, faith-healing and miracles.

To respond to, to assimilate, to work with and to yield to the first mode of grace is what is essential to sanctity. It may or may

---

[1] *Benedict XIV on Heroic Virtue*, translated into English by Thomas Richardson (London. 1882).

[2] A rough translation might run:

Come, Holy Spirit,
Send from Heaven
The radiance of your light.
Come, Father of the powerless
Come, Giver of riches
Come, hearts' Illumination;

Best Comforter,
Sweet guest of the soul,
Sweet freshness,
Coolness in heat,
Rest in labour,
Sorrow's consolation,

O, most blessed Light,
Fill all the depths
Of hearts loyal to you.

Without your Presence
Nothing is in man,
Nothing is innocent.

Bend our stiffened muscles,
Warm our coldness,
Straighten our distortion.
Cleanse what is foul,
Heal our wounds,
Water our dried-up souls.

Grow in your faithful people
Who trust in you
Your seven holy fruits.
Grant us true goodness,
Grant us a happy departure,
Grant us joy perennial.

not co-exist with the second mode according to the temperament and training of the person concerned. Thus, St Thomas More, English, reticent, intellectually active, bred in the discipline of the law with its fine distinctions and clear general principles, showed during his life little evidence of *gratia gratis data*, in so far as these take the form of psi-phenomena or of miracle, though his love, joy, peace, patience and goodness drew even the most difficult and argumentative of men—including his own son-in-law—towards God.

Gratia gratis data may, moreover, as St Thomas Aquinas noted, appear in people without especial holiness. As has already been remarked, if these are encouraged to brood on their gifts they may well become so deeply interested in them, so numb with self-absorption as to atrophy their ordinary human capacity to adore God. Interest in these gifts can also be dangerous even to those who are trying to use this capacity. Psychical research workers anxious to study psi-phenomena from a scientific point of view are often vexed by the discovery that though such and such a religious is said to have produced these phenomena, including levitation, one of the most fascinating and puzzling of them all, the superior of the community involved has drawn no attention to the fact at the time of its occurrence, when their investigations might have yielded the most valuable results. The reason for this is, of course, that among people dedicated to contemplation and intercession for others, the cross-questioning of scientific observers about occurrences which are only incidental to their calling must, at best, distract their attention from their true work and may at worst stimulate a corroding pride in their peculiar experiences, even in their own possible sanctity, which may finally destroy their ability to serve those ends to which they have devoted their lives.

Though the occurrence of "marvels" cannot be adduced in a cause for beatification as primary proof of holiness, it *can* play a secondary part. If a man or woman seems utterly to have been transformed by *gratia gratum faciens*, then evidence that this overflowed in powers of intuitive understanding, prophecy, healing and so on, may be taken to confirm the impression. Usually, of course, the evidence is mixed. What means then should be taken to evaluate, say, the case of a visionary apparently living a life wholly focused on God and showing signs of ecstasy, levitation, prophecy (in which Benedict XIV included "the knowledge of things to come, things past, present events distant in place, and the secret places of the heart"), and possibly of such other strange phenomena as are discussed in detail in the sober and scholarly researches of Fr Thurston, S.J.? It is noted that the first thing to do is to discover what virtues the religious showed in ordinary life and then to investigate his or her health and state of mind. Each kind of "marvel" is then discussed separately.

Benedict observes that ecstasies may be of three kinds. They may be perfectly natural, arising either from disease (catalepsy for instance), from intense intellectual concentration, or even from a particular sort of psychophysical make-up; he raises the question whether the faculty for going into a trance at will is connected with this last. Ecstasies may also be diabolical, induced for show "to excite the admiration of the vulgar". Or they may happen because "God enwraps a man and withdraws him from the senses that he may the more freely meditate on divine things".

Levitation, he writes, may be either diabolical (as in the case of that famous nun of Cordova, Magdalen of the Cross, who proved to be "eaten up with the spirit of pride") or divine. It is worth noting, for our own idiom of thought, that "diabolical" does not necessarily mean that some sort of psycho-kinetic energy was supplied direct by the powers of evil, but that these were involved with the motive at work. It may be hazarded that in the one case a natural though odd and unusual faculty was deliberately cultivated and exploited to attract attention and to induce onlookers to believe in the holiness of the person levitated: while in the other, the whole self being yielded to the love of God, this faculty was unconsciously used to move the body, in a profoundly symbolic gesture, upwards towards the source of light.

That this gesture was determined below the level of conscious-ness, irresistible and irritating as a blush, appears clearly in the case of St Teresa of Avila, who found her levitations most embarrassing and prayed that they might not recur. The phen-omenon is also reported in the lives, among others, of St Thomas Aquinas, St Peter of Alcantara (who was in choir at the time), St Francis Xavier, St Philip Neri and St Joseph of Cupertino, who showed it to a very marked degree. The surprising, the almost comic evidence for it—he seems to have given a "shrill cry" before taking off into flight, in church, out of doors, "under every possible variety of conditions and in many different sur-roundings"—must have been overwhelmingly strong to have convinced, as it did in the end, the *Promotor Fidei* in this case, Prosper Lambertini himself, whose "preliminary animadver-sions . . . are said to have been of a most searching character".[1]

The light that is sometimes seen to surround persons at prayer may, writes Lambertini, arise from natural as well as from supernatural causes. He mentions "natural flames which at times encircle the human head",[2] which sounds like the "aura" perceived by certain "sensitives" who claim to be able to deduce from its brilliance, colour and extent the vigour, temperament and mood of its wearer. Whether this perception is sensory and arises from some sort of hyperaesthesia, or whether it is extra-sensory, the projection in visual imagery of a stimulus received by way of the psi-function, it is very hard to determine. He also mentions "fire" that "may on occasion radiate naturally from a man's whole person . . . in the form of sparks that are given off all round"; possibly some form of static electricity such as is now so common among people wearing nylon fabrics that in certain American hospitals nurses are forbidden to wear such fabrics in the operating theatre lest sparks from them should ignite ether or surgical spirit.

On the theme of prophecy (which, as noted above in different terms, covered for the purposes of his discussion the phenomena

---

[1] Thurston, *op. cit.*
[2] Quoted in Thurston, *op. cit.*

now known as precognition, retrocognition, clairvoyance and telepathy) Lambertini develops the thought of St Thomas Aquinas, sketched in Chapter Seven.

Prophecy, he writes, is a transient thing, cannot be produced to order and occurs in "fools, idiots and melancholy persons, not to mention brute beasts" as well as in such saints as "the Peruvian Rose" (Rose of Lima) who divined secrets she could not have known in any normal way, and Pius V, who told those around him at the day and hour of its occurrence that the battle of Lepanto had been won, a fact verified some time afterwards when couriers travelling at a sixteenth-century speed arrived with the news.

Visions and apparitions he classifies under three headings. They may arise from natural causes, from preternatural causes, or from intellectual vision.

The natural sort can be provoked by fasting, lack of sleep, delirium, by hallucinogenic drugs like henbane (which, he writes, can give visions of "beautiful birds of many colours") and by such a faculty for producing what is now called eidetic imagery as was recorded by Jerome Cardan.[1]

The preternatural sort, which are not explicable in such terms as these, may, like them, be good, bad or irrelevant to sanctity; and "no one is to be considered more holy than another because spirits appear to him and not to the other". Book Three of Prosper Lambertini's work, in which these preternatural visions are mentioned, does not say much about them; but in Book Four[2] there is a note in Italian to the effect that apparitions of the dead sometimes appear by the direct or permissive will of God, so that they may help or comfort those who loved them, or in order to ask for decent burial. To illustrate what is meant Lambertini cites an instance of a ghost who came

---

[1] *De Subtilitate*, Paris, 1550. Cardan, who was writing with modified scepticism about witchcraft and kindred topics, put it on record that between the ages of four and seven he used to watch eidetic imagery projected upon the space above the end of his bed, and he enjoyed it very much, though he realized that it was not really there.

[2] *De Servorum Dei Beatificatione et Beatorum Canonizatione, Liber Quartus Prospero di Lambertinus, Bononiae* 1737.

to tell his son the whereabouts of the receipt for a bill which he was being asked to pay over again out of the dead man's estate. He also quotes a curious instance of a "phantasm of the living" in which one man appeared to another and had a talk to him. *He* later described both the place and the conversation; the other man reported both the conversation and the "appearance". Lambertini's comment is that the man at a distance was seen "only in an imaginary presence, by way of the gift of prophecy". It is to be wished that those who subsequently wrote of such phenomena in the lives of saints could have retained his clarity of thought and expression instead of using such muddled terms as "bi-location".

Lambertini points out that in trying to assess the significance of religious visions it has to be remembered that some people are in all good faith inclined to "think they see what they desire"[1] or fear; one's mouth waters when thinking of a banquet or, when reading of an illness, one thinks one has its symptoms. If "the heart is calm" and if visions are preceded, attended and followed by humility they come directly or indirectly from God. Those which lead to pride and excitement probably come from the devil, even if they appear to be of Christ and His Mother; this is quite certainly so if the percipients boast about them. St Vincent Ferrer goes so far as to say that a definite wish to have visions is associated with "the root and foundation of pride". To sum up, Benedict XIV quotes the following passage from Chapter 71 of the *Dialogues of St Catherine of Siena*, in which she perceived Christ to say: "This is the sign whether the soul is visited by Me or by the devil; when it is visited by Me there is fear at first, and afterwards and at the end cheerfulness and a hunger after virtue; and when the devil comes, at first there is cheerfulness, and afterwards there remain fear and mental darkness."

Perhaps one might append, as a coda, a remark quoted by Fr Conrad Pepler[2] from St John of the Cross: "with regard to all

---

[1] An early recognition of "autism".
[2] *Sacramental Prayer* (London, 1959).

these imaginative visions and apprehensions . . . whether they be false and come from the devil, *or are recognized as true and coming from God* [my italics] the understanding must not be embarrassed by them or feed upon them, neither must the soul desire to receive them or have them lest it should no longer be detached, free, pure, and simple . . . as is needed for union" with God.

Chapter Nine

SPIRITS OR ELECTRICITY

THIS chapter will deal for the most part with intellectual assumptions, scientific preconceptions and arguments, and the state of educated opinion in relation to psi-activity during that epoch in which the industrial revolution got under way, became fully established and was finally taken for granted as the background of life. It should be noted and remembered, however, that throughout this period the illiterate and the un-learned, those who could not read and those not formed in any intellectual discipline, labourers, workmen, peasants, the major-ity of women, continued to accept without question the occur-rence of "warnings", omens, telepathic dreams, and apparitions of the living and the dead just as they accepted without question the facts that a pregnant woman who drank raspberry leaf tea should have an easy labour, that a disappointment in love might bring on a "decline", and that old cobwebs should be clapped on to a bad cut. It has now been shown that raspberry leaf tea re-laxes tension in the relevant muscles; that severe emotional shock predisposes the sufferer to disease, and especially to tuberculosis; and that clumps of old cobweb sometimes contain penicillin.

If intellectual respectability forbade academically distin-guished men to enquire about psychical phenomena in terms of "spirits" or "miracles", three courses were open to them. They could either ignore or deny the fact that they happened; aban-don respectability and the good opinion of their colleagues; or find other terms. Much depends on terms, for in pursuing any investigation the answers you get depend upon the questions you ask and the assumptions on which those questions are based. If you set yourself to enquire what *sort* of green cheese the moon is made of—Wensleydale, Gorgonzola, Stilton—you can accumulate a vast deal of data without finding out very much about the moon, though, to be sure, this mass of material may yield some useful incidental information if it is later re-examined by someone working on a different hypothesis.

Between roughly the beginning of the eighteenth century and the third quarter of the nineteenth, the majority of British philosophers, scientists and thinkers adopted the first course, which is indeed safe, conventional and popular even today. To admit that psi-phenomena could occur would have vitiated their assumptions, their mental habits, the hypotheses on which their work was based, all of which were increasingly conditioned by numerical techniques, dominated by the image of the perfect machine, powerful and infallible in its automatism. Deity itself indeed was honoured in that image. If men would but adopt the principles of *laisser faire*, yield to their own acquisitive impulses, divinely implanted and humanly formulated in the "laws" of political economy (buying everything including labour in the cheapest market and selling it in the dearest, for instance), then the automatic workings of Providence must bring about the greatest happiness of the greatest number since, as Dr Pangloss remarked, "all is for the best in the best of all possible worlds".

The second course, that of abandoning intellectual respectability in the cause of what was contemptuously dismissed as "superstition", was very hard to take. It would involve not only personal ridicule, but the disparagement of good work done in other fields. It might be thought that the Romantic movement would have eased this course, the Romantic movement which yielded a thrilled assent to belief in ghosts, *doppelgängers*,[1] "affinities", gipsy fortune-tellers, omens and telepathic messages between "twin-souls", not to mention vampires, werewolves, enchanters and such black veils as, lifted, might reveal "Clemen-

---

[1] It is interesting that Shelley's professed atheism does not seem to have been based on any materialist philosophy. He appears to have accepted as real, objective and significant his own curious experiences, notably the meeting with his double, and the vision of Byron's little dead daughter Allegra laughing to him from the waves in which he was to drown.

tina's skeleton". But this assent was almost entirely literary and emotional, prompted in part by that same hunger for the wild, the incalculable, the unknown, for freedom from the "mind-forged manacles" of predictability, as is now fed by tales of Triffids and Martian monsters, horrible, vivid, non-human as dinosaurs, or as dragons or the cold demons of Hieronymus Bosch.[1] And emotion, literature, art, all that had to do with the creative play of the imagination, was regarded as ever less relevant to objective investigation into the nature of things. The explicit Moslem theory of the Two Truths, which had disappeared from Europe with St Thomas Aquinas' synthesis of human knowledge in the thirteenth-century, was returning implicit in practice. That rift which it had regarded as necessary between philosophy and theology was extending still further, splitting and widening and deepening into a gulf, an abyss, between scientific thought and human experience. This theory was soon, of course, to be eclipsed by the idea that the truth susceptible of scientific test and proof was the only one, and that the field of the imagination was, precisely, imaginary.

The third course open to the thinker who wished to examine psi-phenomena was, as has been noted, that of attempting to find new terms in which to consider them. In the late eighteenth-century such terms were fatally easy to find in the study of electricity and magnetism (then taken to be one and the same thing); fatally, because this subject, the investigation of energies perceptible to the senses not in themselves but only in their results—the flash of lightning, the crash of thunder, the beautiful patterning of steel-filings around the end of a magnet —yielded analogies so useful to the study alike of psychology

[1] Incidentally, a brief, well-authenticated account of something inexplicable and terrifying as these is to be found in the *Journal of the Society for Psychical Research* for December 1959. A distinguished elderly scientist and his wife each on different occasions, and without mentioning it to the other, perceived coming up the main stairs of their house an incandescent shape with something like pieces of ribbon fluttering from its back, and deep eyes set in a featureless face. The scientist seems to have been much vexed by an occurrence for which no explanation was forthcoming.

and of parapsychology as to be mistaken (as analogies often are) for realities, thus deflecting the attention of successive generations from the real problem involved.

The deflection was all the easier since to look at that problem is as painful as gazing at the noonday sun. It is the problem of experience, of what in all creatures is aware of the external world and of what in man is also aware of his own awareness. The mechanics of sensory perception are understood, but what perceives remains mysterious, given, incomprehensible. It is not only a register of physical stimuli transformed into sensations. It can to a certain extent choose to reject full consciousness of those sensations (as someone sitting writing in a garden may choose to reject full consciousness of the mowing machine's buzz and the smell of new-mown hay). It can on the other hand choose to accept full consciousness of those sensations and, in accordance with its interpretation of their meaning, feel joy, love, fear, rage, pity, awe, feelings intensely real though they cannot be quantitatively weighed, measured or assessed. The perceiving entity can also focus attention upon an idea verbally presented to it, realize that idea in terms of emotion, carry that emotion over into the realm of sensation, and register that sensation as if it had been produced by a physical stimulus; witness A. E. Housman's recognition of true poetry as something which made you feel cold water trickling down your spine. In another context, we have the peculiar "tingling"[1] sometimes associated with the touch of the faith healer who has suggested that cure will follow it, and the actual physical change produced when the skin of someone under hypnosis puffs up into a blister at the spot where he is told he has had a burn.

Whether the facts of which it is cognizant are brought to its attention by sensory or by extra-sensory perception, the conscious identity remains in itself profoundly mysterious. To

---

[1] This "tingling" feeling is also reported in cures obtained by deliberate hypnotic treatment. Cf. G. Ambrose and G. Newbold. *A Handbook of Medical Hypnosis* (London, 1959). It is of course particularly easy to confuse with the "tingling" produced by a weak electric shock.

attempt to consider it is apt to cause extreme intellectual discomfort. It is deeply disquieting to be confronted with a fact whose existence it is impossible either to deny or to comprehend, a relief to look the other way and with an air of universal explanation to talk, according to the idiom of the period, of "animal magnetism", "subtle fluid", "psychic force", "vibrations", "etheric bodies" or "brainwaves". If, as a contributor[1] to the *British Medical Journal* has pointed out, it is all too easy to forget that "an electro-encephalogram . . . a mere sign and index of rhythmical activity in cerebral neurones . . . is no more the neurone activity itself than an electro-cardiogram is a cardiac contraction", it is easier still to ignore the fact that neurone activity is in its turn not consciousness but its accompaniment.

Though the attempt to conceive both of psychological and of parapsychological phenomena in terms of electrical energy was first made in the eighteenth-century, that attempt still continues, partly perhaps as a result of verbal confusion, but very largely from the extreme discomfort of introspection and the consequent desire to avoid confronting any absolute distinction between mind and matter. Those actuated by this desire are now prone to assume that Werner Heisenberg's equation of universal matter with energy[2] somehow fulfils it. "Energy" *sounds* so much more "spiritual" than "matter", a word lichened over with associations of weight, mass, intractable clay, not to mention "gross materialism"; and, since energy and consciousness are both invisible, perhaps they are not really so very different from one another.

This is of course sheer confusion. Awareness and energy are combined in differing proportions in all living beings, from insect communities in their near-automatism to individual

[1] Dr W. Thomson Brown, in a letter to the *British Medical Journal* of 9 January 1960.

[2] "All the elementary particles are made of the same substance, which we now call energy or universal matter; they are just different forms in which matter can appear . . . the matter of Aristotle, which is pure *potentia*, should be compared to our concept of energy, which gets into actuality by means of the form when the elementary particle is created."—*Physics and Philosophy* (London, 1959).

creatures which can supplement instinct by forming conditioned reflexes, from those in whom learning can modify habit to man, whose instincts and reflexes, habits and rituals and training can subserve the capacity to be conscious of the outside world, of himself and of God.

But consciousness and energy remain different in kind. The workings of energy are determined, can be predicted and plotted out and used. They can even be employed to activate computer-complex "electronic brains" reacting with the utmost delicacy to various stimuli, working out mathematical problems, calculating averages, responding to statistical questions. Those "brains" cannot however *experience* stimuli, *choose* from the wide world the data on which they are to work, *reflect* upon their own existence. They have not consciousness.

If this point has been laboured too much, it is because it is so frequently ignored in that flight into automatism which, though it is to be found in all times and places from the African witch doctor with his rubbing board to the Tibetan with his prayer wheel, is particularly easy, respectable, and well sign-posted in our own.[1]

The difference between the "magical" and the "electrical" methods of envisaging psychological and parapsychological phenomena is admirably exemplified in the figures of Cagliostro and of Mesmer.

Cagliostro seems to have had powers both of hypnotic suggestion and of paranormal cognition. He used children under the age of puberty as clairvoyants, telling them, after impressive ceremonies, that they would see visions in a glass bowl of clear water. This they duly did and some of the visions reported do appear to have supplied unexpected information which could

---

[1] Thus, for instance, there is at Oxford a School of Physiology, Psychology and Philosophy, which should shed light on the nature and interpenetration of all human activities, bodily, psychological and intellectual. Those who take it discover that "because it cannot be measured", the consideration of consciousness is explicitly banished from the study of psychology (which is largely devoted to the timing of reactions in rats) and implicitly ignored in the study of philosophy, which is almost entirely linguistic.

not have been received through normal channels. He was moreover taken by Cardinal de Rohan to call on the kind, gentle, elderly Madame du Barry in her exile at Louveciennes; here, to demonstrate his powers, he showed her a "magic" mirror in which she might foresee the future. She looked, and fainted. (What she saw is not recorded; but she was in fact to die on the guillotine.) Cagliostro did not only stimulate and release precognition vicariously, as it were, in other people. There is evidence that he experienced flashes of it himself. A contemporary study of his career[1] notes that "in a letter to the French nation written in London the 20th June 1786, he seems clearly to predict the approaching revolution in France, for he prophesies that 'the Bastille shall be destroyed and become a public walk' and that 'a prince shall reign in France who will abolish *lettres de cachet* [and] invoke the States General'". From the same source comes his own comment on various accurate predictions he is said to have made at St Petersburg: "'I uttered all these predictions,' said he to his judges, 'in consequence of divine inspiration, but I always pretended it was by means of my cabalistical knowledge.'" This has an authentic ring but for the word "divine". He had the "inspiration", the hunch, the given glimpse of the future, but he would neither own to its spontaneity nor acknowledge the fact that he could not explain it. He used it instead to build up his own reputation as a figure larger and more phosphorescent than life, full of strange, esoteric erudition.

He cultivated the art of mystification, partly no doubt to conceal that in earlier life he had been notorious as Joseph Balsamo (a peculiarly repulsive adventurer whose activities had included attempting to make his own wife act as a prostitute) but also because mystification was the stock in trade of magicians, arousing awe and extracting money. Following out this policy, he claimed to have founded a new, Egyptian branch of free-

---

[1] *The Life of Joseph Balsamo commonly called Count Cagliostro* translated from the original Proceedings published at Rome by Order of the Apostolic Chamber (Dublin, 1792).

masonry, with an elaborate secret ritual, and much invocation of a personage known as the Grand Cophte. Egypt, incidentally, seems to have played in the late eighteenth century the same part as Tibet in the late nineteenth as the geographical expression for a numinous Never-Never Land "full of voices" ancestral and ventriloquial, and of gigantic archetypal images.

It is difficult at this distance of time and taste to understand exactly what it was about Cagliostro that made his admirers write and think of him as almost superhuman. Perhaps he identified himself with the Grand Cophte. Perhaps the fact (wearily recorded by his questioners in Rome) that it was "utterly impossible to stop the torrent of his verbosity" produced in receptive audiences a sense of awe-stricken acquiescence in all he said about his own secret powers. This extraordinary figure, dramatizing itself and more than half believing in the drama, exploiting psi and attributing its working to "spirits" or cabalistic learning or a combination of the two, this figure inflated by the emotions induced in its hearers, compelling, hysterical, its wild eyes rolling always in the direction of self-advancement, stands midway between the enchanters of ancient times and the alarming mystagogues of the nineteenth and twentieth centuries, male and female, political and occultist.

Beside it the figure of Mesmer, mistaken in theory and showman in practice though he was, stands out with refreshing sincerity and sanity, the type of an honest and intelligent man acting in good faith on an ingenious false hypothesis to achieve a true alleviation of human suffering. The two had in common an interest in chemistry and alchemy, a belief in certain astrological theories, an aptitude for suggestion, and a gift for stimulating the psi-function. In all else they were different as chalk from cheese; and blackboard chalk from deliquescent Brie, at that.

Franz Anton Mesmer, a Viennese born in 1734, was a doctor of medicine. He held with Paracelsus that "there is a constant mutual interaction between the celestial bodies, the earth, and animated beings",[1] and believed that this interaction was brought about by means of an invisible current which he identified with magnetism, whose study was attracting considerable attention at the time. When, in 1766, he discovered that a Jesuit, Fr Maximilian Hell, was successfully treating sick persons by stroking the skin with a magnet, he concluded that this invisible current could be directed into the body, where it penetrated the nervous system and cured nervous disorders. Ten years later in Switzerland he came across another priest, a Fr J. J. Gassner, healing by touch alone; this led him to modify his theory and to posit that certain people were charged with a natural energy which he called animal magnetism. It was not identical with physical magnetism, but so closely connected with it that the two could reinforce one another.

In accordance with these ideas he devised the procedure of the "magnetic *séance*" for which he became famous. In the middle of a room he placed a tub from which projected a number of magnetized iron rods. Each of a circle of patients in the front row held on to a rod with one hand, and held with the other the hand of a patient standing behind him, who in turn held the hand of a third, and so to the outermost of a series of concentric circles. Dr Mesmer himself, dressed in lilac silk, then pointed a "magnetic wand" (strange symbol alike of traditional magic and scientific theory) at each individual patient, now here, now there. Like their predecessors at Saint-Médard the patients were sometimes convulsed and were frequently aware of a startling alleviation of their symptoms.

After Mesmer had had some success in Paris, a commission, whose members included Lavoisier and Benjamin Franklin, was set up to investigate his claims. Its report presented in 1784 "conceded the phenomena but rejected the theory, imputing the cures and convulsions to the imagination" and rightly concluded that electricity and magnetism were not involved.

Alas, the suggestive powers of Mesmer and the imagination

[1] Quoted by R. Sudre, *A Treatise of Parapsychology*, translated by Celia Green (London, 1960).

of most of his patients were alike geared to the theory. When it was rejected, Mesmer's heyday was over. There was still however a handful of believers whose conviction that some "current" must be at work was based on such incidents as that (observed, recorded and apparently ignored by the commission) of a blind woman who reacted strongly the moment the "magnetic wand", which she could not see, was pointed at her stomach. It now seems probable that she became telepathically aware of Mesmer's symbolic gesture; the influence of a "current" was, however, the only explanation available in the parlance of the time, and that parlance has lingered almost into our own day to ease the mind and confuse the issue. Long after the phenomena of hypnotic suggestion in normal psychology had been recognized, evaluated and used, such terms as "psychic current" and "animal magnetism" retained their pseudo-scientific sway so far as parapsychology was concerned.

By, say, 1845, the majority of those formed in the discipline of the physical sciences, and indeed of medicine, still either subconsciously ignored or deliberately denied the existence of psi-phenomena, though there were a few who, like von Reichenbach, were still attempting to explore the subject in terms of "electricity", "emanations" and what he called "odylic currents". There is probably still some investigation to be done on the lines he indicated, but in connexion not so much with psi as with the electrical activities which may be generated by the normal physiological working of the body.

If one of a number of onions heaped in a cellar begins to sprout, the rest, stimulated by the minute electrical discharges incidental to the process, begin to sprout too, at a faster rate than they would in isolation. If the process of growth in such a small unit of life has electrical accompaniments it is not unreasonable to infer that these will exist in connexion with larger and more complex structures, and that persons of acute sensibility may sometimes become directly aware of them, as bees are aware of the polarization of light. This awareness may be projected and realized in an impression of radiance (or, in self-analytical temperaments, may be simply registered as something given and known but not explained).

Perhaps it is relevant to put on record that on two occasions, within a few weeks of one another, I myself went to see some-one interested, in the von Reichenbach tradition, in the study of what are known as "auras", the light said to dance around the human body as the Aurora Borealis dances above the mag-netic pole of the earth. On the first occasion I was feeling well and cheerful and was told my aura was perceptible so many feet away. The second time I happened to be depressed and physically exhausted; I was informed that this aura had weak-ened and did not extend nearly so far as before. In neither case did I mention my mood or my health, and on each occasion I wore a normal amount of powder, lipstick, etc. Now all warm objects from teapots to elephants' trunks emit infra-red heat waves. It is plain that, in this connexion alone a human being with that sub-normal temperature which often accompanies fatigue and depression must glow with a less powerful "aura" than one in bounding health with a normal temperature.

The faculty for perceiving this psycho-somatic phenomenon is often to be found in people who, in addition, show evidence of a well-developed psi-function (they are probably prone to realize with especial vividness *all* their own perceptions, how-ever these may be caused). This provides many well-taken opportunities for confusion of thought.

Thus, for instance, a normal if hyperaesthetic awareness of electrical phenomena generated by another body and varying in strength in accordance with various physiological factors may well, as has been shown, be projected and realized in terms of radiance. But so may paranormal awareness of some quality in another mind. The difference between these two things may be illustrated (if illustration be necessary) by reference to the Hindu custom of making pilgrimages to "take the durshan", or breathe the blessedness, of some holy man. Now men and women came great distances to "take the durshan" of Gandhi, but not that of another political hero, Jinnah. Jinnah, with all

his vitality and popularity, probably emitted a far more powerful aura of electrical activity than his colleague, but Gandhi's
presence carried with it a sense of living peace.

It is also possible that ordinary light may be liberated as a
by-product of certain little-understood psycho-physical conditions, witness the curious case of "the luminous woman of
Pirano" in 1934.[1] *The Times* of 5 May in that year, reported Dr
Protti, of the University of Padua, as noting that "the radiant
power of her blood is three times the normal"; that her very
strict Lenten fast probably produced "an excess of sulphides"
(a condition sometimes observed in people who cannot wear
silver ear-rings or necklaces because they make dark marks on
the skin so affected); that sulphides become luminous under
ultra-violet radiation; and that, therefore, the combination of
fasting with this peculiar type of blood might well account for
her periodical luminosity.

Thus, someone may be aware of "light" which is an objective
phenomenon brought about by the decision of a woman with a
particular physical constitution and religious devotion to undertake a strict fast: of "light" as the translation into familiar
sensory terms of some hyperaesthetic perception of electrical
activity; and of "light" as an image in which the telepathic
recognition of sanctity is reflected into the conscious mind.

Another instance in which it may be possible to distinguish
between some unknown hyperaesthetic sensory perception and
paranormal cognition is that of dowsing. Geiger counters are
said to show a certain activity above underground streams, and
it may well be that some physical faculty not yet understood is
involved in the experience of the dowser whose involuntary
muscular activities make known to him his own awareness, as
he walks the hill, of hidden water flowing deep below. But in
the awareness of the map dowser, passing his pendulum above
a piece of paper representing unknown ground until it swings
free, an awareness again conveyed to his conscious mind

[1] A fuller discussion of this case will be found in *The Physical
Phenomena of Mysticism.*

by involuntary muscular activity, paranormal cognition is at work.

Although the same psychological mechanism may serve to bring to the attention information received either through what may be called hyper-sensory perception or through extra-sensory perception, it is important to attempt to maintain the distinction between them as far as possible, differentiating for research purposes between, say, the workings of psi in producing telepathic or precognitive hallucinations, dreams and hunches, and what may prove to be phenomena of radiation.

In this connexion it is interesting to consider the experiments which have been conducted with what is called in America a "Faraday Cage".[1] These seem to indicate that there is some connexion of a negative kind between telepathy and such phenomena; it looks indeed as if the latter could distract inner attention from the former.

A "Faraday Cage" is a room-sized hollow cube whose copper walls form a complete barrier against electromagnetic waves and electrostatic effects. A radio set taken inside it will not work. If the outer surface is electrically charged no one inside can find out about this, even by touching the inner walls.

Telepathic teams who achieved statistically significant results in normal room conditions are said to have achieved even better ones working inside such cages, provided those cages were electrically connected with the earth (if the connexion were cut off they reverted to their previous level of scoring). If the outside of the cage carried an electrical charge of twenty thousand volts (neutralizing static electricity, etc., in much the same way as those degaussing devices used during World War II to protect ships' keels against magnetic mines), the teams got still better statistical results and also became aware, it is said, of one another's thoughts.

It is further claimed that if the teams were apart they still achieved a scoring rate higher than the previous statistically

[1] Apparatus of a similar kind has been designed and tried out in England, but I use the American name as it is short and memorable.

significant average if the receiving team were in a Faraday Cage and very much higher if each team were separately in such a cage.

It could be argued from all this that just as there are known to be people with a low "pain threshold" who experience as acute discomfort what others hardly notice, so there are people prone to observe data originally received at a level below that of consciousness; that these may register signals arising either from a sensitiveness to faint electromagnetic phenomena or by way of the psi-function; and that if they are effectively screened against electromagnetic activity they will become more sensitive to extra-sensory perception.

Among radiation phenomena may well be grouped such curious powers as those reported by the Italian Dr Roberto Assagioli in certain persons who claim to be able to "mummify" meat or to preserve flowers, by a combination of touch and will power. This claim, incidentally, does not sound quite so fantastic if it is compared with the old saying that "flowers fade on flirts and flourish on fools", which seems to imply that a quick and lively temperament releases some by-product which more placid natures do not. I do not know whether any planned experiments have been made to test the Italian claims (it might be difficult to find guinea pigs willing to evaluate the English proverb) but it is not impossible that what may be a natural process should in some instances have been brought under voluntary control.

If by the eighteen-forties men of science either ignored or denied the occurrence of psi-phenomena or attempted to account for them all in electrical terms, men of religion still tended to regard them as the result of divine revelation, as the effect of communicating with good or evil spirits, or (especially in Great Britain) as the superstitious delusions of women and uneducated persons. In France alone, Lacordaire was well in advance of his contemporaries in recognizing that the psi-function was part of man's nature, even if he defined it as too narrowly "a last glimmer of Adam's power" before the Fall, "destined to confound human reason, and humble it before God"

Then in America, in 1847, a family named Fox moved into a house at Hydesville in the State of New York, whose owner had left it because they believed it to be haunted. Inexplicable and apparently purposeful knockings and rappings were heard, and the daughters of the family devised codes by which to interpret them, codes which developed from the simplicity of "one knock for yes and two for no" into "one knock for A, two for B" and so on to twenty-six knocks for Z. This enabled whole words, whole sentences to be spelled out, albeit with an intolerable tedium. A cumulative wave of interest in these happenings swept over America and into Europe, generating more phenomena in its course, some genuine, some the work of ingenious persons seizing the opportunity to make money and fame, some genuine at first but eked out by legerdemain as the unknown power to produce them waned. Where spontaneous knockings were not available, various devices were invented by which substitutes could be obtained, notably table turning, which employed the involuntary muscular movements of a circle of people touching a small round table with the tips of their fingers to bring about tiltings which could be interpreted by the same code as the earlier rappings. (With what patience must the sitters have spelled out, letter by letter, at a *séance* near the silent Victor Hugo—who did not take part—verses almost identical with those he was in process of composing!) An advance on table turning, from the point of view of speed, was the invention of a device called a planchette, a small board on wheels with a pencil attached to it, which recorded "messages"; simpler still was the process known as automatic writing, achieved in those capable of it by taking pencil in hand, scribbling or doodling aimlessly for a while and then "allowing" it to write on its own, without the control of the will, in fact in a dissociated state. It is interesting to note the strongly marked blank verse rhythms into which such writings tend to flow, as may be observed in Joan Grant's fascinating novel *Winged*

Pharaoh, much of which was composed in this way. Automatic drawing and painting have also been undertaken. The results, sometimes curiously beautiful, strongly resemble the productions of patients undergoing psycho-therapy; hardly surprising, as all are the work of the subconscious mind, (through which psi-information normally wells up).

There was long a widespread, unquestioning assumption that all the "messages" received and decoded must come from the spirits of the dead, who were continually attempting to attract the attention of the living: such messages were therefore taken to be proofs of personal immortality. A cult of communication with the departed, the benevolent and now omniscient beings who watched over their survivors, began to grow up. Those who followed it soon produced a terminology in which to express their beliefs and a cosmogony into which to fit them. With perhaps unconscious verbal ingenuity they called their movement Spiritualism, a word given a strictly irrelevant ethical flavour by its implied contrast with "materialism". Those who showed a natural aptitude for receiving and transmitting "spirit messages" were called mediums, and "trained for development"; that is, taught techniques of dissociation which liberated the subconscious from the inhibiting power of the conscious mind. Their messages might purport to come through direct from the dead (in which case, drawing telepathically upon the layers of remembrance in those who "sat" with them, they might unwittingly mimic the voice, idiom, gestures of the ostensible sender) or through a secondary personality known as the "control" (a figure which, as already hinted may fruitfully be compared with that of the Totem on which the primitive projects information received by means of psi). This secondary personality may be apprehended as a Red Indian, an Egyptian, a Tibetan, a French doctor, a child, or even, nowadays, as a space man from another planet.

It is easy to see that a total acceptance of this terminology is just as cramping to objective investigation as is the total acceptance of electrical or magnetic terminology in connexion with

Dr Mesmer
1734–1815

"Count" Cagliostro
1743–1795

Dr Mesmer's Tub as contemporaries saw it

From 18th-century engravings: Radio Times Hulton Picture Library

The Mystic Rose from Dante's *Paradiso*

From an engraving by Gustave Doré: Radio Times Hulton Picture Library

the activities of mesmerists and other healers. Much of the Spiritualist cosmogony was mapped out in France, in 1857, by a Monsieur Rivail, who wrote under the name of Allan Kardec, and, as he claimed, at the dictation of "The Other Side", a work entitled *The Book of the Spirits*.

Two years later, in 1859, a very different book appeared, Charles Darwin's *Origin of Species*. It came as a violent seismic shock to the very large number of Fundamentalists, Anglican and Nonconformist, who believed in the verbal, the literal, interpretation of the Scriptures, and who had, furthermore, accepted Archbishop Ussher's carefully worked-out calculation that the world had been created at three o'clock in the afternoon of an October day in 4004 B.C. Here was what looked like proof that the world had existed for unimaginable ages, that the process of creation had been a gradual one, that mammals and birds and fish and reptiles had evolved, generation after generation, into their present forms, and that man himself might trace his physical ancestry back to the same stock as had produced the great apes. Some, like Philip Gosse, the Plymouth Brother naturalist, decided in an agony of mind which prevented their realizing the blasphemy of the notion that God had carefully hidden fossils in the rocks in order to try man's faith. Others refused to deny the evidence before them and felt that they must in honesty renounce belief in a religion incompatible with it. A whole generation of intellectuals brought up in the evangelical tradition turned, as they thought, to gaze into the void, where there was no God, no survival, no meaning. Those who followed High Church teachings were less perturbed; the early Fathers had, after all, outlined an evolutionary doctrine of creation. There was, however, a general sense of jolted uneasiness as of having stepped on a non-existent stair.

It is probable that this uneasiness had much to do with that growing enthusiasm for amateur and professional attempts to induce psi-phenomena which marked the 'sixties and 'seventies. Here, for the critical, was the evidence that the materialist philosophies might not be quite so firmly entrenched as their supporters claimed. Here, for the uncritical, were not only the personalities of the loved dead but also of the authoritative "controls" in charge both of them and of the living; kind Nannies of the soul in the vast, slow, cold, uncharted universe. "Spirit-rapping" was the craze of the day. The Empress Eugénie and Elizabeth Barrett Browning, among many others, were intrigued, as well they might be, by the extraordinary occurrences connected with D. D. Home, tuberculous son of a Methodist family, whose presence seemed to trigger off a regular machine-gun fire of knocking and to set heavy pieces of furniture rising six feet or more from the ground, an example he occasionally followed. Lord Adare, an intelligent, responsible and sane young man, was convinced that he had seen Home float out of one window and in at another, and set down his observations in telling detail. Browning cast doubts on his genuineness in "Mr Sludge the Medium"; but young William Crookes, after careful investigation, wrote (rather pontifically perhaps) "that certain physical phenomena such as the movement of material objects and the production of sounds resembling electrical discharges occur in circumstances in which they cannot be explained by any law of physics known at present, is a fact of which I am certain".

Table-turning, simply to see what would happen, became a game at parties, and in families, such as that of the four Macdonald sisters, who "turned" all sorts of objects including "a very communicative tea-urn", not to mention a *large* round table which on one occasion after "awakening" in its usual way "gradually quickened its pace until we had to run to keep up with it", and continued its gyrations even after Macdonald *père* had jumped on top of it.[1] One of these sisters, Alice, produced two children in whom extra-sensory perception was strong. Her daughter, Trix, developed a talent for crystal gazing and automatic writing and took part in the Verrall Cross Correspondences, of which more later. Her son, Rudyard Kipling, showed odd flashes of clairvoyance in his work, basing, for

[1] A. W. Baldwin, *The Macdonald Sisters* (London, 1960).

instance, two of the stories in *Puck of Pook's Hill* on the existence of an "imaginary" well-shaft in Pevensey Castle; a well-shaft which, unknown and unsuspected at the time when the book was written, was in fact discovered some ten years after its publication.

(In parenthesis, it is worth noting that precognition, sometimes personal and sometimes, as in this case, impersonal, may happen fairly frequently in imaginative writing, recalling the traditional connexion between prophecy and poetry. Other examples are to be found in the work of H. G. Wells—many of whose stories were founded on his peculiarly vivid dreams—who, for instance, described the use of tanks in warfare long before World War I, two years of which went by before they were even invented. The whole subject would make a good theme for a literary thesis.)

In 1869 the London Dialectical Society began an investigation of spiritualism. Its cautious report, published two years later, agreed that inexplicable sounds, vibrations and movements of heavy bodies seemed to occur at spiritualist *séances* and that answers given by the coded raps to questions put by the sitters might contain information known only to one person present and unknown to the medium. 1882 saw the foundation of the Society for Psychical Research in England, and 1884 that of its American counterpart. For a detailed history of their activities the reader should consult Rosalind Heywood's thorough and brilliant survey *The Sixth Sense* to which reference has already been made.

Among the points that should be noted here, one is that the founders of the original society were scientists and philosophers, who brought with them traditions of intellectual discipline, combining an eagerness to receive evidence and to experiment and an ability to form and test hypotheses, with willingness to suspend judgement until all the relevant facts had been discovered and examined. Both in England and in America lively and original minds were brought to bear on the problem of considering "without prejudice or prepossession and in a scientific spirit those faculties of man, real or supposed, which appear to be inexplicable on any recognized hypothesis" (to quote the Society's statement of its aims). Long before Freud, F. W. Myers formulated the concept of what he called the subliminal self; long before Jung (and long after Averroes) William James posited the existence of "a collective spiritual reservoir" in which are stored the experiences of all who ever lived, and wrote that individual human lives are like trees whose roots interlace inseparably in the ground whence they spring.

The field of investigation open to the new Society was enormous. There was hypnotism, then little understood, and mysterious still where it interacts with telepathy. Pierre Janet, at the Salpêtrière, quoted an instance in which a hypnotized woman in one room herself experienced all the sensory impressions of her hypnotizer in another, "even to burns and pinches in exactly the same part of the body".[1] Myers supervised and verified the results of a series of experiments made by Janet and Gibert, in which suggestions were telepathically transmitted over a distance of two kilometres to a middle-aged subject with whom a general hypnotic contact had already been established, and who duly went to sleep, woke up again and walked down the road in accordance with commands that could not have been received by normal sensory channels. (Today, when more is known about post-hypnotic suggestion, one may speculate as to whether she became telepathically aware at the time of the original contact of what was to be asked of her later.)

Instances such as these serve to confirm the idea that communication between living persons rather than information conveyed by spirits could account for much of the material obtained at *séances*, and showed, moreover, that "crisis apparitions" (seen by one person of another in danger or at the moment of death) tended to occur between people deeply concerned with one another, husbands and wives, parents and children, brothers and sisters, lovers and friends. It is interesting to compare with this tendency Ronald Rose's findings as

[1] Sudre, *op. cit.*

to the relative frequency of telepathic impressions among the Australian aborigines of whom he wrote in *Living Magic* and the Samoan community which is the subject of his later book.[1] They occurred far more often in the former group, and he attributes this in part to the fact that family ties and individual affections were very much stronger there than among the Samoans, whose children seemed to "belong" as much to grandmothers, aunts, cousins and even remoter relations as to their own parents, and who ate cheerfully in any household near which they happened to find themselves hungry. It is possible that the provision of school dinners may have something to do with the apparent decline in conscious extra-sensory perception in this country and that the dispatch of three year olds to all-day nursery schools may accelerate the process.

Experiments in what was then called thought-transference or thought-reading were undertaken. Some were between people of undeniable integrity close to one another, one telling a group of people the themes on which her thoughts were to run, the other coming in from another room well out of earshot and "guessing" them. It has already been noted that Gilbert Murray and his daughter, who shared many memories, many interests and the love of many of the same books, produced especially striking results. In another series a woman tried to transmit at a given time a series of thought pictures to a friend at a distance, recording them as she did so; just over a third were recognizably received. Mrs Alfred Sidgwick began to investigate the associations and memories of mediums and to compare them with those of their controls in the trance state, and found they were held in common, a process later elaborated by Whately Carington by means of a word-association test. Those of the ostensible "communicators" were different, which would, of course, be the case whether they were the spirits of the dead or the subconscious minds of the living "sitters".

Theories of telepathy were formulated; the part of the "agent" who was believed to initiate the process and to send a message

[1] *South Seas Magic* (London, 1959).

in some way, was at first stressed much more than that of the percipient who received it. Today it is sometimes suggested that the percipient's part is the only significant one, that he (or more often she) dwells unconsciously upon the thought of a loved person, and that this process, which goes on all the time, becomes known to the conscious mind only at moments of crisis. In support of this theory it is pointed out that there are well-authenticated instances in which the percipient seems to be precognitively aware of some misfortune of which the "agent" knows nothing until it happens, and that "messages" are apparently received from pets of which the owner is very fond. The first contention may carry some weight, but surely not the second. If, as Konrad Lorenz submits, the dog is liable to regard its owner either as a parent or as the leader of his pack, nothing is more likely than that telepathic distress signals should be put through to him. It seems most probable that a two-way process is involved, with agent and percipient both engaged.

Sitting with mediums went on, but it became clear, as the understanding of telepathic processes increased, that it was almost impossible to obtain *watertight* proofs of survival in this way. If a piece of information, a characteristic phrase, a reference to the past made by a "communicator" could be recognized by a sitter, then it could also have been drawn from that sitter's unconscious memories. (I once saw this tapping of such memories done by a gypsy at a fair in Mundesley, who told a girl visitor with me—she had never seen either of us before—that that girl lived in a house at the bottom corner of a triangle and that her grandfather was an architect. This was true, but neither the house in London nor the grandfather in Gloucester was in the girl's thoughts at the time.) The slow and reluctant acceptance of the uncomfortable fact that small-scale flashes of precognition do in fact occur completed the *impasse*. A neat illustration is to be found in the *Proceedings of the Society for Psychical Research* for 1925, which contains an account of the following incident. In 1922, Dr Soal was told at a *séance* with a medium, Mrs Blanche Cooper, that a spirit communicator named Gordon Davis, with whom he had been at school, was present. He said he had been killed in the 1914-18 war, and gave convincing evidence of his identity. At a later *séance* the same medium described in vivid detail the house at Southend in which he had lived. Three years later Dr Soal learnt that Gordon Davis had *not* been killed, and found that the house in Southend where he was actually living corresponded accurately, inside and out, with the description furnished by Mrs Cooper. He also found that in 1922, when she had given it, Mr Davis had been living in London and had had no idea of moving to Southend at all.

As to the "materializations" produced by certain mediums, several opinions are possible. The least tenable is that put forward by spiritualists. According to this, the medium exudes a substance known as ectoplasm, whence the spirits of the dead can mould themselves shapes resembling those of their bodies during life. When the spirits leave the medium she reabsorbs the ectoplasm. Since this is a living substance attached to her in some way, the medium is given a painful shock if investigators attempt to touch, handle or examine it. It is curious that this undifferentiated, infinitely plastic matter, which can be sculptured into faces, hands and mobile muscles, should apparently have an elaborately organized nervous structure of its own, much more sensitive than that of the parent body.

Several French investigators, while believing that ectoplasm has an objective existence, hold that the unconscious mind of the medium models it (by a process perhaps analogous to that of growth) into the likeness of an image she has perceived telepathically in the minds of her sitters; just as, with a similarly unconscious dramatization, another may act the part, use the voice, idiom, jokes of some dead person whom their hearts remember.

Research workers in England do not seem to accept the evidence for ectoplasm as very reliable. Those mediums who have produced it on the Continent do not appear to be able to do so under the stringent precautionary conditions insisted upon in this country; they ascribe their failure to the off-putting character of these conditions, which they find inhibit all spontaneity. Many attempts have been made to fake materializations. I have myself seen photographs of these which, put in an epidiascope and projected on to a screen, show very clearly in this enlarged form the slightly irregular weave of what no housewife could fail to recognize as butter muslin. That these attempts are made does not of course prove that there is in fact no such thing as ectoplasm, but it does suggest that in some cases, at any rate, the resemblance that materialized figures seem to bear to the dead may arise simply and sadly from the fact that people tend to perceive what they long for, especially if it appears to "make sense". Significant here are those experiments in "wishful seeing" reported at the British Association meeting in September 1959 (to which reference has already been made) and M. L. Johnson Abercrombie's[1] stress upon "the part that our past experience and present attitude play in determining what we see". A most striking illustration of this fact is an account of how a group shown (among other objects) a card bearing a red six of clubs automatically "saw" it either as black or as a six of hearts; because (of course!) there *is* no such thing as a red six of clubs. Somewhere between sight and perception came denial. They did not even get as far as the child who saw a giraffe and said he did not believe it; they simply could not envisage what was actually there.

Though it may justifiably be thought that certain spontaneous hauntings (those classified by Benedict XIV as likely to comfort or to help the living, rather than those which seem to go on and on repeating themselves like films shown over and over again) may arise from telepathy between the dead and those who loved them, only one set of occurrences in the history of organized psychical research presents features whence survival might logically be deduced. It is known as the Verrall Cross Correspondences.

After Myers' death in 1903, Mrs Verrall, anxious to give

[1] *Op. cit.*

some opportunity for him to prove his continued existence, took up automatic writing and presently succeeded in obtaining what seemed to be messages from him. A year later similar scripts were being written by a medium in America. Later, Kipling's sister began to receive them. And there were others. The correspondences continued on and off for thirty years. The erudite classical allusions to be found in the scripts meant little or nothing to some of those who put them on paper, and only when the pieces of the jigsaw were, so to speak, fitted together was the full meaning of the series apparent.

Even in this case, however, there are those who feel that an alternative explanation is possible on scientific lines. They suggest that Mrs Verrall, herself a classical scholar, unconsciously chose and transmitted the material, and that the whole affair was one of "mutual telepathy".[1] But though the psi-function, working as it does through the unconscious, might perhaps choose material, and so brood on it that it reaches other minds, it does not usually undertake activities which need careful, detailed planning; and the "selective" transmission of material, this bit to one person, that to another, is very difficult to reconcile with the way in which psi is usually observed to occur. In spontaneous telepathy between two living persons both are interested in one another, and an impression, a vision, an emotion comes through. But to attract the attention of one medium to one group of data and of another to another, and to see that the results fitted in in a finished product does not look like the work of the unconscious, but of deliberate and careful thought whether on the part of Myers or of some other entity.

In spite of all this activity, there was little general interest in the facts that had been established. Evidence provided by long and careful experimental work conducted by persons of complete integrity tended to be dismissed without examination as the result of coincidence, illusion or even collusion. Many lumped psychical research, the detached investigation of psi-

[1] Sudre, *op. cit.*

phenomena, together with spiritualism, the theory and practice of a cult of the dead, and ignored both as a morbid phantasmagoria of chance, twaddle, self-deception, fraud and mental instability, a phantasmagoria reinforced by the massacres and griefs of World War I, massacres and griefs such as had not been known in England for more than three generations.

The Somnambulist Age was setting in, as a result of that gulf between scientific thought and human experience whose beginnings have already been described, a gulf torn deeper still by the Darwinian controversies. The whole idea of a synthesis of knowledge dimmed and faded. Those trained in the methods of the physical sciences tended to find vague, emotional and unreliable the thoughts and ideas of those who expressed themselves in other ways. These in turn found scientific terminology completely inadequate for their own purpose, and, moreover, became more and more subjective. Communication began to fail. Research scientists continued to pursue their work, focusing attention so closely upon it as to bring about near-blindness to its implications in other fields and to the uses to which their findings might be put. In writing, the "stream of consciousness" method became popular, and then the stream of unconsciousness. D. H. Lawrence felt and inspired a passion for "thinking with the blood" rather than the brain, a passion echoed in the Nazi movement. Painters and sculptors, impatient of all intellectual approach to their work, attempted to convey purely sensory impressions, to regard exterior objects less as things existing in their own right than as stimulants to feeling. Inspiration was better than reason, and anything emerging from the unconscious must *ipso facto* be inspired.

It was, oddly enough, in the field of psychical research that a step was taken towards translating the language of experience into a terminology common to the sciences—that of statistics. As early as 1874, the great French physiologist Charles Richet had suggested[1] that the calculus of probability might be

[1] In an article, "La Suggestion Mentale et le Calcul des Probabilités" published in the *Revue Philosophique* for that year.

used in connexion with a series of experiments with playing cards to show whether statistical proof of the existence of what he called "lucidity", or clairvoyance, could be obtained. Although he reverted to this idea several times in his busy life, no considerable attempt seems to have been made to carry it out until 1912, when it was tried in a small way at Stanford University in the United States. Fourteen years later a similar attempt was made at Harvard. Rhine's work with the simplified Zener cards, which was to bring the whole matter to public attention, began in the Psychology Department of Duke University, North Carolina, in 1927.

Its nature and scope have already been sketched in the first and third chapters of this book, and it is now so well known that there is no need to give a detailed account of it here. Attempts have been made to deny the efficiency with which the experiments were conducted and the validity of the statistical methods used to evaluate them. New series of experiments, carried out with all possible precautions, have, however, yielded similar results, and the statistical methods are those already in use in such different disciplines as civil engineering and biology. A quotation from the English summary of an article by Professor Dr Emilio Servadio, the Italian psychiatrist, may help to account for the strength and persistence of these attempts.

> Rational thought, which was imposed with great difficulty on primitive, magical methods of thinking, is maintained in contemporary man by an efficient psychological defence mechanism, alerted directly it is faced with any phenomenon which looks like a regression to the former level of consciousness. Parapsychological phenomena with their archaic structure are felt to menace the very basis of individual personality. These mechanisms of denial have to be taken into account in the same way as the opposite tendencies towards uncritical credulity.[1]

[1] *Zeitschrift für Parapsychologie und Grenzgebiete der Psychologie* (Freiburg im Bresgau, September 1958).

There are three main reasons for which Dr Rhine's achievement is of cardinal importance.

First, in our epoch the majority of men assume the language of the exact sciences, with its mathematical symbolism, to be the only valid means of testing, assessing and formulating objective truth. Rhine has demonstrated in this language the existence of the psi-function, whose workings had previously been discussed (and sometimes acknowledged) for the most part in the more vivid but less precise vocabulary of humanism. He has translated the knowledge of a vital fact from one intellectual idiom into another.

Second, that psi has been shown to exist implies the inadequacy of those ideas about the nature of human personality which have slowly been crystallizing ever since the age of Locke, and demonstrates that among its components is something not wholly dependent upon time, space and the immediate reports of the senses.

The third and most important feature of Rhine's findings is that they may serve to provide a basic framework of thought upon which there may one day be built such an integrated synthesis of knowledge as has not existed since the thirteenth century.

Some of his own deductions are open to criticism, notably of course his idea that because the psi-function may be described as "spiritual" all its manifestations are necessarily "good". His attempt to argue from the existence of psi to the existence of God is, moreover, innocent of any knowledge of formal logic, of philosophical thought and of any theology but that of guilt and release. But that such an argument can be framed in the language of those who trust no other, and that it can bring them to regard God not simply as a source of subjective feelings but as an Object of thought to be considered without uneasy intellectual reservations, this is of the greatest possible significance for the present and the future.

Chapter Ten

A NEW INTERPRETATION

I HAVE attempted to discuss the working of the psi-factor in various forms, spontaneous, cultivated and experimental, and in various contexts, biological, cultural and historical. This last chapter will recapitulate some of the points which have been made and rough out a theory of its provenance and purpose.

It has been argued that in animals psi seems to be a function of the "form and behaviour design" of each species, interacting with that group mind which builds "itself up from the unconsciously shared experience of all"[1] its members and is operative in each of them. It appears as inherited instinct, impelling the spider to make its web, the bee its octagonal cell, in accordance with a given, unchanging norm. It appears as telepathy, synchronizing and co-ordinating the specialized activities of the different workers in the termitary. It appears as precognition in certain migrants making their way unerringly through the sea currents or the winds from where they were hatched to place they have never seen, known only to generations dead before they came into being. In producing an overriding impulse to follow out the appropriate behaviour pattern, it subserves the reproduction, the survival and the perfection of each kind of creature.

As species develop the ability to form conditioned reflexes, and then habits, and then learnt judgements, the part played by the group mind becomes increasingly important. It may modify, by its reaction to changing exterior circumstance, the workings of the original "form and behaviour design". This reaction may be expressed either as a more and more elaborate self-defence

[1] Hardy, *op. cit.*

or as a flexible adaptation to the new conditions. It has been suggested, indeed, that the degeneration and extinction of species such as those prehistoric monsters whose armoured bony carapaces became so cumbrous that they could hardly move, may be attributable to the psycho-somatic influence of a group mind preoccupied with self-protection against all change.

In man, individual reasoning and separate personal choice became possible. As a result of one conscious and profound choice—to cut himself off from spontaneous dependence on God, live separate in unalterable pride—his group mind did not merely degenerate, with something analogous to sloth, from the form and behaviour design of his species. It split away. Both survive in him, the latter maintaining his ineradicable sense that, like it or not, some behaviour patterns should be followed and others rejected; that, in human parlance, some actions are right and some are wrong. Different cultures, different modes of upbringing, different creeds may modify his judgements as to which are which; but nothing will alter his conviction that the two sorts exist. As has already been noted, brain washing itself can do no more than reorientate conscience; it cannot destroy it.

The group mind, the collective unconscious, tainted by the ancient and continuing experience of evil, seeps into the being of every individual self, a self which is simultaneously drawn towards the original design for its species. The constant tension between the two is eased by the formulation of legal codes; the law of nature for the species is projected and rationalized in natural law, external, rigid, easy to recognize, hard to follow.

The Incarnation fulfilled and transcended with joy this projected, external law, showing it to be not a series of arbitrary decrees but a means to an end, and bringing into being a group mind renewed, spontaneous, free, in which the individual reborn could ultimately achieve that end, carry out the purpose for which he and his species were made; to know, love and serve God and to enjoy His Presence for ever. Psi would still link each human being with his contemporaries and his forebears, with the collective unconscious of mankind, whose impulses, good, bad, and neutral, would flow into him as before. But it could also link him with the new group, with the springs of grace welling up through those who were members of one another in the Mystical Body of Christ. Through that individual, moreover, the impulses of the new group could flow back (without his necessarily knowing it), into the old, changing its colouring, revitalizing it deep below the level of consciousness. Hence the overwhelming importance for all mankind of those dedicated to contemplative prayer. Hence the stress and exhaustion and glory of their calling.

It has been argued that in animal species the psi-factor is to be found at work in instinctive processes subserving reproduction. Ancient tradition and modern observation can both be adduced to support the hypothesis that in man too there is a close connexion between psychical and sexual activity.

One aspect of this is to be seen in the insistence upon virginity, chastity, or at the very least upon periodical spells of continence in those who deliberately attempt to cultivate and to use the psi-function, as in the traditional employment of a child under the age of puberty for scrying in the inkpool or the crystal.

If sexual activity inhibits the workings of psi, so also it seems can psi-activity inhibit biological processes connected with reproduction. Reference has already been made to Ronald Edwin's remark that during the long periods in which his clairvoyant powers were at their height he was completely free from physical desire. Women clairvoyants and mediums have noticed that in similar circumstances the menses do not occur.[1]

Persons of great vitality appear often to swing between the one impulse and the other, as seems to have happened in the cases of Rasputin, and of those late nineteenth-century occultist figures involved in sexual scandals. When such persons have carefully trained themselves to dissociate the unconscious mind, through which psi works, from the inhibitions of the conscious

[1] Personal communication.

self, they have no means of resisting a temptation as violent as vision has been vivid. It is no coincidence that this kind of instability is associated with the cultivation of psychic powers.

Deliberate attempts have of course been made from time to time to stimulate the psi-function by means of orgy. The cult of Dionysus and the life of Alasteir Crowley afford concrete and revolting examples of this, and Arthur Rimbaud, writing in the 1870's, provided a prescription and a theory: "The poet makes himself a *seer* by a long, vast, and reasoned *derangement of all the senses*—every form of love, of suffering and of madness." It seems probable that if these attempts succeed it is because they are exceptionally forceful methods of dissociation; commending themselves especially to minds tightlaced into Greek rationalism, into the rigid doctrines of the Plymouth Brethren, or into the strict logic of the French educational system.

A form of dissociation akin to Rimbaud's "reasoned derangement of the senses" which has aroused much recent interest is that to be achieved by the use of hallucinogenic drugs like lsd. These sometimes permit detachment, the swallower remaining aware, throughout a series of overwhelming experiences, that they are subjective, in a state perhaps akin to that "dual functioning of consciousness" which enabled Lily Yeats to be aware simultaneously of her surroundings and of veridical hallucinations. *Pace* the opinion of the late Mrs Eileen Garrett who once told me that such drugs *must* release psi-activity in those who take them "because those experiences show us our *real* selves", it seems to me that they can at best act, so to speak, as snorkel masks, enabling or compelling people to sink into their own depths, there to perceive "under the glassy green translucent wave" all that can hardly, or very dimly, be seen from above the surface: the sand, the glimmering shoals of fish, a crab going sideways, the brilliant anemones, the fronds of seaweed, red and green and brown, stirring with the movements of the current or of some octopus emerging slowly and horribly from a cleft in the rocks they cover. But nothing can be seen that was not already there all the time; psi-activity may be revealed, but not stimulated.

I have already touched upon the way in which extra-sensory is linked with sensory perception, knowledge intuitively received expressing itself through such a network of associated images as carries remembrance, but with much greater vividness. Sometimes the percipient projects this imagery upon the outside world (as a magic lantern projects large and clear on a white sheet the picture, tiny and obscure in the lantern slide), and then becomes aware of it reflected back to himself as say an exterior "vision" or "voice".[1] Sometimes he is conscious of it as an inner experience of peculiar intensity. This may happen in connexion with telepathy with the dead. Which form it takes is probably determined by the temperament and conditioning of the percipient. Thus one woman, completely absorbed in sorting out the personal papers of a lately dead father who could not bear to have his personal possessions touched, might be so roused and shocked by the sudden unexpected sense of a furious presence as to say to the empty soundless room, "Darling, I'm terribly sorry, but as you're dead it's got to be done, and I'm the best person to do it"; another might "see" or "hear" the dead man; or yet another project a similar awareness in the form of poltergeist disturbances.

It has also been indicated that religious experiences follow similar patterns; this is hardly surprising if, as is postulated, the same function, using the same psycho-physical mechanisms, is at work. Some temperaments, especially in those culture patterns where it seems normal and natural so to do, see visions, hear voices, which express to them their inner awareness of God and of His will for them, as happened in the quiet everyday pastures of Domrémy to that breathless child who was to deliver her country, to be burned at the stake and to be canonized as St Joan. Others use sensory imagery, recognizing it as no

---

[1] For a fascinating discussion of the fact that "the sporadic spontaneous experiences reported to parapsychologists are generally different in quality and in frequency from the hallucinations associated with (mental) illness and abnormal physiological states", the reader is referred to Dr Donald J. West's article "Visionary and Hallucinatory Experiences" in *The International Journal of Parapsychology*, II, 1 (Winter, 1960).

more than an analogy of their experience and yet finding that analogy more real, more significant than even the original that the senses knew. Witness St Augustine: "And yet when I love my God, I do love a light, a voice, a fragrance, a food and an embrace—the light, voice, fragrance, food, embrace of my inner being, where there is the inshining into my soul of That which space cannot contain, and where there is a sound of which time cannot deprive me, and where there is a fragrance whose sweetness the wind cannot blow away, and a taste which cannot be diminished by eating, and an embrace never sundered by satiety."[1] Yet others can speak only of "a dazzling darkness" and cry with Henry Vaughan:

> Oh for that dark, that I in Him
> Might live invisible and dim.

And others still can say no more than *Neti*, *Neti*; He is not this, not that; but a Presence which cannot be defined in words or ideas or concepts, which can only be known as existent, as That which Is, known as mysteriously but as certainly as a man knows himself to be.

And so back, full circle, to the body again: the body, first means of perception, continual source of that imagery in which its owner may become fully aware of his own intuitions: the body, the living symbol through which his feelings, his desires, his whole self may be imaged to the world in varying degrees, from the blush to the stigmata, from the sweat of fear to the odour of sanctity,[2] from jumping for joy or trembling with fright to the phenomenon of levitation: the body, generator of that energy which can be used to subserve either the reproduction and survival of the species, or psi-activity.

And if, as has been suggested, the psi-function in man is the means of contemplation, a quantity of apparently heterogenous

---

[1] *Confessions*, X, 6.
[2] For well-authenticated instances of this odd, but objective occurrence, cf. Thurston, *op. cit.* It seems to have been observed with especial frequency in living and dead members of the order of Discalced Carmelites.

teachings, from those dealing with the celibacy of the priest-hood to those forbidding fortune-telling, fall neatly into pattern.

As the vision of God is the fulfilment of man's being, it is plainly necessary so to regulate sexual activity that he is neither swallowed up in this by way of simple animal enjoyment nor distracted from his main Object by a series of absorbing and passionate love affairs with one person after another. A certain amount of energy must be left for psi, whether its workings come into consciousness or not. Hence the prohibition of polygamy; hence the enjoinment of pre-marital chastity; hence the three possible kinds of life open to the individual Catholic.

In the first of these, marriage, the spouses give themselves to be part of the splendour of creation, bringing into being through the sacrament of bodily love unique new lives, new mirrors of God, new selves "struck from nothingness to know eternity". Since these new humans have to be fed, warmed, washed, trained, taught and clothed, their parents will have little time or energy for contemplative prayer while they are young; if psi appears—as it often does between mother and small child—it will be linked with family love. It is interesting, though, to consider in this connexion the ruling that if a spacing out of births is to be attempted this should be either by sexual abstin-ence or by the use of the infertile period; each of these modes of behaviour ensures that some fund of energy may be available for other uses. In the main, however, though the wills and bodies of those who choose this way of living may joyfully serve the purposes of God, not until they grow old will they have much leisure to think about Him.

The second kind of life is, of course, that of the priest. It is plain that the celibacy of this state is not only a device for en-suring that those who serve God at the altar should not be dis-tracted and encumbered by human obligations. It is also, and primarily, an attempt to divert the energy that might have been used for reproductive activity to the uses of psi, psi to be dedi-cated to prayer and to a knowledge of the needs of their people.

The third is the life of the hermit and of the religious orders, wholly dedicated to contemplation, in which psi may be given full fruition in union with God, and thence radiate into the collective unconscious, so that the contemplative's prayers, insight, adoration will be used for all men.

Each state will obviously have its own difficulties. The first may tend to the placid satisfaction of biological fulfilment, the habit of concentrating all attention upon the needs of the family rather than upon the Presence of God. Those called to the second and third states will be tormented when sexual desire threatens to filch away the fund of energy they wish to devote to contemplative prayer, though sometimes, as happened to St Hugh of Lincoln, they may succeed at a comparatively early age in using that fund for prayer alone. Those in the third state may also find themselves overwhelmed with the fear, gloom, terror, loneliness, temptations of people known and unknown, which have been transferred to their shoulders to bear with Christ.

It becomes plain, moreover, why Catholics—like their spiritual forefathers the Jews—are forbidden to try to develop and use the psi-function for any but religious ends. It is not only that others who attempt to cultivate it are frequently committed to beliefs which they believe to be erroneous. It is not only that the modes of cultivation employed almost always involve dissociating the conscious from the unconscious mind, with a consequent suspension of judgement, reason and integrated choice. It is that such an attempt is fundamentally distracting, focusing attention not upon essentials but upon trivialities, on the one hand linking a man more closely with the tainted collectivity of his species, and on the other encouraging him to excited pride rather than to calm, matter-of-fact humility. By the cultivation of psi I do not of course mean engaging in prolonged (and often boring) scientific experiments in card guessing and so on, or perfecting and using a talent for dowsing or mapdowsing; but the deliberate, professional attempt to yield the mind, whether awake or in an induced trance state, to record and transmit any vivid extra-sensory perceptions it may receive.

It is a very different thing if these perceptions are received unsought. The psi-function is morally neutral and can, like most human functions, operate in an automatic way above or below the threshold of consciousness or be used for good or for evil ends in accordance with the bent, and sometimes the will, of its owner.

It may rightly be remarked that very little has been said about how the psi-function works, whether in interaction between living minds, in interaction with matter, or in interaction with time. This is because, though various tentative hypotheses have been put forward, no one knows. It remains profoundly mysterious. As has already been reiterated, the analogy with electricity, and especially with radio, is both tempting and extremely misleading. Radio is not selective. Anyone can listen to any programme available in his locality. Spontaneous psi-activity is selective. Telepathy occurs between those linked by personal relationships and common interests. It might be hazarded that some weak electrical activity not yet understood, emitted by one person at a moment of stress, could stimulate the temporal lobe of the brain in another closely connected with him, reviving memory and its associations so vividly as to produce an hallucination of his presence; but this theory does not serve to explain how *new* information could be transmitted. It does not, moreover, account for crisis apparitions, or telepathic impressions, of people a very great way off, even at the other side of the world. Wireless waves weaken in accordance with the inverse square of distance from the place of their origin. Spontaneous psi is not affected.

There are many fully documented and evidentially satisfying cases on record in which someone was telepathically aware, clearly or dimly, of the feelings of a friend thousands of miles away. Perhaps I may be allowed to cite an instance known to me. One Monday morning a young relation told me that he had had a most curious, uneasy, vivid dream of being back at school among a small group of boys being coached by the history master, a dream in which something was very wrong, though he did not know what. He had liked this master very much and was gratefully conscious that he owed a great deal to his teaching. Since his schooldays, however, he had spent three years at Oxford, taken his degree, and gone into the Army to do his National Service, while the history master had left the school, and taken up a university post in New Zealand. It was at least five years since they had met and he was not in the foreground of the young man's life. "I haven't thought of him for years, I do hope he's all right," the latter said as he finished telling me the dream. This was about half-past eight in the morning. As I left my office about six o'clock that evening, I bought an *Evening Standard* and saw that an aeroplane carrying the former history master and a number of other university men from New Zealand and some South-East Asian countries to an educational conference had crashed and that there were no survivors.

The connexion between psi-activity and matter, living or inert, is just as difficult to explain and even harder to accept. Where what is called "psychic healing" is concerned, it is clear that psycho-somatic processes initiated by very powerful suggestion are at work; but how odd it is that one mind should be able so powerfully to impress another that a suggestion should be transmitted to the autonomic nervous system which co-ordinates and determines, deep below the level of consciousness, even of sensation, all the non-voluntary activities of the body. Inedia, the power to do without food, for very long periods, of which there are reliable records both among ordinary people and among those dedicated to a religious life[1]; levitation; and the sudden loss of weight said to have been observed during the course of *séances* in mediums, specializing in physical phenomena: all these are odd enough, but do at any rate concern the reactions of the living body-mind, in which consciousness and energy co-exist and are correlated in everyday experience.

Odder still are those poltergeist phenomena in which objects are observed to move in a peculiar and characteristic curve,

[1] Cf. Thurston, *op. cit.*, for accounts of the nineteenth-century American Mollie Fancher, as of St Catherine of Siena and others.

quite unlike the trajectory of something thrown, for they apparently imply that the unconscious mind can exert physical force at a distance. Yet there is evidence for it, evidence supported, as noted in Chapter Three, by the fact that the pattern of scoring in psycho-kinesis experiments is the same as that observed in those testing ordinary extra-sensory perception, in that significant results usually occur towards the beginning and tail off in a "decline effect" as the subject gets bored, which is totally unlike that shown by someone learning a skill.

The oddest and most unpalatable of all aspects of psi lies in its peculiar relationship to time as we experience it. It is not too difficult, to be sure, to allow that retro-cognition (otherwise post-cognition) may occur; perhaps because the process of remembering one's own past, so vividly *there*, though invisible, provides a familiar analogy, perhaps because one can think of a film being played over and over again, or can imagine say the "ghost" of Lady Macbeth re-enacting for ever, in a timeless repetitive automatism, the guilty gesture of attempting vainly to wash her hands. It is possible moreover to talk—and to be understood—about a place being "full" of a certain emotional atmosphere to whose survival everyone conscious of it will contribute more vitality. And so on. Though these are no more than analogies, they afford a comfortable feeling that something points towards a rational explanation, an explanation that may one day be made completely plain.

But there is no ordinary experience, no convincing analogy to make comfortable the notion that people are occasionally aware of what has not yet happened, whether it is a card one ahead of that being proposed for guessing, or a railway accident twenty years in the future. Myers' query, "Are we regarding as a stream of consequences what is really an ocean of co-existencies?"; William James' kindred notion of an eternal present; the concept of other dimensions whose effects we can observe but whose nature we can no more comprehend than the Flatlanders could comprehend the nature of a cube; Dunne's theory of a Serial Universe, with a time behind our time, and another behind that, and so on to infinity: all these weave a discreet curtain of speculation over the skeleton in the cupboard, but in no way ease acceptance of the fact that it is there, or not at any rate by the non-mathematical type of mind. This may however be given some inkling of what is meant by considering instead of Dunne's mathematical arguments and symbols his likening of consciousness to a searchlight exploring a four-dimensional world.

There are those who find the small "time-displacement" phenomenon to be seen in the precognitive card guesser less strange than the long-range prophecies which are occasionally recorded and verified. This is not simply because the irregularity is "only a very little one", but because there is not such a vast multiplicity of causes and choices at work between the seer and the seen.

I am no more competent to discuss the problems of pre-destination and free will than I am to explain those of the higher mathematics, but, since it may be useful to people who share my incompetence, I shall put forward some considerations that seem relevant to the strange way in which the psi-function, like Friar Bacon's brazen head, may be aware of how "Time Is, Time Was, Time Will Be".

"Ask me no more", sang the poet:

> Ask me no more where Jove bestows
> When June is past the fading rose,
> For in your beauty's orient deep
> These things, as in their causes, sleep.

St Thomas Aquinas, discussing the problem of precognition, held that it sprang from the capacity to perceive future events "as in their causes, sleeping" in the present. The percipient, telepathically aware of all the relevant factors at work, came intuitively to a correct conclusion as to their outcome (rather as a man working on some problem may sleep on it and wake to find his subconscious has brought the solution into focus).

He then projected his conclusion in the form of vision, voice or dream, so that it appeared to come from some external source.

Although the methods employed are entirely different, and the materials available are chosen and manipulated by the reasoning mind, sociological attempts to deduce future developments from present conditions are continually being made, and with some success. Neither in the case of the conscious nor of the subconscious process can it be inferred that there is any implicit or explicit derogation of the principle of individual free will. Thus an expert in demographical statistics will try to predict, by correlating the age of the present population, the birth rate and the infant mortality in a given area, how many children will be passing through its schools in fifteen years' time and what buildings should be planned to accommodate them. He will probably be able to give a reasonably accurate overall estimate, but this estimate will take no account of individual lives and choices, of who will take vows of chastity as priest or nun, of who will marry whom, or of who will live in promiscuity producing illegitimate babies.

It is interesting that Werner Heisenberg[1] should maintain the existence of two types of causality, which seem to operate the one on a large scale, the other on a small. In the former, a strict determinism prevails. In the latter, there is "potentiality", the possibility of unpredictable, spontaneous activity (and even, at the level of nuclear physics, of "time reversal", of a situation in which it is not possible to know which of two events is the cause of the other and which the effect). He contends moreover that "the causality governing man is of the weaker type, and he embodies both mechanical fate *and* potentiality". In large-scale matters, sociologists will be justified in basing their plans on the assumption that a number of developments are predetermined, in personal matters the individual can pray for grace to help him make a free and a right choice.

If that individual becomes aware, through hunch or dream or warning "voice", of some disaster to which present causes

[1] *Op. cit.*

outside his control are building up, he may be free to choose, ahead of schedule as it were, whether he will be involved in it or trust his intuition, even if this brings him temporarily into ridicule. The odd way in which some trivial veridical detail of the achieved disaster—a newspaper headline, a soldier's uniform—may present itself to him with especial clarity can be paralleled by the common experience of remembering just such details of past events, details charged with some strong emotional significance not always understood.

I do not myself find this attempt to interpret the process involved precognition very satisfying, for precognitive experiences are usually so vividly of something "given", independent, existing in its own right, and containing chunks of objective and, so to speak, irrelevant data, which neither telepathy as to present circumstances nor intuition as to their outcome could be expected to provide. It should, however, be considered as well as the mathematical theories which have been put forward, and perhaps in connexion with them.

There are two other hypotheses in which time and causality are involved. Both are characterized by a careful, painstaking avoidance of what would seem to any theist to be the obvious explanation of the problem involved. One seems to imply that occasional reversals of the temporal process can occur, as if part of a stream were, here and there, to be diverted and pumped at high pressure round a looped channel to flow backwards into the main current. This was first formulated nearly sixty years ago by a French thinker, Gabriel Tarde, in an article entitled "The Effect of Future Events".[1] "Purposiveness," he wrote, "plays a role in the phenomena of life perhaps more important than that of heredity. The embryo is explained by the adult creature. Evolution . . . shows changes occurring not at random but apparently in accordance with a directing idea . . . when several events converge towards one important event, *this future event has exerted an influence*" (my italics) on the present.

Perhaps the contemporary blaze of Bergson's thought so

[1] *Revue de Metaphysique et de Morale*, IX (Paris, 1901).

dazzled Monsieur Tarde that he did not realize that he was seeing, and reiterating in other words, Aristotle's theory of teleology. Perhaps it was simply such a distaste for the whole concept as, according to Dr Denis Hill,[1] leads medical students who have been conditioned to consider disease in terms of strict physical causation to shy away from psychiatry as "non-scientific". Was it however an emotional reaction against some all too anthropomorphic concept of the Divine, or an assumption that there could be no contact between the disciplines of science and of theology that made him construct a very difficult theory of time rather than accept the fact that "directive ideas" exist not in the void but in a mind; that forced him and his followers to postulate an abstract "purposiveness" working itself out in biological development rather than realize that purposiveness and purposes are not autonomous entities, but can only be conceived, held, and co-ordinated in an Intelligence alive and aware of Itself and of Its own activities ?

The other hypothesis is that put forward by Jung in the theory of synchronicity which is, as has already been noted, an attempt to reconcile with what he calls the iron law of causality the occurrence not only of psi-phenomena but also of significant coincidences, events in the outer world which suddenly express, symbolize or perfect psychological developments in this or that individual. He instances an occasion on which he was carefully explaining to a worried patient, reluctant to accept what he said, that an insect of which that patient kept dreaming was a scarab, the Egyptian symbol of rebirth and renewal. His remarks were met with a sort of glum resistance until suddenly there flew into the room where they were sitting the nearest European equivalent of the scarab, a glowing green and gold rose beetle. It settled before them, and the arrival of this external image of his own thought in some odd way jolted the patient into realizing its meaning, and set him on the way to recovery.

[1] "Acceptance of Psychiatry by the Medical Student", *British Medical Journal* (26 March, 1960).

Where Tarde wrote of purposiveness, directive ideas, and the effect of future events to explain what he had observed, Jung uses the word Tao to indicate the source alike of temporal processes and of synchronicity: Tao, the self-caused, self-existent activity, which cannot be contained in human thought. It is clear from his other work that the Name of God carries for him at best the definition of an archetypal idea at work in the psyche and at worst the sense of a threatening, capricious, and implacable tyrant.

For those who associate that Name with "the unfathomable mystery, the incomprehensible Being" of whom Bede Griffiths writes in *The Golden String*, and with that passage from St Augustine quoted there which broods upon the Power "most secret, most present, most beautiful, most mighty . . . ever in action and ever quiet . . . upholding, filling and protecting, creating, nourishing and perfecting all things" there will be no difficulty in accepting that the continuous glory of creation in matter, life and consciousness, and our power of recognizing it by reason and intuition, in time and in eternity, spring all alike from God.

Appendix

THE EVIL EYE

IN connexion with psycho-kinesis one ought perhaps to consider the phenomenon known as the Evil Eye. In Italy, where belief in it is still very much alive, it is considered to be of two kinds. With the first, *malocchio*, I am not concerned here; it is thought to be a voluntary and deliberate piece of ill-wishing, and is probably to be explained in terms of suggestion. The other kind, the *jettatura*, is very much more interesting. It is conceived as an involuntary power over which its unfortunate possessor has no control, and its effect is to bring bad luck to his neighbours. It used to be thought superstitious to speak of certain people as "unlucky", attracting misfortune to themselves; but it is now intellectually respectable to do so provided that the current verbal fashions are followed and that one uses the term "accident prone". Accident proneness is officially recognized as a risk among factory workers, and industrial psychologists have investigated the subject in some detail. It springs from various unconscious sources, including the need to purge away guilt in self-punishment.

It is not far from the idea of the accident-prone individual to that of the Jonah, the man who makes the boat dangerous, the man whose own personal ill-luck is believed to involve his companions. It is easy to see that, say, an accident-prone worker in an atomic power plant might be an outsize in Jonahs, bringing disaster not only on his work-mates but upon the surrounding countryside.

Now the possessor of *jettatura* need not himself be accident prone. He projects his accident proneness on his surroundings. He is unlucky by proxy, a Jonah whose misfortunes occur only to those around him, unknowing or unwilling scapegoats in whom his conflicts are worked out. On a journey, it is his friend's luggage, not his own, which falls inexplicably off the dockside into the water. Pots of azaleas carefully arranged on a shelf for a party topple on to somebody else's head when he comes into the room, and so on.

It looks very much as if this sinister misfortune—life is understandably difficult for the man believed to possess the quality of *jettatura*—were a combination of accident proneness and psycho-kinesis, and thus closely connected with poltergeist activity. Both varieties of phenomena are associated with given individuals. Neither is primarily associated with the conscious mind of those individuals. Both may affect physical objects.

There is room for considerable research in both subjects. It has been claimed that poltergeist phenomena clear up when the conflict in the unconscious mind of the person in whom they are centred is resolved, though not much evidence on the point has been published, partly perhaps for reasons of professional etiquette. In 1942, I was told myself, in circumstantial detail, of an elderly cook around whom poltergeist activity developed at a period of acute war-time tension and who lost several jobs through no fault of her own, because her employers could not stand the strain, let alone the expense, of seeing saucepans float gently off stoves and crockery crash from the table to floor without her touching any of them. She was then given psychiatric treatment for some other condition, and the poltergeist trouble cleared up at the same time. This, however, is purely anecdotal. It would be interesting to know if any systematic records of such cases have been made in England and whether Italian psychiatrists have thought of investigating and treating instances of *jettatura* on these lines. Those to whom it is attributed are not always peasants living in remote villages; at least one distinguished academic character is said to be afflicted in this way and to be uncomfortably conscious of the fact. Men of intellectual ability might well be willing to co-operate in experiments designed not only to illuminate this condition but to rid them of it.

It would also be interesting to know whether this particular form of the Evil Eye is recognized in other parts of the world as well as Italy and the Near East, or whether it develops particularly easily in people born into those mental and physical climates, just as the peculiar precognitive phenomenon of "false arrival" seems especially prone to develop in Sweden and Finland. In this—which occasionally occurs in England as well, though not nearly so often—all the sounds of a man's coming home, front gate banging, feet running up the steps, key turning in the lock, front door slamming—are unexpectedly "heard", say, an hour, half an hour, twenty minutes, before his actual coming repeats them in every detail, like a delayed echo. It is an alarming experience in countries where it is unfamiliar, and apt to be deceptive to anyone who is cooking; no explanation has been put forward, except under the general heading of telepathy between those involved. I have known three first-hand instances of this. In each the home-coming was of an unpredictable person so vague about time that no expectation could be formed of when he was likely to arrive.

Index

Aaron, 106
Abercrombie, M. L. Johnson, 21 n., 232
Abraham, 102
Abrams Boxes, 56
accident proneness, 65, 253
Achnutschik, 73
Adam, 49
Adare, Lord, 226
Adelard of Bath, traveller and scholar, 169
adolescents and psychokinesis, 80
Afnan, S. F., 170 n.
Agabus, 153, 173, 197 n.
agent, part played by in telepathy, 79, 80–1, 230
Age of Enlightenment, 189
Agrippa, 182
Akbar, Emperor, curious powers of, 54
Alexandria, University of, 159
Alkindi, 182; on dreams, 166; on senses, 168
Allah, 106, 166
alternation of emotions, 239
Ambrose, G., 212 n.
Amos, 106
Ananias directed to St. Paul, 154
Anawree, Eskimo diviner, 77
angokoks, 69, 72–3, 75–6, 78; see also medicine man, shaman
animal soul, 45, 49, 113, 134
animals, in relation to psi, 33, 34, 37, 42–5, 53, 54, 55, 56, 165; Chap. II passim; see also migration
animal-tamers, 58
Antony of Padua, St., 58
Apostles, Acts of the, 140, 153, 155
apparitions, animal, 33, 34; classified, 206; crisis, 245; of the dead, 127, 188, 206, 241; telepathic, 80; Torrington, 34
Apuleius of Madaura, 158
Aristotle, 213 n., 251
d'Ars, Curé, see John Vianney, St.

Ascension, the, 152
Ashurbanipal's library, 84
Asivak, Eskimo fortune teller, 77
Assagioli, Roberto, 93, 222
association, theory of, 50; word-, 229
astrology, 90, 99, 162, 163 n.
Aubrey, 185
augurs, 88–9
Augustine, St, 161, 172 n. 252; quoted, 242
auras, 205, 219
autism, 186 n., 207 n.
automatism, 214; muscular, 26; see also dowsing
autosuggestion, 118
Averroes, 169
Avicenna, 169
Azande tribe, 77, 95

Babylon, 90, 100
Bacon, Francis, 183
Bacon, Friar, 248
Balaam and Balak, 104–5
Baldwin, A. W., 226 n.
Balsamo, Joseph, see Cagliostro
Barry, Madame du, 215
beatification and psi phenomena, 199, 200–3
Belloc, Hilaire, 55
Bendit, Laurence, 18
Benedict XIV, 199–202, 204–7, 232; see also Prosper Lambertini
Benedict, Ruth, 86
Bergson, Henri, 250
Bhagavad-Gita, 126
Blackwood, Algernon, 33
Blofeld, John, 117
body-image, 33, 75; body, "mind-made", 118–19; see also doppelgänger
Boeldeke, Alfred, 68
bones, oracle, 94
Boniface, St, 201
Boredom, effect of, 247
Bosch, Hieronymus, 211

brain, electronic, 29
brain, mind and, 28–30, 50–1
brain-washing, 70, 238
Briggs, K. M., 185 n.
Brown, W. Thomson, 213 n.
Bruno, 182
Buchan, John, 185 n.
Buddha, 117, 126
Buddhism and Buddhist practices, 115–19, 122–4
Bushmen of South Africa, telepathy in, 62

Cagliostro, 214–16
Caiaphas, 172
calcium, depletion of body, 75
Campanella, 182
canonization, 199, 200, 201
Carbonnel, Mrs, 34
Cardan, Jerome, 206
Carington, Whately, 20–1, 21 n., 23, 39, 42, 47, 50–4, 58, 229
Carpenter, Edward, 73, 75
Carracioli, Marchese, 199
Catherine of Genoa, St, 114
Catherine of Siena, St, 246 n.
Catholics, forbidden to cultivate psi, 244
causality, two types, 249
causation, 190; primitive ideas of, 65
Celsus, 161
Ceremonies, initiation, 77
chakras, 28
chamayo, 68
Champdor, Albert, 84
chance average scores, variation from, 61
Chester-Beatty papyrus, 85
chickens, used for divining, 89
Choupan, 75
Christ, misinterpretations of, 140; Mystical Body of, 49, 131; preaching, 136; nature of, 134; suspended animation and, 139 n.; visions of, 207
Chu Hsi, 126
Ch'u Ta Kao, 126 n.
chumfo, Amerindian term for psi, 9
Cicero's distinction between spontaneous and organized extrasensory perception, 157
clairvoyance, 68, 235; defined, 132

cognition, paranormal, 120–1; *see also* psi activity
collective mind, Chapter II *passim*, 149, 182
collective unconscious, 48, 113, 160, 181, 238, 239, 244; *see also* group mind world soul
"communicators," nature of, 230
conflicts, interior, 80, 196
Confucius, 127
contemplation and physical phenomena, 114 and *passim*
contemplative life, corruption of, 116
contemplatives, 113, 115
contraries in dreams, 167
Conze, Edward, 117–19
Cooper, Blanche, 230–1
Cophte, Grand, 216
Corcyra, Council of, 176, 178
Crehan, S. J., Joseph, 114 n., 148 n.
Crookes, William, 226
Crowley, Alasteir, 240
cures by Mesmer, 217–18; miraculous, 201; at Saint-Médard, 190
currents, odylic, 218; psychic, 218

Dalai Lama, 123
Dalmazzo, Francis, 144
dances, bee, 37
Darwin, Charles, 225
Darwinian controversy, 234
datura, 76, 86, 105
Davidoff, 73
Davis, Gordon, 231
Day, J. Wentworth, 34
death, portent, phenomena interpreted as, 193; presumption of, from apparition, 188; survival of, 232–3, 234
definitions, 15
Delphi, 19
Demdike, Mother, 178
Deren, Maya, 75 n.
Descartes, René, 28
devil, legend of pact with, 178
Devil's Advocate, function of, 199, 205
dharmas, 118
Dialectical Society, London, 227
dice, use of in p-k experiments, 24, 81

Dingwall, E. J., 130 n.
direction-finding, 40
Discalced Carmelites, 242 n.
Dispensation, Old and New, 189
dissociation, 19, 29; some techniques of achieving, 76
distractions, psi phenomena as, 124
doppelgänger, 75, 210
dove as symbol, 160–1
Dowsers, British Society of, 10
dowsing, 10, 24–5, 220; map, 132
drawings, telepathic, 46
Dreams, Calpurnia's, 92; classified by Philo, 160; interpretation, 83–5; Pharaoh's, 67, 84, 85; precognitive, 167; telepathic, 97; waking, 154
drugs, hallucinogenic, used in hope of stimulating psi function, 68, 76, 86, 105, 177, 240
Duke University, 235
Dunne, J. W., 10, 167, 247–8
durshan, taking the, 219
Dyaks, 73

ears burning, popular interpretation of, 78
Eccles, Professor, 29
ecstasy, collective, 106
ectoplasm, 231
Edge Hill, Battle of, 23
Edwin, Ronald, 71, 73, 157, 239
egg-sexing, 24
Egyptian dream interpretation, different schools of, 85
Electricity, 15, 151, 211, 218, 245
electro-encephalograph, use of, 29
Eliseus, 171
Elves, etc., 185
energy, 212–13; diversion of, 243–4; electrical, 151
epilepsy, cures of not to be considered miraculous, 201
Epworth Rectory, 192
Evans-Pritchard, E. E., 72 n., 77
experiments, qualitative and quantitative, 22
Eye, Evil, 24, 253 ff.

fairies, 185
Falkner, Thomas, 73

false arrival phenomenon, 255
familiars, belief in, 178, 184
Fancher, Mollie, 246 n.
Faraday Cage, 221–2
Fathers, early, 225
Faust legend, 178
Fell, William, 34
Ficino, 181–2, 183 n.
firewalking, 76
Fitzherbert, Joan, 109
fortune-tellers, 19, 77
Fox sisters, 223
Francis of Assisi, St, 58, 59, 134
Francis Xavier, St., 205
Franklin, Benjamin, 217
free-will, 26, 115, 163 n., 248
Freuchen, Peter, 77–8

Galen, 158
Gandhi, 219–20
Gassner, Fr J. J., 217
Geiger counters, in connexion with dowsing, 25, 220
Gerard of Cremona, 166, 169
Gerasimus, St, 58
Gibbon, Monk, 74 n.
gland, pineal, believed to be seat of soul, 28
Glanvill, F.R.S., Joseph, 188–9
gnosis, 165
Gnostics, 115
God, 112–13, 115; awareness of, 241; existence of, 236; Holy Spirit of, 65; light of, 148; longing for, 114; and man, 238; Name of, 252; Presence of, 121, 244; service of, 124, 133, 162, 243; as source of creation, 252
gods and goddesses, 88, 91, 180
Golden Sequence (The) quoted, 202 n.
Gorer, Geoffrey, 64–5, 143
Gospel of St Matthew, 141
Gospels, 134
Gosse, Philip, 225
grace, 49, 132, 156, 202
Grant, Joan, 223–4
grappin, the, 197
gratia gratis data, 202–3
gratia gratum faciens, 202–3
Graves, Robert, 92 n.
Gregory, St, 202

Griffiths, Bede, O.S.B., 252
group-mind, 48–9, 182, 238; *see also* collective unconscious, world soul

hallucinations, 16, 74, 187; auditory, 18; of memory, 186; of muscles, 25; veridical, 16–17, 114, 150, 158, 172
Hardy, Professor Sir Aleister, F.R.S., 39, 46, 48, 52, 58, 237 n.
Harrison, R. J., 45
haruspices, 19, 89
Harvard, 235
Hastings, Fr Adrian, 106
hauntings, 24, 52, 80, 127, 129–31; *see also* poltergeists
Haynes, Oriana, 84 n.
head-ghost, 78
healers, 55, 84
healing, faith, 142; miracles of, 138; paranormal, 136; psychic, 246
Heard, Gerald, 139 n.
heat phenomena, 114, 117
Heisenberg, Werner, 213, 249
Hell, Fr Maximilian, 217
heraldry, 32
Heredity in connexion with the psi function, 71, 72, 73, 226
hermits, 58, 116, 243–4
Herodotus, 164
Hewitt, Osbert Wyndham, 57
Heywood, Rosalind, 56, 58, 80 n., 195 n., 227
Hill, Denis, 251
hippie groups, 177
Hippolytus, 158
Hobbes, Thomas, 98
Home, D. D., 226
Homer, 69
homonyms, subconscious use of, 86; *see also* punning in prophecy
Housman, A. E., 212
Howland, A. C., 188 n.
Hugh of Lincoln, St, 58, 244
Hugo, Victor, 223
Hume on miracles, 190
"hunches," 17, 39, 62–3
Huxley, Aldous, 115, 117, 126
Huxley, T. H., 16, 189
Hypatia, 161
hyperaesthesia, 205, 219

hypnosis, 184, 228
hysteria, mass, 175

imagery, 146, 174; archetypal, 105; auditory, 148; cryptic, 84; eidetic, 71; limitations of, 120 n., projection of, 118; in connexion with thought-processes, 181; *see also* totemism
Incarnation, 151–2
Industrialization, effect of, 93
inedia, 246
Inferiority, inferiority-feeling and compensatory development of psi function, 71–4
instinct in relation to psi function, Chapter II and *passim*
interaction of psyche and body, 28
Isidore of Seville, St, and his classification of diviners, 163–4, 172
Islam, 106, 166–7, 181
Israel, 101–7, 244

James the Deacon, 160
James, Montague, 98
James, William, 228, 247
Janet, Pierre, 228
jettatura, 253–4
Jews, 101–4, 107, 176, 244
Joan, St, 241
Jobling, Mr Justice Geoffrey, 167
John Bosco, St, 144
John, St, Apostle, 137
John of the Cross, St, 207
John Vianney, St, Curé d'Ars, 144, 196–8
Jonah (or Jonas), 137–8, 253
Joseph of Cupertino, St, 114, 205
Julian, Emperor, 161
Jung, C. G., 15, 65, 173, 252; anticipated, 169; hypothesis, 251
Justinian, Emperor, 159

K-ideas, and objects, 52, 75, 162 and *passim*
Kardec, Allan, 225
Kingsley, Mary, 73
Kipling, Rudyard, 226; sister, 226 233
Kirk, Robert, 185, 189
knockings, 193; coded, 223

Knox, Mgr Ronald, 141, 190
Koestler, Arthur, 119 n.
Krishna, 126
Kubla Khan, 106

Lacordaire; interpretation of psi phenomena, 222
Lambert, G. W., 130, 194
Lambertini, Prosper, 198–9, 205–7; see also Benedict XIV
Langton, Stephen, 202
Lao Tzu, 121–2
Lapps, 67
Lavoisier, 217
law on apparitions and hauntings, thesis on, 188
Lawrence, D. H., 234
Layard, John, 103
Lazarelli, 182
Lazarus, 139, 139 n.
Lea, H. C., 188 n.
Lepanto, Battle of, result telepathically perceived by St Pius V, 206
lepers, healing of, 138–9
levitation, 114, 117–19, 203, 205, 242, 246
Lewis, Dr C. S., 59, 143, 180
Lob-lie-by-the-fire, 185
Locke, 236
Lorenz, Konrad, 36, 42, 50, 54, 230
luck, beginners', in connection with experimental work, 81

Maddox, John Lee, 73, 74–6, 78
Magdalen of the Cross (Cordova), 204
magic and magicians, 84, 87, 100, 124, 158, 162, 176, 178
magnetism, 211, 217; animal, 218
magpies (as symbols), 96–7
Magus, Simon, 156
Malebranche, 187
malocchio, 253
mana, 66
mandala, 173
Marais, Eugène, 43
Mare, Walter de la, 152
Mari Llwd, 34
materializations, 231–2
Mead, Margaret, 87 n.
medicine-man, 69, 72; see also angokok, shaman

mediums, 24, 91, 159, 229
Meier, C. A., 195 n.
memory, hallucination of, 186
menopause in connexion with poltergeist phenomena, 195
menses, suspended at times of psi activity, 239
mescalin, 105, 130
Mesmer, Franz Anton, 214, 216–18
migration, 31, 39–40
mind, 29, 244, 254, group, see group-mind
mind-brain relationship, 29
minds, collective, Chapter II, passim, 182
miracles, Chapter VI passim; assessment of in relation to canonization, etc., 200–7
Mohave tribe, 86
Mompesson, J. P., 82
Monica, St, distinguishes between ordinary and significant dreams, 172
Montet, P., 85 n.
morph, concept of, 48, 70, 132, 149, 156
Moses, 102
mummification, report of, 222
Murphy, Professor Gardner, 46, 79
Murray, Gilbert, 20, 229
Murray, Margaret, 176
Music, use of, 171
Myers, F. W., 228, 232, 247

Neel, Alexandra David, 117
Newbold, G., 212
Nietzsche, 86
Nirvana, 115
Nonnus, Bishop, 160–1
Northrup, F.C.S., 121 n.

obi-men, 72
Old Shuck, 33
Olivier, Edith, 32
Omen-Priests, 84
omens, 32, 90, 102, 158
oracles, 19, 77, 88, 91–2, 94
Orpheus, 59
Otto, Rudolf, 66
Oxenham's bird, symbol of approaching death, 32

Paracelsus, 216
paranormal, the, 132; phenomena, 128; knowledge, 77; cognition, 18; 220-1; *see also* psi-activity
Paul, St, 49, 150, 153, 154, 156, 175
Pelagia, 160
Pentecost, 148
Pepler, Fr Conrad, O.P., 207
perception extra-sensory, 21, 28, 221; trained, 73; hyper-sensory, 221; primitive, 64; *see also* psi-activity, precognition, telepathy
percipient, part played by, 230
percipients, human and animal, 56, 230
Perry, Rev Michael, 149
persecution of witches, 176
personification of feelings and concepts, 180
Peruvian Indians, 68
Peter, St, 153, 154, 155
Peter of Alcantara, St, 205
Pevensey Castle, 227
Philo Judaeus, 161; classification of dreams, 160; theories quoted, 166
Pirano, "luminous woman" of, 220
Pius V, St, 206
planchette, 223
Pliny, 158, 164
Plotinus, 161
Plutarch, 88, 92, 157
poltergeist phenomena, 10, 24, 80, 119, 188, 196, 254; drumming, 81, 82; occurrence in clerical households, 198; trajectory of moving objects, 186, 246-7; *see also* haunting, psycho-kinesis, tele-kinesis
Pomponazzi, 182
Post, Colonel van der, 62, 67
post-cognition, extra-sensory, 23, 247; *see also* retrocognition, hauntings
potentiality, concept of in atomic physics, 249
powers, psychic, incidental development of, 115-17
prayer, 113, 166, 244
precognition, 9, 23, 26, 76, 89, 158 167-8; by animals, 31; of death, 32
predestination, 248

prediction, demographical, 249
presence, sense of, 56-7, 129
Priestley, Dr, 194
prisca magica, 183
probability, calculus of, 234
Promotor Fidei, 199, 205
prophecy, 10, 106, 170, 173, 206; communication of, 174; degrees of, 172; natural, 10, 170; punning in, 91
Protti, Dr, of the University of Padua, 220
psi-activity, 80; animal, 31, 35, 39, 48; awareness, 88; chosen as colourless term, 27; comparative study needed, 66; consciousness of, 60; definition, 15; development of, 69, 72; early experiment devised by Bacon, 183; experiments by Carington 20-1, 51, 229, Murray 20, 229, Rhine 21, 60, 81, 167, 235, Tyrrell 21; exploitation, 107; family, 110-11, 243; induced, 20, 68; ignored, 222; probably in all living species, 180; projected, 77; in religion, 123; St Paul's view, 156; specialists in, primitive, 78; spontaneous, 92, 245; and time, 247; in symbolic or psychosomatic form, 79, 97; transmission, 79
psi-function, methods adopted to stimulate; ascetic practices, 75, 158, 243-4; hallucinogenic drugs, 68, 76, 86, 105, 177, 240; projection of attention, upon cigar smoke 69, crystal ball 173, 239, ink blobs 20, livers 90, 96, oil drops 84, tea leaves 20, muscular movements of fingers 10, 24-5, 132, 220, 223, of foot 77, of head 78, of legs 164, 173, and in mime 153, 173, 197 n.
Psychical Research Society for, 9, 11, 39, 186-7, 227
psycho-kinesis, 10, 24, 28, 80, 82, 119, 254; *see also* levitation, *and* poltergeist phenomena
psychons, psychon systems, 51, 53, 54
psycho-somatic phenomena, 27, 55, 78, 117, 141, 158, 194, 219

psychometry, 52
Pyrrhus, a healer, 158
Pythagoras, 159

Quakers, 70, 184
Queen, function of termite, 43–4

rain-makers, 81, 143
Rasputin, 135–6, 239
rationalizations of methods of releasing psi, 95–6
Reclus, Elie, 75
Redcap, Mother, 179
reflexes, conditioned, 38, 237
Réginald-Omez, O.P. Fr, 30, 159 n.
Reichenbach, von, 218–19
religious orders, 243–4
Resurrection, 138, 145, 152; a contemporary theory, 149–50; appearances, 149
retrocognition, 9, 123, 247; see also post-cognition; hauntings
Rhine, J. B., 21, 60, 81, 167, 235–6
Richardson, Thomas, 202 n.
Richet, Charles, 234
Rickaby, S. J., Fr Joseph, 169 n.
Rilke, quoted, 108
Rimbaud, Arthur, 240
Rio, Martin del, 182
Rites, Congregation of, 200
ritual, protective, 100–1; secret, 216
Rivail (Allan Kardec), 225
Rocard, Prof Yves, 24–5
Rohan, Cardinal de, 215
Rolle, Richard, 114
Rorschach "objects", 90, 94–5, 97; test, 20, 68
Rose, Ronald, 9, 32, 67, 228
Rose of Lima, St, 206
Royal Society, 184
Rupert, Prince, his poodle, 184
Russell, Bertrand, 189
Russell, E. S., 47

Sacrament, the Blessed, 152
Saint-Médard, 190, 217
St Trivier-les-Moignons, priests at, 197

salisatores, 164, 173
Samuel, 105
sanctity, recognition of, 199, 202
Sargent, Dr William, 70
Saul, 106
Schmeidler and McConnell, on relationship between temperament and extra-sensory perception, 61, 71, 88, 167
Schroedinger, Erwin, 51, 62 n.
Schwartz, Berthold, 109
science, Christian, 64; primitive, 87
scorers, negative, in experiments, 61, 167
Scriptures, Buddhist, 117–18
Scrying (or crystal gazing), 19, 173, 239
séances, 158, 217, 227, 228
Seneca, 95
sensations, 145, 212
sense-perception, 208
Servadio, Emilio, 109; quoted 235
Shackleton, Basil, 22–3
Shakespeare, 171
shaman, 69, 72, 75, 86, 91, 163, 173; see also angokok, medicine man, obi man
Sharp, Cecil, 34
Shekinah, 148 n.
Shelley, 210 n.
Sheppard, Lancelot, 196 n.
Shipton, Mother, 179
Shug monster, 33
Siddhis, 117
Sidgwick, Alfred, 229
sight, second, 117, 185
sin, original, 48, 70, 132
skin, 78; psychosomatic condition, 133; marking, 220
sneezing, 78, 158
Soal, S. G., 22, 22 n., 23, 230–1
Socrates' daemon, 158
somnambulism, 26, 74, 173
soothsayers, 90, 100, 162
soul, animal, 45, 113, 134; world, 160
Southey, Robert, 192, 194
Spectres, thesis on, 188
Spencer, Herbert, 16
"spirit" activity, 73, 183, 185, 191–2, 224, 226
Spirit, coming of the Holy, 145

spiritualism, 224, 225, 227
spiritus mundi, 181; *see also* world-soul
Stanford University, 235
Steegmann, Philip, 31
Stewart, Gloria, 22
stigmatization, 133, 242
Sudre, René, 228, 233 n.
Sufi mystics, 166
suggestion, 55; direct, 82; healing by, 183; power of, 246; self, 118; *see also* healing
superstition, 93, 96, 98–9
symbiotic relationships, 42, 54
symbols, 96–7, 103, 160
synchronicity, theory of, 15, 65, 251–2
Synesius, Bishop, 161

Tabitha revived, 153
table-turning, 223, 226
Taoism and Taoists, 115–16, 121–2
Tao, the, of Jung, 65, 252
Tao Tê Ching, 121, 126
Tarde, Gabriel, 250–1, 252
Tedworth, Drummer of, 81, 188
telekinesis, 10; *see also* psychokinesis
teleology, 251
telepathic apparitions, 80; drawings, 21; dreams, 57, 182, 245; interaction in groups of individuals, 52–3; transmission to son in America of results of treatment to mother in England, 190
telepathy, 9, 50–1; 79–81, 110–11, 178, 181, 182–3, 206–7, 228–30, 232–3, 245, animal, 44, Chap. II *passim*; animal and human, 53–8; emotional ties in, 79, 245; and Faraday Cage, 221; *see also* psi-activity
Teresa of Avila, St, 205
termitary, workings of, 43–4
theology, and biological concepts, 49; and language, 236; discipline of, and discipline of science, 251
Theosophists, 28
Thèrése of Lisieux, St, 143
Thomas Aquinas, St, 9, 115, 165, 169 n., 173–4, 205–6, 211, 248; on Avicenna, 169, 170–1; synthesis of thought, 174
Thomas More, St, 115, 203
Thomas the Rhymer, 124
Thorndike, Lynn, 95 n., 99 n., 160 n., 166 n.
thought, Catholic, 132; non-Christian, 132; scientific and religious, 191; -transference, 28, 182, 229
Thurston, Fr Herbert, S. J., 114, 204, 205 n., 242 n., 246 n.
Tiberius, Emperor, 100
Tibet, 99, 214, 216
Time, -displacement, 9, 23, 65, 248; primitive experience of, 64; reversal-hypothesis, 249; theories of, 247–50
totemism and totems, 32, 67, 75, 180, 224
traditions (religious) in relation to psi-activity, 123
training of shamans, etc., 73–6
trance, inducement of, 118; in Lazarus, 139 n.; -medium, 91; *see also* dissociation
Transfiguration of Christ, 144, 146, 147–8
trickery by children, 193–4
Trithemius, Abbot, 182
Truths, the two, doctrine of, 169, 211
tso-wang, 121
Tyrrell, G. N. M., 21, 67

unconscious (mind), 19; collective, 48, 113, 160, 181, 238, 239
Upanishad, the Isa, 125–6
Ussher, Archbishop, 225

Vaughan, Henry, 242
Vedantists, 139 n.
Verrall, Mrs, 233
Verrall Cross correspondences, 226, 232–3
Vincent Ferrer, St, 207
Vision, Beatific, 112; intellectual, 174
vision(s) classification, 206; experienced by Cornelius, 155; kinds of, 172; religious, 206–8
Voltaire, 199
Voodoo, 75

Waley, Arthur, 121
Walker, D. P., 181 n.
Walpole, Horace, 199
Walsingham, Lady, 34
wand, "magnetic", 217–18
warts treated by suggestion, 55
water, walking on, 143; -divining, see dowsing
weather, Queen's, 143
weight, reputed loss of by "physical" mediums, 246
Weisinger, Abbot, 30 n.
Welch, Holmes, 121–2
Wells, H. G., and precognition, 227
Wendell, H. L., 25
werewolf, and body image, 33
Wesley, John's beliefs as to psi phenomena, 192, 198; Mrs Wesley, 192–3, 195, 196; Wesley, poltergeist, 191–7
West, Donald, 241 n.
White, O. P., Fr Victor, 115, 171
Wickes, Frances, 195

Williams, C. B., 40
Williams, Charles, 120 n., 161
wishful seeing, 186 n.; see also autism witch coven, 76; craft, 176–7; cult, 177; doctor, 72, 77; -doctor apprentice, 74; -hunts, 175–8; -persecutions, 187; -shot (hexenschuss), 71; substance, 72; witches, 55, 192
wizards, 73, 104
Woolley, Sir Leonard, 94
world-soul (spiritus mundi), 160
writing, automatic, etc., 223–4, 233

Yeats, Lily, 74 n., 240
Yeats, W. B., 74
Yoga, 80, 121; exercises, 116

Zaehner, R. C., 124 n.
Zener, Dr, 21; cards, 235
Zodiac, 99
Zuni Indians, 86

DATE DUE

OCT 29 2002